PRAISE FOR PETER EDWARDS

"This is history that is as well paced as a novel, despite its depth of research. Edwards is a thoughtprovoking and entertaining guide through the Fenian movement, its attempts to conquer Canada, the spy who helped bring it all down and the fall of Parnell. It raises the question of what the back-story of the recent troubles will reveal. A real page turner of a book!"
Liam Clarke, *The Sunday Times*

"Edwards grabs the facts of Irish-American intrigue and skulduggery and makes from them a first class thriller that is a masterclass of how to make history relevant and engaging to a modern audience. The skulduggery, quixotic schemes and double-dealing of Parnellite era, Land Reform and Home Rule are brought to light."
Manchán Magan, *The Irish Times*

"The Infiltrator opens a window into the fascinating world of 19th century espionage and intrigue."
Declan Power, security journalist and author

"I applaud Edwards' skill at weaving a rousing narrative . . . I congratulate him on creating an entertaining book that reads more like a novel than a work of non-fiction. He successfully brings Henri Le Caron out of the shadows of history so that readers can decide for themselves if he was one of North America's greatest liars and scoundrels or one of the new Dominion of Canada's first heroes."
The Beaver

"Peter Edwards is to be commended for bringing the Le Caron story back to life."
- *The Globe and Mail*

D1121266

Yours truly,

H. Le Caron

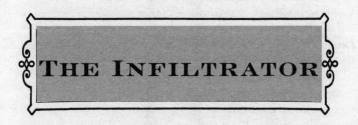

THE INFILTRATOR

Henri Le Caron; The British Spy
Inside the Fenian Movement

PETER EDWARDS

First published in 2008 as *Delusion* by Key Porter Limited.
This edition published in 2010 by Maverick House Publishers.

Maverick House Publishers, Office 19, Dunboyne Business Park, Dunboyne, Co. Meath, Ireland.

info@maverickhouse.com
http://www.maverickhouse.com

ISBN: 978-1-905379-67-5

For Barbara, Sarah and James, Pauline and Amund Hanson, and
Winona and Ken Edwards

Thanks a million

To-day is recorded the death of a brave, able and resolute man, who had done much good to the service of his country. We mean Thomas Beach, otherwise Henri le Caron, the Spy. The term is sometimes one of reproach; in a case like this it ought to be one of the highest praise. If you honour a soldier for risking his life in the excitement of the battlefield, what are you to say of the cool daring of the man who, for five-and-twenty years slept and waked, so to speak, with a rope around his neck and a knife at his breast?

—The St. James Gazette

Le Caron! He is a living lie!

—Sir Charles Russell, future British lord chief justice

We are now preparing for . . . the cost of making a rigorous campaign with "delusion" [dynamite].

—1886 Irish-American revolutionary circular

CONTENTS

ACKNOWLEDGEMENTS

There are a number of people who helped me greatly in my research, including Jack Gumbrecht of the Historical Society of Pennsylvania; Debbie Vaughan of the Chicago Historical Society; Karen L. Jania of the Bentley Historical Library in Chicago; Roger McCarville of the Gaelic League of Detroit; the library staff at the University of Michigan; David Weston, keeper of Special Collections, Glasgow University Library; Coleen Payette, Information Services at the Cornwall Public Library in Ontario, and Giacomo "Jack" DeStefano of the Paterson Museum in Paterson, New Jersey.

I was truly fortunate to be able to draw upon the expertise and goodwill of Glynis Morris, a researcher in Essex, England, who was efficient, pleasant, and speedy in investigating Le Caron's Colchester roots. David Patrick O'Connor of Hamilton, Ontario, whose letters to the editor of various newspapers and calls to CBC Radio are lively and intelligent additions to Canadian journalism, ably pointed out differences in the mindset of Canadian and American Irish transplants. It's with sadness that I note that Mr. Justice Archie Campbell passed away before this book was published. I was hoping he would get a chance to read it. His encouragement was one of the great bonuses of my work, and he is missed.

I took it as a given that my agent, Daphne Hart, of the Helen Heller Agency of Toronto, would be pleasant, efficient, and encouraging, and she was true to form once again. I'm thankful to Jordan Fenn of Key Porter Books for seeing the value of the project, and it was a fresh pleasure to work with Carol Harrison, my editor at Key Porter.

I'm also extremely happy with John Mooney, Jean Harrington and their co-workers at Maverick House for giving this astounding story new life.

My wife, Barbara, accompanied me in my travels to sites mentioned in the book. I marvel at her patience for the many times when I was bunkered in my office or on my reading chair and treasure her support, encouragement, and insights. James and Sarah continue to make me proud.

The idea of writing a book on one of the great spies of the Western world came to me after the horrific events of 11 September 2001. Fears of terrorism and hidden enemies within our midst were almost palpable after that awful morning. In the aftermath, I found myself wondering about earlier groups who were considered "The Enemy," even before Osama bin Laden, the Soviets, the Germans, Mussolini's Italy, and the Japanese.

My research into the life of Henri Le Caron stretched for several years, and as I worked on this project, relations between Ireland and the British government underwent a seismic shift. There was little fanfare on 1 August 2007, when the British Army withdrew from what had become the longest sustained operation in the force's history. More than three hundred thousand soldiers had served in Northern Ireland since 1969, and numbers only hint at the pain of what was known as "The Troubles." An estimated 3,524 people were killed, including 763 British soldiers. The withdrawal of British troops followed the Good Friday Agreement of 1998, which allowed the Republic of Ireland to become involved in Northern Ireland affairs. Peace was certainly a long time in coming, and is never a guaranteed thing. Still, the fact that such horrors could be brought to a peaceful conclusion offers at least a few rays of hope for other conflicts.

Even negotiated peace has its critics. Generations of residents in Northern Ireland grew up defining themselves by violence and conflict, a sad parallel to Le Caron's time. When The Troubles finally seemed over, there was an odd but real sense of loss for some of the combatants. *The*

Times of London reported on 6 September 2007 that this emotion was especially strong in the community of Ballymurphy in West Belfast, the homeground for Gerry Adams, who was a leader in the Provisional Irish Republican Army before he moved on to head the IRA's political arm, Sinn Féin. *The Times'* story called to mind the old English idiom "Better the devil you know than the devil you don't." The article was based on a mental health study in Ballymurphy, and its chilling comments included "We felt more safe during The Troubles," and "I could cope with the war; it's the peace that I cannot manage."

Despite such anxieties, by late summer of 2007, the Irish peace initiative was such a success that former IRA commander Martin McGuinness was meeting with Sunni and Shia factions in Iraq in an effort to help forge peace there as well. Just a few years earlier, the idea of someone considered a former terrorist being utilised as an expert on international peacemaking would have seemed laughable.

The deeper I was immersed in my research, the more I wondered what constituted the biggest threat to a revolutionary movement. Bold government action? Implosion? Public revulsion? Respectability? Success? Time itself? It also dawned on me that Irish revolutionaries of Le Caron's time still saw the United States as a revolutionary movement more than a century after the fact, while officials in the American government had already moved far beyond these perceived ideals.

Espionage and terrorism were sharp features in the political landscape, but they weren't inventions of the Victorian age. Neither were foreign intrigue and government duplicity. Indeed, the website for the British Foreign Secret Intelligence Service, or MI6, notes that "the history of British intelligence organisations, engaged in foreign intelligence collection and in the interception of mail and messages, goes back at least to the second half of the 15ᵗʰ Century. Thomas Cromwell ran secret agents in Europe on behalf of Henry VIII. Sir Francis Walsingham developed expertise in secret interception, as well as maintaining a network of fifty secret agents abroad while Private Secretary to Elizabeth I."

While there was no Central Intelligence Agency in Le Caron's day, the American government was actively involved in undermining the

British government, including its Canadian colony. This shouldn't be surprising since the Americans and Britons shed each others' blood during the War of 1812, which closely followed the mutual bloodletting of the Revolutionary War.

Benjamin Disraeli, British prime minister from 1874–1880, once observed that "nations have no permanent friends and no permanent enemies, only permanent interests." Those words from Le Caron's time ring just as true today. While America covertly supported military action against Canada in the post-Civil War years, the CIA has been onside with the Canadian Security Intelligence Service and MI6 in more modern times.

Sometimes historic events seem totally detached from the present and so offer a kind of refuge for researchers and readers. This wasn't the case for me with this story. Instead, I found that Le Caron's life and activities helped bring context to current events as he operated for a quarter century at the epicentre of the complex, volatile emotions that were later manifested in The Troubles. It's also easy to regard White House support of the Fenian raids of the 1860s as the precursor of modern, covert CIA operations like plots to assassinate foreign leaders in countries such as Guatemala, the Congo, Cuba, and Chile, and participation in the domestic political burglaries like the 1970s Watergate scandal.

This project involved more than thoughts about revolution and terrorism. Any time someone sets out to write about a person, that story is also an account of the time and place in which that person lived. The central character becomes a tour guide of sorts. Following Le Caron led me into reading about events and issues like the treatment of African-Americans and the Irish during the American Civil War, the often boozy birth of Canada, and the almost giddy belief in science and progress in the second half of the nineteenth century. Without Le Caron, I'm confident I never would have spent much time thinking about the connection of grave-robbing to modern medicine.

I also thought a lot about the impact of dynamite and its inventor, Alfred Nobel. The newly invented explosive is central to Le Caron's story, both metaphorically and literally. This was a time when there was an explosion of possibilities, for good and evil, in engineering and science and politics. In far too many of these cases, humankind proved far better at unleashing wild energy than in harnessing it for any particular general benefit.

The Irish revolutionaries of the 19th century referred to dynamite attacks as "the delusions." We now tend to think of "delusions" in a psychiatric sense, as false beliefs that are firmly held. Both the British and revolutionary Irish people in these pages would have considered the other side to be deluded. Delusion can also refer to the act of deceiving, and Le Caron's entire adult life was built upon deception.

The longer I looked into the remarkable life story of Henri Le Caron, the more I realised how his story, like so many things Canadian, was framed by the influences of the United States, Great Britain, and, to a lesser degree, France. I travelled to key locations, including Manhattan, Chicago, Dublin, Colchester, London, and Paris, to try for a further sense of place.

Throughout this journey, my opinions of Le Caron as a person changed frequently. It would have been easier, and far less interesting, had he been strictly a hero or a villain. The deeper I delved into the lives of other key characters in this story, the more I realised how all of them, and not just Le Caron, had to choose between society's superficial rules and deeper primal blood ties. Under the surface, many of the warring characters in the book turned out to be very similar, struggling to be loyal to the idealised views of their parents and homelands, while fighting to survive in the here and now. It called to mind the old Woody Allen joke, "Why are we fighting? We both want the same thing."

This is a bizarre, sweeping, and altogether true story, and because it appears so far-fetched, I have included footnotes. That way, sceptics can check my sources, and then feel the same flashes of wonder that I did when discovering events in and around Henri Le Caron's life. Footnotes also allowed me the freedom of recording little asides, which didn't belong in the main text, but which were too precious to be thrown out altogether. Bob Dylan fans might enjoy reading in the footnotes how some locales connected to his musical roots are also tied to the roots of Irish revolution in America. This includes a mention that the brick Greenwich Village apartment building on 4th Street where Dylan lived in the early 1960s housed British government offices in the 1860s. It was here where Dylan wrote about the sting of betrayal in "Positively 4th Street," and it was also here, a century before, where at least one Irish nationalist decided to betray his cause and become a paid informer for Britain. I've also used the footnotes as a place to record conversions of money in Le Caron's time into modern terms.

While researching Le Caron's story, I also took a little time to probe deeper into my own. My veins course with English, Irish, Welsh, Scottish, Catholic, and Protestant blood. I also have relatives on both sides of the Canadian-American border. I feel this gives me an opportunity to tell the remarkable story of Henri Le Caron with no overwhelming bias, and considerable curiosity.

No conversations have been recreated and what appears between quotation marks in these pages are the words of central characters, as recorded at the time. Le Caron's own letters, which I found in Canada, the United States, and Britain, and his memoirs, *Twenty-five Years in the Secret Service: The Recollections of a Spy,* were of particular use here.

CAST OF CHARACTERS

THE AUTHORITIES

Anderson, Sir Robert (1841–1918): The spymaster for British agent Thomas Billis Beach (a.k.a. Henri Le Caron), he was lord-lieutenant of Ireland and secretary to the Prison Commission, responsible to the secretary of state regarding political crime. In August 1888 he was promoted to head of the London Metropolitan Criminal Investigations Division, more commonly known as Scotland Yard. His cases included the 1888 Jack the Ripper investigation into the murder of prostitutes in London's East End Whitechapel district. In his free time, Anderson wrote books on Christian spirituality that are still read today.

Beach, Thomas Billis (1841–1894): He infiltrated the Irish revolutionary movement in North America for of a quarter century under the name Henri Le Caron and was known in Canadian and British intelligence services by a series of aliases that included Informant B, Thomas, Mr. McKay, and Dr. Howard. He was the first superspy for the new Dominion of Canada, and operated mainly out of Braidwood, Illinois, a small mining community on the outskirts of Chicago. Irish nationalist John Devoy grudgingly called him "the champion spy of the century."

Gladstone, William Ewart (1809–1898): The British prime minister from 1868 to 1874, 1880 to 1885, 1886, and 1892 to 1894, his successes included introducing public elementary education and vote by secret ballot. He also eloquently spoke out for justice around the world. The Liberal leader's failures included an inability to have an Irish Home Rule bill passed.

Grant, Ulysses Simpson (1822–1885): As a Union Army Civil War general, his ruthless nature earned him the nickname Unconditional Surrender Grant. He rose to become commander of all the Union armies. A Republican, he was elected president of the United States in 1868 and again in 1876.

Johnson, Andrew (1808–1875): He was appointed Tennessee military governor in 1862 during the American Civil War, after the Union Army recaptured parts of the state. A Democrat, he became American president after Abraham Lincoln was assassinated on 15 April 1865 and soon afterwards struggled to hang on to power as Congress tried to impeach him.

Macdonald, Sir John Alexander (1815–1891): He led the Conservative Party in Canada for 24 years (1867–1891) and was Canada's first prime minister, serving from 1867 to 1873 and 1878 to 1891. He set up Canada's first border police, whose agents included the spy Thomas Beach, a.k.a. Henri Le Caron.

McGee, Thomas D'Arcy (1825–1868): His father was a Dublin bookseller who took part in the 1798 insurrection in his native Ireland. McGee followed his lead, fighting as part of the Young Ireland movement of 1848, which called for Ireland's separation from Britain, by force if necessary. In time, he renounced his old views and became one of Canada's Fathers of Confederation. He was assassinated early in the morning of 7 April 1868, six days before his 43rd birthday, by a Fenian sympathiser.

McMicken, Gilbert (1813–1891): The Canadian Conservative Party loyalist was head of Sir John A. Macdonald's border police, and the Canadian handler of spy Henri Le Caron.

Millen, General Francis (1830 or 1831–1889): Called Agent X in British government documents (and sometimes wrongly as Miller in the press), the soldier-turned-journalist-turned-agent for the British government pretended to plot to blow up Queen Victoria at her Golden Jubilee celebrations at Westminster Abbey on 21 June 1887.

Monro, James (1838–1920): Commissioner of the London Metropolitan Police, more popularly known as Scotland Yard, his files included Irish independence fighters and also the 1888 Jack the Ripper case. Monro was known for his extreme discretion, which stood out even in the ultra-secretive world of Scotland Yard.

Queen Victoria (1819–1901): She assumed the British throne on 20 June 1837 at age 18, and within five years she had survived two assassination attempts. As assassination plots against herself and her family continued, her views on the treatment of revolutionaries hardened.

Taché, Alexandre-Antonin (1823–1894): Roman Catholic Archbishop of the Canadian province of Manitoba at the time when the Métis people organised to protect their rights against the advance of white settlers.

THE REVOLUTIONARIES

Cronin, Dr. Philip Patrick Henry (1846–1889): Born near the town of Mallow, County Cork, he was taken by his family to New York City as an infant, where he lived for five years before moving to Baltimore and then St. Catharines, Upper Canada. A doctor by training, Cronin was an enthusiastic Irish nationalist, who was aligned with leading Irish independence fighter John Devoy. His Chicago neighbour and fellow revolutionary, Alexander Sullivan, was one of his enemies.

Davitt, Michael (1846–1906): Born in Straide, County Mayo, Ireland, in the depths of the Great Famine, he was just four years old when his family was evicted from their home, which was then torched to prevent their return. Soon after his family relocated in Haslingden, Lancashire, near Manchester, England, until they were evicted again. At age 11, his arm was mutilated in a cotton mill accident and had to be amputated. He served seven years in prison after being arrested in 1870 for smuggling weapons to Irish rebels. His family moved to Pennsylvania and he often travelled from Ireland to America to visit them and for Fenian affairs. He was elected to Parliament, where he championed Irish Home Rule and passive resistance in his 'No Rent' campaign against absentee landlords.

Devoy, John (1842–1928): A native of Kill, County Kildare, he attempted to undermine the British Army by secretly drawing Irish soldiers in its ranks into the Irish independence movement. After serving seven years in British prisons, he relocated to New York and fought for Irish independence for the remainder of his life. In some letters his code name was Duval, while others knew him as Joncares.

Dillon, Luke (1850–1930): He was born in Leeds, England, at the end of the Potato Famine and became a leading Irish-American nationalist while working in Philadelphia as a bank teller. He was sentenced to life in prison on Queen Victoria's birthday in 1900, after being found guilty of attempting to blow up the Welland Canal, between Lake Erie and Lake Ontario, to disrupt Boer War grain shipments. He served more than fourteen years in Kingston Penitentiary in Ontario, Canada, after being convicted under the name Karl Dullman.

Egan, Patrick (1841–1919): Born in Ballymahon, County Longford, Ireland, he was considered something of a wizard with money. He was closely associated with Irish nationalists Michael Davitt and Charles Stewart Parnell, and was closely watched by British authorities. He escaped arrest by fleeing Ireland for Paris and eventually settled in Lincoln, Nebraska, where he remained a force in Irish revolutionary politics. He found time to father 14 children and to work in mainstream American politics, serving as American envoy extraordinary and minister plenipotentiary to Chile from 1889 to 1893.

Ford, Patrick (1837–1913): His parents died shortly after his birth in Galway, Ireland, and family friends brought him to Boston when he was four. By 1859 he was editor and publisher of the *Boston Sunday Times*. After serving for the Union Army in the Civil War, he founded the *Irish World* newspaper in New York City, which he used to promote Irish independence. He considered the Irish Home Rule reforms proposed by British prime minister William Ewart Gladstone to be a dangerous compromise. Michael Davitt called him "the most powerful support on the American continent of the struggle in Ireland."

Lomasney, William Mackey (Michael) (1841–1884): Nicknamed The Little Captain, the Cincinnatti-born man sailed to Ireland in 1865 to aid in an anticipated uprising. He was briefly imprisoned on charges of stealing weapons and shooting a police officer, then briefly joined the Toronto circle of Fenians in 1866. Within a few years, he settled in Detroit, running a downtown bookstore and unwittingly befriending British spy Henri Le Caron.

Marx, Jenny (Jennychen) (1844–1883): The Paris-born journalist and eldest daughter of Karl Marx, she wrote under the pseudonym Jenny Williams about harsh prison conditions for Irish revolutionaries, including O'Donovan Rossa.

O'Neill, General John (1834–1878): Born in the town of Drumgallon, parish of Clontifret, County Monaghan, O'Neill's family fled Ireland for America during the Potato Famine of the 1840s, relocating to Elizabeth, New Jersey. He was a soldier throughout his adult life, first fighting Indian bands in the American West before the outbreak of the Civil War. As a member of the Union Army, he served as an officer in the 15th U.S. Coloured Cavalry. After the war, he twice led Fenian troops in invasion attempts of Canada.

Parnell, Charles Stewart (1846–1891): A Protestant landlord's son from County Wicklow, Ireland, Parnell spent most of his adult life battling landlords on behalf of Catholic tenants. As leader of the Irish Party, he was known for long, seldom eloquent, and frequently disruptive speeches in Parliament.

Rossa, Jeremiah O'Donovan (1831–1915): A native of Rosscarbery, County Cork, Ireland, his real name was Jeremiah O'Donovan and his nickname of O'Dynamite accurately captured his politics. His treatment in English prisons became an international scandal after it caught the eye and pen of Jenny Marx, the journalist daughter of communist theorist Karl Marx.

Stephens, James (1824–1901): Born in County Kilkenny, Ireland, he was a central member of the Young Ireland independence movement of 1848 and with Thomas Clark Luby, founded the Irish Republican Brotherhood on St. Patrick's Day 1858. His friend John O'Mahoney started the Fenian movement in the United States at the same time. Stephens fled Ireland for France, disguised as a lady's maid, and the French refused to extradite him. This made him one of the "wild geese," or Irish nationalists, who were driven out of the country.

Sullivan, Alexander (circa 1847–1913): An Irish revolutionary leader and leading member of the Irish community in Chicago, the lawyer was a head of The Triangle, which secretly directed violent Irish independence operations from within the United States.

OTHERS

O'Shea, Katharine (1846–1921): Her divorce from Captain William O'Shea of the Irish Party and remarriage to Irish Party leader Charles Stewart Parnell was an international scandal, with enormous historical ramifications. Enemies called her Kitty, slang for "prostitute," although she was a faithful and loving companion to Parnell.

O'Shea, Captain William (1840–1905): He was officially a member of the Irish Party, but cultivated contacts in the Liberal Party, especially British prime minister William Ewart Gladstone. He used his wife's love of Charles Stewart Parnell to advance his own political career.

REVOLUTIONARY GROUPS

Clan-na-Gael/Clann na nGael: The goals of this secret Irish brotherhood were to attack English politicians and landmarks to force Irish Home Rule. In Irish, its name means "Clan or Family of the Gaels" or "Irish Kinfolk," and the group worked closely with the United Brotherhood of Ireland. The Clann na nGael was created in 1868 by Irish-Americans who wanted a change from Fenianism, which was wracked by factionalism. Its founders included *New York Herald* scientific editor Jerome Collins, who died in 1880 whilst exploring the Arctic.

Fenians: The organisation pre-dated the Clann na nGael, and sought to forcibly separate Ireland from England. Leaders of its North American arm hoped to take over Canada, and then swap it with Great Britain for Ireland. Its name was taken from an old Irish legend about an army called the Fianna who protected Ireland against foreign invaders.

Invincibles: A short-lived, particularly extreme terrorist group responsible for the 1882 murder of two English politicians in Dublin's Phoenix Park. The killing horrified Irish Party leader Charles Stewart Parnell.

Land League: A passive resistance movement in Ireland in the 1880s aimed at breaking the landlords' grip over farmland.

New Departure: This Irish nationalist movement was created in 1878 by Michael Davitt and John Devoy in an attempt to wed the revolutionary spirit of the Irish Republican Brotherhood and Irish-American Clann na nGael with the parliamentary action of Charles Stewart Parnell's Irish Party in a united call for land rights. Its proponents felt the need to accomplish something beyond bloodshed or, as John Devoy bluntly said, "We must come out of the rat-holes of conspiracy."

The Triangle: This was a particularly secretive Irish revolutionary leadership group in the United States, which was made up of three Clann na nGael members led by Chicago lawyer Alexander Sullivan.

Young Ireland: Leading journalists, lawyers, historians, and poets who were radicalised by the Great Potato Famine of 1845 to 1848 made up this nationalist movement. They felt betrayed by England as millions starved while Irish-grown produce that could have saved them was exported for profit. They argued that force was justified, if necessary, and sought a separate Parliament for the Irish, based in Ireland. Many were transported to Australia or fled to America, where some of them joined forces in the Fenian independence movement

CHAPTER 1

INFORMANT B

White House, Washington, April 1868

I was written down as the black sheep of the family, from whom no permanent good could ever be expected.

—Spy Thomas Billis Beach (a.k.a. Major Henri Le Caron)

A hard look into the stranger's flashing black eyes might have forced the American president to pause uncomfortably. Those sharp eyes, with their ferret's stare, weren't the only unsettling things about the neat, alert, rigid man in his late twenties. The visitor's slender body appeared almost ready to explode with energy, even as he sat in his chair with his arms tightly coiled across his chest like a skinny Napoleon.[1] A further study of the visitor's face would have offered President Andrew Johnson no comfort, and it would later be described by a newspaperman as "one of the boniest faces in or out of the New World, like a death's head with a tight skin of yellow parchment."[2]

The hard-eyed, bony-faced visitor to the Oval Office didn't seek attention, and the president focused instead on General John O'Neill, the other White House guest that day in early 1868. General O'Neill clearly enjoyed the attention and was a man impossible to ignore, with a shock of facial hair that made the wild beard of Karl Marx look groomed and effeminate by comparison.

O'Neill's hairy countenance was a friendly and familiar sight for the president as their connection dated back to 1862 when Johnson was military governor of Tennessee during the Civil War and O'Neill was in his command. Now, Johnson was well into his fourth year in the White

House, easily long enough for him to know how lonely Washington could be. The assassination of President Abraham Lincoln on 14 April 1865 at Ford's Theatre in Washington, D.C., by actor John Wilkes Booth made Johnson the first vice-president to ascend to the presidency through assassination. It had to sting when Johnson heard snickers calling him His Accidentcy, a pathetic contrast to Lincoln's affectionate nickname of The Great Emancipator. There had been rumours that Johnson had been drunk when he gave his inauguration address, and now there were rumblings that he was about to experience another sad historic first, and become the first American president to undergo the humiliation of impeachment proceedings. Long before his visit from O'Neill and his unsettling companion, Johnson realised he must take his friends and support when and where he could find them.

Like Johnson, O'Neill's past included flashes of brilliance, wild mishaps, and no small measure of alcohol. O'Neill had pulled himself up from the rank of private, fighting Native Americans on the Plains and Confederates in the Deep South while wearing the blue of an American cavalryman. In his heart, however, Irish-born O'Neill was always first and foremost an Irish revolutionary, which explained the sprig of green pinned over his heart. Thoughts that America had won her freedom from Britain less than a century before inspired O'Neill, who was further buoyed by the realisation that he had a friend in the White House. Now, at age 34, in a rich voice that told of his roots in the town of Drumgallon, parish of Clontifret, County Monaghan, Ireland, General O'Neill told his old friend of a plan that was even wilder than his beard.

O'Neill commanded a newly formed group called the Fenians, a collection of idealists, wasters, adventurers, and plotters drawn from the nearly two hundred thousand men of Irish parentage who fought in the American Civil War. Some of them still wore their Civil War uniforms, with buttons they added after the war displaying the embossed letters IRA, for the Irish Republican Army.

The general planned to lead them across the largely undefended, 1,300-mile border between the U.S. and Canada, and seize the young dominion. Then he would swap captive Canada for Ireland with Great

Britain, and the Irish would finally be masters of their own land. It was a wild idea, but was it any wilder than America's victory over Great Britain less than a century before, and its promise of government by and for the people? In that struggle, the rebel American colonies had been aided enormously by the Dutch and the French. Was it so unnatural now for the Irish to expect American aid in a similar struggle?

By the time he visited Johnson in the Oval Office, O'Neill had already survived defeat, and more than a little ridicule, because of his previous efforts to invade and conquer Canada. However, if the wildly bearded general was humbled by the setbacks, he certainly didn't show it. The post-Civil War years were a time of expansion for railways, industry, science, population, and dreams, when the only boundaries seemed those set by one's will and confidence. The general reflected that spirit as he told his old friend, the American president, about his eagerness to launch a northern assault that would be so precise, powerful, and pure in its purpose that it was preordained to make Ireland a free republic, just like America.

For his part, Johnson wasn't about to suggest that he had no time for ragtag revolutionaries. He already knew the sting of Irish disfavour. Immediately after the failed 1866 invasions of Canada, Johnson issued a public proclamation against more Fenian hostility, and for this, he was damned by his Washington rivals as a "dirty tool of the English government" and a "toady." The year 1868 was an election year, and Johnson knew he needed Irish-American votes for any chance to cling to office.

TWENTY-SEVEN YEARS EARLIER

Boyhood fantasies of military service and travel are as natural and commonplace as oxygen in Colchester, Essex, the garrison town 60 miles east of London where Thomas Billis Beach was born on 26 September 1841. The original community was the capital for the ancient British Catuvellauni tribe in AD 43, when conquering Emperor Claudius rode into town on an elephant, and claimed it as part of the Roman Empire. The town was later liberated by an even more flamboyant warrior, legendary Queen Boudicca, whose name comes from the Celtic word bouda, which translates into "victory."

Britain's Queen Victoria considered Boudicca both a namesake and an inspiration, and commissioned poet laureate Alfred Lord Tennyson to write a poem about the warrior queen, which includes the lines, "Burst the gates, and burn the palaces, break the works of the statuary." Victoria's loving husband, Prince Albert, commissioned a bronze statue of Boudicca, standing proud and tall on a chariot beside her daughters, her hair flowing to her waist and her stare fierce and defiant, like a lioness. The statue was prominently placed next to the Westminster Bridge and Houses of Parliament in London, a reminder of the patriot queen who died defending her island from invaders and imperialism. Ironically, Irish nationalists now considered Queen Victoria to be a fresh symbol of imperialism and the invasion of their own island. If Her Majesty was amused by this observation, she disguised it well.

A military tradition continued in Colchester, long after the death of Boudicca and the retreat of the Romans. As a toddler, Beach would have undoubtedly heard two children's nursery rhymes written in Colchester that referred to the community's military past. "Old King Cole" harkens back to the legendary founder and namesake of Colchester, and "Humpty Dumpty" refers to a cannon from the seventeenth-century English Civil War, with its passage about "all the king's men" describing supporters of King Charles I. As a boy, Beach would certainly have seen bullet holes in the Tudor-style Siege House on East Street, fired in the Wars of the Roses in 1648, two centuries before his birth.[3]

The Colchester of Beach's childhood was a place of tradition, history, and order, where the town hall stood on the same spot for seven centuries. The castle in the heart of the city was even more durable, rebuilt in the 1070s by William the Conqueror, using bricks recycled from a temple constructed a thousand years before by Roman Emperor Claudius.

Beach grew up in a proudly English household at 12 Magdelan Street, along the city's old fortress wall. He was the oldest son and second oldest child of thirteen children of John Joseph Billis Beach and Maria (née Passmore) Beach.[4] The father was listed in the 1861 census as a master cooper, a trade that made watertight vessels for pots and barrels to hold perishables like food and gunpowder. He wasn't a rich man, but earned enough to employ two tradesmen and three apprentices. A man of strong and unbending beliefs, John Beach found time to moonlight as an independent Methodist preacher, and forbade alcohol, even on holidays, in his loving, strict, crowded, conservative, and thoroughly English home.

In Beach's childhood, he would have often seen troops drilling in the local parade square, where there had once been Roman chariot races, as soldiers prepared to fight overseas for the glory and advancement of the British Empire. Beach later said he often imagined military service abroad as a bold little drummer boy, far from the confines of his crowded house and provincial town. A local history later described him as a choirboy who was turned down in his attempt to become a drummer boy.[5] For his part, Beach later recalled that it was "but natural that the glory of the redcoat life should affect me, and that, like so many other foolish boys, I should feel drawn to the ranks."[6]

One of his brothers was a commissioned officer who fought for the British Empire against the Zulus in South Africa. The bones of another brother dried on the sands of Tel-el-Kebir, Egypt, in 1882 after he served under Lieutenant-General Garnet Wolseley against the military insurrection of Pasha Said Ahmed Arabi.

Beach was also restless to see the world. He later recalled that he wasn't much past his 12th birthday when one morning, he "packed up his marbles, toys, and trophies, and in the early light slipped quietly out on to the high-road en route for that Mecca of all country boys—the great glorious city of London!"[7]

He blundered by telling a school chum of his scheme, and soon afterwards, his anxious parents nabbed him. The taste of adventure was intoxicating, and he soon bolted again, this time managing two weeks of freedom before he was discovered. "The natural consequences attended these attempts of mine, and soon I was written down as the black sheep of the family, from whom no permanent good could ever be expected."

His parents apprenticed him to a Quaker draper, but young Thomas did not see his future in window coverings. The draper was equally unimpressed, kicking him out 11 months into a seven-year apprenticeship. By May 1857, at age 15, Beach snuck off again to London, where relatives in the great city helped him secure work in a prominent drapery house. This employment also ended prematurely after he accidentally set fire to his workplace.[8]

Still restless, Beach drifted from London to Bath, and then again to Bristol, where he was hit by fever and left penniless. He was taken to St. Bartholomew's Hospital in London, which was legally known as the "House of the Poore in West Smithfield in the suburbs of the City of London of Henry VIII's Foundation," and popularly called Barts. There, he was horrified by the death of a patient in a bed next to him. Renewed strength for Thomas meant a return to restlessness, and soon he was striking out for Paris via the French port of Havre. Perhaps seeking to embellish the tale, he later said that he left England in a hurry after stealing a box of pennies that a sister had saved to donate to missionary work. Even if this is true, he was close to penniless when he arrived in Paris, with no ability to speak French. Not surprisingly, he gravitated to the British Embassy in the Faubourg St. Honoré district, close to the Tuilleries Gardens and Palais de l'Élysée, where he found quarters in a hotel run by an Englishwoman. One Sunday, while walking a few blocks from the hotel near St. Michael's church on the Rue d'Aguesseau, he was drawn inside by the music of the service, and especially by the comforting sound of English voices from the small, unpretentious building. It seemed only natural for the former choirboy to sing here as well, and he quickly struck up an acquaintance with a man in the choir, who invited him to share his comfortable lodging in the house of Withers, a la Suisesse, 52 Faubourg St. Honoré. Beach sang well enough to be paid as a ringer, and over the next two years, he got work at a draper's shop and banking house.

There was plenty of fun to be had in Paris, even for a teetotaller who sang in the choir. It was a time of rebirth and prosperity in the French capital as Louis Napoleon encouraged his dictatorial urban prefect, Georges-Eugène Haussmann, to wrench the city from the Middle Ages into the present. In Haussmann's unapologetic words, "We ripped open the belly of old Paris, the neighborhood of revolt and barricades, and cut a large opening through the almost impenetrable maze of alleys, piece by piece, and put in cross-streets whose continuations terminated the work."[9]

In an explosion of destruction and renewal, some twenty thousand houses were demolished and another forty thousand built. Streets were widened, straightened, macadamised, and lined with telegraph lines, while gold arrived in Paris from new mines in California and South Africa. The newborn middle class was only too happy to spend its money on comfort and mass-produced cheap goods.

France and England now saw each other as friends. Just a few years earlier, the two countries fought alongside each other in the Crimean War and in 1855 Queen Victoria arrived for a visit, making her the first English monarch to set foot in Paris since Henry VI in the early 15th century. By the time of Beach's arrival, the *entente cordiale* was still in full glow.

It was also a time when order and hedonism somehow were both in vogue, each feeding off the other. Women modestly covered their faces and virtually bared their breasts at the masked balls so loved by Emperor Louis Napoleon. Syphilis burned a horrific swath through the city's artists, claiming writer Guy de Maupassant, poet Charles Baudelaire, and Impressionist painter Edouard Manet; indeed, the great Impressionist painter Pierre-Auguste Renoir lamented that he might not ever be considered a genius as his penis was disease-free.[10]

A shot fired on the other side of the ocean on 12 April 1861 forever changed the lives of Beach and his teenaged friends in the Faubourg St. Honoré district. It was fired by rebel forces on Fort Sumter in Charleston Harbor, South Carolina, and signalled the beginning of the American Civil War. Beach knew precious little about the causes of the conflict, but he did feel its magnetic pull. "That shot echoed all over the world, but in no place was the effect more keenly marked than in the American colony in Paris, which even in these days was a very numerous one," Beach later recalled.[11]

News of the American conflict came in bits and pieces, making each fresh dispatch all the more tantalising. Beach's friends in the American colony in Paris were rushing home to join the conflagration, and Beach didn't want to be left behind. Later describing his emotions, he didn't talk about freeing African-American slaves or holding the American union together or any other great idea. Instead, he spoke of adventure and travel and youthful bonding. It wasn't long before the 19-year-old was on board the Great Eastern, sailing for New York City and Union Army recruiting halls.

CHAPTER 2

WAR FEVER

New York City, 1861

We are slaughtered like sheep.
   —*Irish American* newspaper on Civil War losses

The term "slumming" was coined in 1841, after 29-year-old author Charles Dickens ventured into the largely Irish, totally poor Five Points section of Manhattan, closely flanked by bodyguards. After his safari through the squalor, Dickens wrote in American Notes of "poverty, wretchedness, and vice," where livestock strolled past grim brothels. "Many of those pigs live here. Do they ever wonder why their masters walk upright in lieu of going on all-fours? And why they talk instead of grunting?"[1]

Life for the pigs and humans of Five Points only got worse over the next few decades with each boatload of desperate, penniless, sick Irish immigrants docking in New York harbour. The new arrivals were pushed to America's shores by an impossible-to-see airborne fungus, which destroyed Irish potato crops, the staple of their already meagre diets. As the Irish starved or fled, the British government did next to nothing beyond collecting taxes for Irish grain sold abroad. An estimated 1.5 million of Ireland's population of eight million starved while Britain continued to export Irish-grown corn abroad. There was an awful consistency to such indifference. In 1729, Irish novelist Jonathan Swift had tried to jar the British into caring about Irish hunger when he wrote "A Modest Proposal; for Preventing the Children of Poor

People in Ireland from Being a Burden to Their Parents or Country, and for Making Them Beneficial to the Public." In his satirical article, Swift noted that British laws prevented the Irish from manufacturing goods for export, and suggested both the English and Irish would be better off if Irish people were redefined as cattle and fed well, until their slaughter, for meat. Realising that readers might be squeamish about such an idea, he continued, "I have been assured by a very knowing American of my acquaintance in London, that a young, healthy child well nursed is at a year old a most delicious, nourishing, and wholesome food, whether stewed, roasted, baked, or boiled."

It was a masterpiece of satire, but bold, clever words don't fill bellies and starvation continued. Irish who survived passage in the steerage holds of "coffin ships" arrived in America with hollow eyes and their souls filled with a profound hatred of all things British. By the time the American Civil War began in April 1861 there were more than 1.6 million people with Irish blood living in North America. New York was nicknamed New Cork for those newcomers who were crammed into its Five Points and Hell's Kitchen neighbourhoods.[2] The young Irish immigrants who lined up in New York City's recruiting halls for the Union Army had grown up hearing tales of Irish eating grass and even corpses during the famines of the 1840s. Their hatred of England was nourished by stories of mass graves in the south of Ireland, where bodies of hundreds of men who were hanged in the 1798 rebellion were buried. They also grew up knowing that the Irish were denied their own schools and universities while many of Ireland's most prosperous citizens were sucked into London, where laws controlling Irish lives were drafted. Meanwhile, the poor who hadn't yet starved or migrated wallowed in Dublin tenements on streets with telltale names like Dirty, Murdering, Dunghill, and Cut-throat Lanes.[3]

The newest of these New Yorkers also had raw recent memories of life in America, including how it felt to walk past signs reading "Irishmen need not apply" while seeking work. Many of the insults were from the Know Nothings, a virulent American-born, anti-immigration, and anti-Catholic society that feared the Pope was scheming to take over America with an influx of Catholic immigrants. The Know Nothings got their name because members were prone to reply, "I know nothing," when asked about their intensely secretive organisation. The motto of their movement was "I know nothing but my Country, my whole Country and nothing but my Country." While the inner workings of their group were closely guarded, their political views were public and ugly, like the argument that immigrants should wait 21 years before gaining citizenship or that only Protestants should be allowed to attend public schools. Now, the outbreak of the Civil War gave Irish Catholic immigrants an opportunity to prove their loyalty to America by fighting for the Union Army. War also meant that they would be clothed and fed.

When 19-year-old Thomas Billis Beach enlisted in the Eighth Pennsylvania Reserves in New York City on 7 August 1861, it seemed little more than a three-month adventure. He decided on a whim to register as Henri Le Caron, taking the name of a family who ran a Paris restaurant. The name change meant that his family wouldn't accidentally learn that he was in the military and worry about him. In a few months, he reasoned, he would be out of the service, and could joke about the deception with them, if he wished. Before seeing any action, he transferred to the Anderson Fifteenth Cavalry of the Pennsylvania Volunteers, commanded by Colonel William J. Palmer. There's no reason to believe that his reasons for the transfer were well thought out or deep; rather, he would later note that the Anderson Cavalry had particularly handsome blue uniforms.

On 30 August 1862 Henri Le Caron was finally mustered into service, and less than three weeks later, he was at Antietam (or Sharpsburg), Maryland, on the bloodiest day in young America's history as General Robert E. Lee attempted to carry the war into the North. On 17 September when the fighting stopped at Antietam, 12,410 Union and 10,700 Confederate troops lay dead, and neither side could claim a decisive victory. No one felt the horrors more than the Irish brigades within the Union ranks, who were involved in the assault on the aptly named Bloody Lane, where the Sixty-third and Sixty-ninth New York regiments absorbed 60% casualties.

For the Irish fighting alongside Le Caron, there was the chilling suspicion that Union leaders considered their lives particularly expendable. At the Battle of Fredericksburg, Virginia, on 13 December 1862, 545 of 1,200 Irish brigade members lost their lives, were wounded, or went missing in a failed attack on Marye's Heights. The day after the slaughter, Captain William J. Nagle of the Eighty-eight New York Regiment wrote a letter to his father, which was reprinted in the Irish American newspaper of New York City: "Irish blood and Irish bones cover that terrible field to-day... We are slaughtered like sheep..."[4]

Le Caron was among the forces of the Western Army that advanced into Tennessee in October 1862 under General William S. Rosencranz in a push toward Nashville and Murfreesboro. This southern march included engagements at Tullahoma and Winchester, and the capture of Chattanooga and Chickamauga. Some of the battles were described in the searing, haunting anti-war prose of novelist Ambrose Bierce, a fellow Union soldier. Among other things, Bierce noted that spies could expect to be shot or hanged within a day of capture. Le Caron's recollections of these campaigns were far lighter as he still seemed consumed by nothing more than his boyish need for adventure.

Le Caron would later describe how, on Christmas Eve 1862, he rode his horse up to a house some fifteen miles from Nashville. He was 21 years old now, old enough to be an officer commanding a party of 30 men. As Le Caron told the story, they were engaged in a scouting duty, and stopped to buy food. In the time it took to dismount, they found themselves surrounded by a band of Confederates. Le Caron was locked in a log smokehouse, and could hear raucous sounds from inside the main house as their captors sat down to dinner. "Our position was anything but a happy one," he later wrote. "Death was very near."[5]

Late that night, Le Caron heard the bolt of the smokehouse door pulled open. Instead of facing a firing squad, he saw the farmer's young blonde niece Nannie Melville. They had only met for a few minutes and now she was risking her life to save the Union soldiers. Le Caron and his troops walked 15 miles to rejoin their comrades, who had given them up for lost. He could only hope his young saviour wasn't discovered and punished for her kindness and bravery.

In later years, Le Caron didn't talk about how he refused to report for battle two days after he said he met Nannie Melville. However, army records note that on the morning of 26 December 1862, Le Caron was a private in Company B of the Anderson Cavalry. This refutes his later claims that he was an officer commanding a group of 30 men. According to army records, Le Caron and some six hundred others simply refused to risk their lives at the front near Nashville. By this time, they had been in the military for four months, long enough for bitterness and fear and doubt to fester. Their weapons were poor and their officers inexperienced, and if they didn't do something, their deaths seemed inevitable and pointless. And so, when they were ordered to march to the front on 26 December Le Caron and fellow soldiers instead stacked their weapons in front of their tents and refused to budge.[6]

There were too many malcontents, with too strong political connections, for them to be shot for this defiance. Instead, the rebels of Company B complained all the way to Secretary of War Edwin M. Stanton on 31 December 1862, writing: "In justice to ourselves, we consider it to be our imperious duty, under the peculiar circumstances by which we are now surrounded, to decline performing any duty until provided with a sufficient number of officers to enable us to battle with credit to our State and Government."[7]

Their complaints were partially supported by N.H. Davis, assistant inspector-general, U.S. Army, who concluded "as a class they are very intelligent young men, but have been unfortunate in not having their organization completed by the appointment of a sufficient number of company officers, in consequence of which, and other causes, such as the interference and influence of friends at home, they have become demoralized, and wanting in discipline."[8] There were enough improvements and promises for the troops in the Anderson Cavalry to be mollified, and sent back into battle.

A 1906 history of Le Caron's unit includes an article by a veteran named Frank M. Crawford, who recalled Le Caron as a pleasant, if somewhat odd man, and an accomplished chief bugler. Crawford recalled that the young man liked to tell tall tales, even though he kept his secret about his true identity to himself. "He gave out that he was a

Frenchman, and in some vague way the rumor got abroad that he was in some way connected with and related to the Orleans princes," Crawford wrote. They considered his "odd foreign ways" to be French, and were always a little confused that he spoke with an English accent. Crawford wrote that Le Caron had a hard time pronouncing the letter h, which made him hard to understand for his American comrades. "I remember one of our night marches when a good many things happened to him," Crawford recalled. "'Hi was asleep on my 'orse,' he said, 'when my 'at fell off, and when hi got hoff to get hit someone stole an 'am hi 'ad, and while hi looked for my 'am, my 'orse walked off and so hi lost my 'at and my 'am and 'orse, all in five minutes.'"⁹

As Crawford recalled, Le Caron "was a good-natured, jolly fellow, keen to appreciate a lively remark, which always brought a laugh to his face." This was particularly true in the winter of 1863 after the cavalry's East Tennessee campaign, when they were camped between Missionary Ridge and Chattanooga, and their colonel had given them a couple of weeks of complete rest from all drills. Le Caron had been transferred, on 1 November to Company S, and promoted to full chief bugler. When the drills finally resumed, Le Caron took his position in the open space between the line of officers' tents and the enlisted men, and composed his face to begin bugling. This meant that he couldn't laugh or even smile. Crawford recalled that "Some of the men nearby had an inkling of the coming call, and began making good-natured, facetious remarks, at which Le Caron grinned, and postponed the call. As soon as he could get his face straight, up came the bugle, and his lips took on that severe expression necessary to produce sound, and then another remark by some other soldier brought out the grin and the call was again postponed."

Soon Le Caron couldn't stop smiling despite his best efforts, and Crawford speculated that "perhaps he never would have got it all out had not the Adjutant, who orders all calls and was wondering why he did not hear this one, come to his rescue, drove off his persecutors, and then at last the call was sounded."

As Le Caron later told the story, it was in April 1864 in Nashville when he once again met Nannie Melville, the young woman who had risked her life to save him by freeing him from the smokehouse back on Christmas Eve, 1862. Melville, the daughter of an Irish Virginia planter and a German mother, lived in Nashville now as her uncle's farm had been destroyed by war. Her skills on a horse were dazzling, and her bright eyes promised adventure. Le Caron was quickly smitten. "I ignored all the articles of war and subscribed to those of marriage, entering into a treaty of peace freighted with the happiest of results," Le Caron later recalled.[10]

In Crawford's version of the story, he doesn't mention Nannie as having saved Le Caron's life. Perhaps he didn't know of this, or perhaps Le Caron later embellished things with the rescue story to make a good story better. As Crawford later wrote, "It was in the summer of 1864, while we were at Nashville waiting for a new set of horses, that Le Caron wooed and won a lady residing there, and his marriage in the Catholic Church and the reception afterward at her home was an eventful occasion to many of us who were there."[11]

Not long after his wedding, Crawford and Le Caron were both promoted to leadership over the Thirteenth Reg. U.S. Coloured Troops. Le Caron was elevated from bugler to second lieutenant on 13 September 1864, and it's perhaps a comment on the lack of stature of the African-American unit that Le Caron failed to mention it when later describing his wartime years.[12] The 13th Reg. had been organised in Nashville on 19 November 1863, and guarded the Nashville & Northwestern Railroad in Tennessee and Alabama, and chased rebel forces away from Nashville and across the Tennessee River in December 1864. It was necessary, gruelling, dangerous work, with 86 enlisted men and four officers killed in battle, and another 265 men dead from disease.

Le Caron did later tell of how he was hospitalised for a month after his horse was shot out from under him, while the man riding next to him was killed. In the spring of 1865 he was a full lieutenant, first class, with the assignment of scouting the enemy and keeping tabs on Confederate guerrilla bands. He was riding ahead of his men, near Duck River, when he saw a man, in the grey uniform of the Confederacy, fleeing from the rear of a farmhouse. Le Caron shouted for him to stop, then ordered his men to head him off. The fugitive didn't speak, instead he fired at Le Caron and missed. Le Caron ran the man down with his horse, and stunned him with a blow from the butt end of his revolver. They stripped off the man's grey uniform, and saw the blue coat of their own regiment, with a mark where there had been corporal's stripes. The men recalled that a few days earlier a corporal in their unit was slain by a southern soldier. Lying before them was the corporal's killer. Realising this, Le Caron's troop filled the man with bullets. A search of his pockets yielded some two hundred dollars in bills, the man's identity, and an oath of allegiance to the U.S. government. Le Caron figured he had used the document numerous times to trick his way to freedom. Now the false papers were stained with the dead man's blood.[13]

Inside the farmhouse, two women and a half dozen small children wept. The oldest of the women was the mother of the dead man, who was identified as William M. Guin, a nephew of ex-U.S. Senator Guin of California, and considered the leader of a particularly vicious rebel gang. Standard practice called for Le Caron to burn to the ground the house of anyone who harboured guerrillas. However, as he looked at the crying women and their sad-eyed children, Le Caron relented.

Crawford considered Le Caron a close friend by the end of the war, later writing that their "casual acquaintance ripened into an intimacy which continued for many years after the war closed." Despite this, even he didn't know Le Caron's real name or nationality. As Crawford later mused, "He was an odd character while in the Regiment, and was still odd all the years I knew him, but the oddest thing of all was that with all our intimacy I never knew or suspected what he really was."[14]

Le Caron was mustered out of the military on 10 January 1866 settling in Nashville with Nannie and their 1-year-old son, Henry, an Americanisation of Le Caron's *nomme de guerre*. Although the shooting had stopped, the former soldier did not revert to Thomas Billis Beach. His future was in America and his name would remain Henri Le Caron.

CHAPTER 3

A Spy is Born

Office of the Britsh Home Secretary, London, 1865

My Son is surrounded by Fenians in Nashville.

—**John J.B. Beach**

There was something about England that soothed John A. Macdonald, the attorney-general of Canada West during the time of the American Civil War. England was a safe refuge for the often-troubled Canadian, a welcoming place of retreat when the pressures of political and family life felt like they were going to consume him. Macdonald had the ability to laugh at problems, and liked to joke that "When fortune empties her chamberpot on your head, smile—and say 'we are going to have a summer shower.'"[1] However, there were many times when his quick wit and deep liquor cabinet simply weren't enough. He remarked at least once that "I had no boyhood," which was sadly accurate. He was just seven when he saw his four-year-old brother, James, beaten to death by a drunken family friend, and there were innumerable times when he suffered roughly at the hands of his alcoholic father.[2]

Adulthood changed but didn't lessen pressures for Macdonald. A son borne by his first wife, Isabella, died in infancy, and Isabella's physical and mental health declined until her death in 1856. Sometimes when memories and reality couldn't be ignored or drowned in gin, Macdonald simply refused to budge from his bed. Once, during a particularly down time, there were published rumours that he might have killed himself.

39

The reports weren't true, but the fact that knowledgeable government insiders believed the suicide rumours was an indication of how low his moods could sink. His best solution for riding out his darkest days was to retreat to England, and lose himself in an audience at the Drury Lane theatre or the bookshops of Chancery Lane until he mustered up the power to return to Canada and laugh and scheme again.[3]

During the American Civil War, Macdonald feared that Union Army leaders might lead a combined Irish-American and Union Army force north to Canada to seize the British colony once the Confederacy was defeated. These worries were easily understandable given the uneasy early history between the Americans and the British colonies. Many of the elite in Canada were the descendants of United Empire Loyalists, who had fought against Washington in the American War of Independence less than a century before. During the War of 1812, Canadians had torched the president's home in Washington. During its restoration, it was painted white, and eventually became known as the White House. An American victory at Baltimore inspired Francis Scott Key to write "The Star Spangled Banner," which became the American national anthem. Cotton from the Confederacy fuelled the textile mills of England, and the economic ties between the Confederacy and England remained tight throughout the Civil War. Union officials bristled at reports that the rebels were allowed to build war ships in British ports, while Confederate fugitives routinely hid out in Quebec. The presence of the Southerners was so strong in Montreal that writer Cheryl MacDonald notes that one of the city's hotels boasted the best mint juleps north of the Mason-Dixon Line.[4]

Macdonald was troubled during the Civil War by the aggressiveness of Union Army recruiting agents, who were alternately called "crimps," "scalpers," "bounty jumpers," and "substitute brokers." Crimps flashed money about in Upper Canada communities like London and Windsor in what is now southwestern Ontario in attempts to lure civilians and members of the British military into the Union Army ranks. Canadian boys were plied with drinks so that they would sign Union Army enlistment papers, and then were rushed onto the battlefield. Such victims included Charles Lloyd, who was job-hunting in Buffalo when he accepted a soft drink from a stranger and quickly fell unconscious. When Lloyd woke up, he was a member of the Union Army. John Bland Allison, aged 15, was knocked out on a Niagara Region street and deposited on the Michigan, a Union Navy ship. Lloyd managed to desert and Allison was rescued by a Canadian consul, but countless other young Canadians weren't so lucky and didn't live to tell their stories.[5]

Canadian-American tensions reached their nadir on 18 October 1864 when a band of Confederate soldiers left the hospitality and fine mint juleps of Montreal to ride into St. Albans, Vermont. They robbed a bank and killed a man before fleeing back to Canada. There, they were arrested and promptly released with the bank's loot by a Montreal judge. It was all American Secretary of State William Seward could do to keep enraged Union generals from riding into Canada and hitting back hard.

In response to the tensions, Macdonald stationed some two thousand volunteer British militia members along the border, and quietly established the Western Frontier Constabulary to patrol rail lines and border points between the southern Ontario cities of Toronto and Sarnia. In Canada East, similar policing responsibilities were given to the Montreal Water Police. Without any debate or public notice, the colony's Secret Service was born.[6]

The Canada East branch of the secret force was placed under the direction of Montreal police officer William Ermatinger, who had previously specialised in handling crowds in labour disputes. When Macdonald chose a leader for the agency in Canada West, he didn't look to policing or the military, but instead chose an ambitious political ally with a reputation for guarding dangerous secrets. His choice, Gilbert McMicken, a Conservative member of the provincial Parliament for Welland in the Niagara Region of Upper Canada, had worked as a merchant, entrepreneur, inventor, customs collector, warden, land speculator, and mayor of the tiny Niagara community of Clifton, tight against the New York border.

Perhaps an explanation for how McMicken landed the plum post lies in the three years he served for Zimmerman's Bank in the Niagara region. Macdonald was a friend of the bank's chief officer, Samuel

Zimmerman, who was also a railway contractor, ship builder, and hotel owner. McMicken had left Zimmerman's employ in 1857 immediately before the bank became the focus of an enormous fraud scandal. Macdonald must have appreciated that McMicken didn't betray any damaging secrets about his friend Zimmerman to the press, opposition, or police. Macdonald certainly also welcomed McMicken's political support in 1858 and 1859 when he stood up to defend Macdonald in the Legislature no fewer than twenty times.[7]

Macdonald privately described McMicken as a "shrewd, cool, and determined man who won't easily lose his head, and who will fearlessly perform his duty." Sounding oddly like a modern mobster, Macdonald also called McMicken "a friend of ours" as he gave him the title of "stipeniary magistrate."[8] The appointment was not publicly announced, but McMicken was clearly thrilled nonetheless, as shown by a gushing letter he wrote to Macdonald: "I shall do my best to fulfil the duties of the office and act to merit your approbation. . . " McMicken, in his early fifties, bubbled on: "I feel I have 10 good years work in me yet, and if I can only get a foothold on the world again I shall shine. This foothold I. . . receive at your hands and to no one would I sooner be indebted to."[9]

McMicken remained true to his word and answered his call to duty with gusto. By the end of the Civil War, he had recruited about fifteen undercover agents to travel the border regions, seeking out "the existence of any plot, conspiracy or organization whereby peace would be endangered, the Queen's Majesty insulted, or her proclamation of Neutrality infringed." Macdonald's spies were to report to McMicken on Wednesdays and Sundays, and were encouraged to maintain regular jobs to avoid suspicion. It was hardly the first spying done by the British on the Americans or vice versa, but it did bring more structure to the practice of deception. Edward Bancroft, a confidante of top U.S. diplomats during the American Revolution, was in fact a top British spy and his contemporary, Sir Joseph Yorke, the British ambassador to The Hague, kept abreast of political and shipping intrigues with what celebrated historian Barbara Tuchman called "the most organized secret service in Europe."[10]

As the Canadian colonies tightened their border security, a new group of Irish nationalists were making loud noises in America and Ireland. They were more prone to violence than the dreamers of the failed 1848 Young Ireland uprising, and adopted the name Fenians, after an old Irish legend about an unbeatable army called the Fianna that defended the evergreen isle of Éireann against foreign invaders. The Fenians didn't consider themselves as an underground movement, but instead conducted themselves like a government in exile, and raised money by selling bonds, which looked much like American currency. Many of these bonds were bought with funds scraped together by servant girls who cleaned New York's brownstones and ditch-diggers who carved out America's new canals. Once Ireland was a nation once again, they believed they would be repaid with interest in a free republic to call their own.

The Civil War, so horrible for young America, gave weapons, training, and confidence to this new wave of Irish nationalists. When the Irish brigades of the Union Army disbanded, members bought their carbines for a nominal fee, and trained their sights on their real enemy, Great Britain. They were eager to line up once more behind battle-hardened leaders like Thomas Francis Meagher, a hero of the Union Army's Irish Brigade, who had been known since his youth as Meagher of the Sword for his eloquent defence of the use of force to further a righteous cause. Now, with the Civil War over, Meagher and thousands like him yearned to attack Britain, or at least something British.

One faction of the Fenians, led by Young Ireland exile John O'Mahony, advocated armed rebellion in Ireland. The other group, called the Senate wing and led by New York merchant William Roberts, saw Canada as a plump and inviting target, slumbering on the other side of the world's longest unguarded border. Irish-Americans prided themselves on living in a nation without a monarchy, and saw an attack on Canada as a liberation rather than an invasion. What self-respecting Irish man or woman in Canada would not welcome being freed from the British Crown?

Le Caron's old war friend General John O'Neill was a Fenian, and wanted to attack Canada, then swap the colonies with Britain for Ireland.

In 1865, O'Neill told Le Caron about Fenian plans to invade. Seizing and then exchanging colonies, as a child might trade marbles, might seem insane, but far crazier things had been tried countless times in warfare and in the name of patriotism.

The words from O'Neill's lips shocked Le Caron even though he could have read the same scheme in newspapers or heard it in public speeches. Suddenly feeling very English, despite his French name, Le Caron wrote home to his father, with whom he had re-established contact after the Civil War. Presumably, he had explained the youthful deception that had led him to adopt the alias, and the patriotic reasons he had for continuing with the ruse. In the letter, Le Caron described O'Neill's plots to his father in what he called the "careless spirit of a wanderer's notes."

By this time, John J.B. Beach had left his cooper trade to work for the government as a bonding agent and rate collector for the third ward of Colchester. Collecting taxes was a very English job for a very English man. The elder Beach was a patriot who had never travelled more than fifty miles from his home, while his 24-year-old son was at heart an adventurer who craved his father's approval. The Fenian invasion plans gave them a point of connection. On 23 March 1866 Beach wrote a letter in his best handwriting to Edward Cardwell, British secretary of state for foreign affairs:

> *I have a Son who is 1st Lieut. and Adjutant in the Army of the U.S. of America stationed at Nashville Tennessee from where I am continually receiving communications on general events some of which connected with Fenianism are of a startling character especially a correspondence which I received by Post to day dated from Nashville on the 8th [illegible] which I now consider it to be my duty to communicate by way of confirming the accounts which are reaching you from the other side of the Atlantic as to the Power and Magnitude of Fenianism.*
>
> *Fenianism is a Fact, and requires thorough and energetic action to at once extinguish it.*
>
> *My Son is surrounded by Fenians in Nashville, was personally acquainted with the late Genl. Secretary of the 16th [illegible] but now dismissed by the Government for attending a Fenian Congress at New York is also intimate with Capt. O'Neill and are men of standing.*

There is not one Man enrolled in the two Companies mentioned but what has given $200 [worth more than 2,400 dollars U.S. in the early twenty-first century] to the Cause.

My son is acquainted with the Fenian Head Centre of the City of Nashville and he positively informed him that Blood will be shed before a Month.

There are Fenians Hats Coats Songs and Plays with a priminency of Green and almost every thing... calculated to excite and enflame [sic] these ungrateful fanatical bloodthirsty Fenians.

If I can be of any service in obtaining information from some of the Hot Beds of Fenianism in the Southern States expecially, I shall be happy to do so
and remain
Yours Obediently,
John J.B. Beach
Bonding Agent +
Collector of Poor Rates
for the 3rd Ward of
Colchester[11]

Beach was headstrong and confident like his son, and didn't seek his son's permission before he sent the letter off to the home secretary, just like his son didn't ask his permission to sail to America and join the Union Army. Like his son, the elder Beach also didn't seem too concerned by the dangers of espionage work. The elder Beach stopped short of volunteering his son to serve as a spy, but that was the obvious next step in his approach to the government. For Henri Le Caron/Thomas Beach, this meant the chance to please his father, serve his country, and charge himself with surges of adrenalin. If he thought more calmly about it, it also meant placing his life and the lives of his young family in danger.

CHAPTER 4

"ON TO CANADA"

Canadian-American Border, June 1866

I regret to tell you that you are not going to be hanged.
—Fenian leader William Roberts writes to Fenian prisoner

The Fenians planned to fuse speed, power, trickery, and more than a little flair when they seized the Canadian colonies. Some three thousand men stationed in Chicago and Milwaukee would sail across the Great Lakes, march through the smaller communities of Stratford, Paris, Guelph, and Port Colbourne, and then strike simultaneously in London and Hamilton. "This would compel the enemy to concentrate his forces about the meridian of Toronto, uncovering Montreal," reasoned T.W. "Fighting Tom" Sweeny, a one-armed veteran of the Mexican and American civil wars, and now secretary of war for the Fenian Brotherhood.

That would set Phase Two of the Canadian conquest plan into motion. All communication between Upper and Lower Canada would be ruptured by the destruction of St. Ann's Bridge, at the junction of the Ottawa and St. Lawrence rivers, and by attacks on the Grand Trunk Railroad and Beauharnois Canal in southwestern Quebec. A misinformation campaign on the whereabouts of Sweeny would further befuddle the enemy.[1]

The Fenians reasoned that British forces would also be hit hard by attacks from Fenian loyalists inside their own lines. The Fenians were an illegal organisation in the Canadian colonies, but that didn't prevent 17 lodges from being established in Canada West, including nine in Toronto. The most prominent of these underground Canadian members seemed to be Michael Murphy, who ran a bar on the Esplanade in Toronto, and whom the *Globe* newspaper unkindly described as "a vain, excitable, untrustworthy man, not wanting in talent, but without education; vigorous and active, but lacking discretion, and quite incapable of influencing any large body of his countrymen."[2] The invaders fully expected that Murphy and fellow Fenian supporters on Canadian soil would enthusiastically join in the fighting once the invasion began.

McMicken had plenty of intelligence reports from his agents that an attack on the Canadian colonies was in the works for the spring of 1866. Such information wasn't hard to get as Fenians openly bragged about marching on Canada, and about their well-placed friends in Washington. Indeed, Le Caron later noted that John F. Finerty, the editor of the Chicago Citizen, "declared with great glee that Andrew Johnson, the then President of the United States, openly encouraged the movement."[3]

Canadian officials reasoned the likely invasion date was 17 March 1866—St. Patrick's Day. When that day came and went with no invasion, there was a collective sigh of relief.[4] A few weeks later, however, O'Mahony's branch of the Fenians botched an attempt to seize tiny Campobello Island off the coast of New Brunswick. Few people in Canada even knew that the island existed, and the failed invasion attempt did precious little to put it on the map.

Meanwhile, O'Mahony's rivals in Roberts's wing of the Fenians, including O'Neill and Sweeny, went on scheming on a grander scale. Their plan called for 3,000 troops in Chicago and Milwaukee to be joined by 13,000 fellow patriots for a triumphant march across the border into Canada's largest cities, Toronto and Montreal. It was to be a tour de force, a glorious day of conquest for the history books of future generations. "But judge of my surprise on arriving at the front... to find that scarcely 1,000 men had reported to the general commanding the right wing of the army," Sweeny later recalled.

Things only got worse for O'Neill and Sweeny. While there weren't many Fenian troops, there were even fewer rifles for them to fire, even though pains had been taken to deposit weapons along the border at American points like St. Albans, Malone, and Potsdam. The seller of the guns and ammunition was none other than the United States government. However, Sweeny later recalled, the invaders were rudely surprised when they moved to collect their weapons and march on the border: "The United States Government, in selling these stores to my agents, was perfectly well aware of the purpose for which they were intended, and their willingness in allowing these sales to be made, together with the sympathy expressed for us by individuals in eminent positions at Washington, caused me to be totally unprepared for the treacherous seizure of our arms and ammunition, which rendered a successful movement into Canada hopeless, at that time."

In other words, one arm of the American government sold the weapons, while another arm seized them. Sweeny suspected that the White House connived with the British government to stop the invasion after first collecting money to arm the invaders. By the time the frustrated Fenians reached the border at Buffalo, New York, at 3am on June 1, 1866, there were just 700 soldiers—about 15,300 less than the force predicted by Sweeny. Many of those who did report for duty were, in Le Caron's words, "full of whisky and thirsty for glory."[5] Meanwhile, McMicken's agents had filed so many reports predicting their arrival that the British would only have been shocked if they did not invade.

There was a hiccup of glory, however, for Sweeny's men. An hour after their arrival at 4am, the Irish flag was planted on British soil near the tiny Niagara Peninsula community of Ridgeway. The Fenian fun ended a few miles further inland when they were confronted by volunteer soldiers from Toronto, including University of Toronto students, and O'Neill's forces fled back across the American border.

Sweeny was among those arrested in the U.S. for violating America's neutrality laws. As he stewed in jail, he naturally felt betrayed, both by the Americans and members of his own ranks. Later he wrote, ". . . our success would have been certain, even with the number of men that we had, if they had received their arms, ammunition and equipments, as reinforcements were coming rapidly to the front. But even this was paralysed by the [American] Government, as it took possession of the railroads leading to the points of rendezvous, and also the telegraph lines, cutting all our supplies and means of communication, several of our men being turned off the cars while travelling as passengers without arms or equipments."

Officials in the British Home Office were queasy about Canadian plans to hang the rebels captured on colonial soil. They weren't particularly bothered by William Roberts's bold threats that he would muster 21,000 Fenian avengers to swoop into Canada, should such executions be carried out. What worried the Home Office was the prospect of creating martyrs in North America, as Ireland was already full of them.

Governor General Monck was gently asked if the prisoners might be pardoned and sentenced to 20 years of penal servitude instead of the gallows. Roberts was crushed when the Canadians agreed, as is shown in his letter of 30 November 1866 to a condemned man with the unfortunate name of Robert Lynch. One might expect some joy in a letter that tells a man that he would not be hanged by the neck until dead, but this was far from the case. "I regret to tell you that you are not going to be hanged," Roberts wrote. "So great a crime upon a non-combatant like ourself would make every Irishman in America a Fenian, and furnish our exchequer with the necessary means to clear Canada of English authority in short order."[6]

The Fenian attacks accelerated a push to mould the colonies of Canada West and Canada East into a single nation, and they were joined together as the Dominion of Canada on 1 July 1867. John A. Macdonald, the man who had mobilised the secret police force, became Canada's first prime minister. The Fenians, who plotted to conquer a colony, had helped forge it into a nation instead.

Le Caron's amateur intelligence-gathering activities stimulated his sense of patriotism and provided a bonding experience with his father, but spying didn't pay the bills. He needed a stable income to support Nannie and baby Henry, and an old army comrade suggested that he become a physician. This was during the time of the "barber surgeon," when an MD degree could be earned in two years. It didn't matter that Le

Caron had dropped out of school before his teenage years, and he was soon accepted at Rush Medical College in Chicago, where many other aspiring doctors of the time were equally, or even more, uneducated. In these days before anaesthetics, physicians were not expected to have a sweeping knowledge of science. It was far more valuable to possess the stomach of an abattoir worker and the quick sawing skills of a lumberjack, as pre-anaesthetic operations were routinely held in basements or attics of hospitals, so that the loud screams of patients would not disturb others.

The Clerkenwell House of Detention sat in northern London, in a built-up residential area of concrete and brick known to Charles Dickens's readers as the lair of fictitious arch-thief Fagin. A Clerkenwell cell was home in the late 1860s to Irish-American Richard Burke, a weapons supplier for the Fenians. By late 1867, details of a plot to spring Burke from Clerkenwell reached the desk of Robert Anderson in Dublin Castle, the nerve centre for the British government in Ireland for eight centuries.

Anderson was born in 1841 and, like Le Caron, drifted into espionage, in large measure through his father's influence. Anderson's father, Matthew, was a Crown solicitor in Ireland, prosecuting state trials in 1865 against Fenians charged with treason. Matthew Anderson trusted his eldest son, Samuel, to help out and, in turn, Samuel enlisted his brother Robert, sharing with him all the confidential reports and secret information that crossed his desk. While Robert Anderson got his job through nepotism, like countless other British civil servants, he was nonetheless a competent man, able to work with the quiet patience and efficiency of a spider.[7] Intelligence gathering was interesting stuff for Anderson, but not his chief passion. That remained his evangelical religion. Cool and analytical when assessing police intelligence reports, he was, beneath the surface, a passionately religious man. He was sure, among other things, that his Bible studies had allowed him to calculate the exact date of the next coming of Christ.

Irish nationalists profoundly distrusted "castle rats" like the Andersons. English invader Oliver Cromwell, whose forces killed some four thousand Irish in the town of Drogheda alone, was a former resident of Dublin Castle. Months before reports of the Clerkenwell plot reached Anderson's desk, hundreds of Fenians had been herded into the castle square to await executions, deportations, and imprisonment after a failed uprising. It didn't escape notice that a statue in the castle courtyard of a woman who supposedly represented impartial justice didn't have her eyes totally closed, or that the scales of justice that she held seemed to tip with just a little rain.

There was no formal secret service organisation or intelligence department at Dublin Castle when Robert Anderson began his work there. Instead, he found an unruly pile of documents on Irish affairs in an office cupboard. Anderson had the paperwork of the Irish file well under control by late 1867 when the reports crossed his desk about the plot to spring Burke from the Clerkenwell House of Detention. He wrote a detailed description of the scheme for the Home Office and Scotland Yard. Meanwhile, the secretary of state forwarded a further warning to the House of Commons that on 12 December 1867: "The rescue of Richard Burke from prison in London is contemplated. The plan is to blow up the exercise walls by means of gunpowder; the hour between [illegible]; and 4pm; and the signal for all right, a white ball thrown up outside when he is at exercise."

So there was no surprise, at 4pm on 12 December when a white ball was lobbed over the wall of the Clerkenwell exercise ground. Authorities watched keenly as Burke immediately feigned that there was a stone in his shoe, and retreated into a corner of the yard. He braced himself for the explosion, and was shocked to hear... nothing. The bomb's fuse was damp.

The next day, police secretly watched again as another white ball was tossed over the stone wall at Clerkenwell as another warning to Burke. They kept watching as a barrel of powder was rolled up outside the detention centre. Again, Burke retreated quickly to a corner of the yard. Police continued to watch mutely as the bomb demolished much of the prison wall, as well as a nearby row of tenement houses, killing 12 people and injuring an estimated 120.

With that explosion, apathy about terrorism was suddenly replaced by what Anderson called "unreasoning panic." Communist thinker Karl Marx, then a resident of London's gritty downtown Soho district, noted the blast had a profound effect on the British working classes, writing: "The London masses, who have shown great sympathy towards Ireland, will be made wild and driven into the arms of a reactionary government. One cannot expect the London proletarians to allow themselves to be blown up in honour of Fenian emissaries."

There was an emergency British Cabinet meeting the day after the explosion, a Saturday, and by Monday, plans were afoot for the enrolment of 50,000 special constables in London alone. Twice as many officers were dispatched to the outlying regions. Cabinet also set up a secret service department, although this was only intended as a temporary measure, and Anderson was summoned from Dublin to serve in it. "When I came to London the following week, the scheme submitted to me was that we should take up our quarters in a private house in some quiet street and 'work underground,'" Anderson later recalled. "To this I objected, not only for professional reasons, but because I believed that secrecy on such lines would be impossible. In Mexico, it is said, people speak the truth only when they wish to deceive; and a display of openness is always a good screen for secrecy."

Coincidentally, Le Caron was in England at the time for his first visit with his parents since he ran away from home to Paris as a teenager. Now, he was 26 years old, a war veteran, a father, and a medical student.[8] He was also a potential professional spy. His father was now clearly proud of his formerly restless, troublesome son, who had balked years before when pushed to accept less glamorous, but more safe and secure, work as a draper. John Beach showed his son the letters he had recently received from government officials concerning his warnings about Fenianism. Le Caron clearly relished his new hero/patriot status in the family. "Poor old father!" Le Caron later wrote. "Never was a Briton prouder than he of the service he had been enabled to do his country—services unpaid and as purely patriotic as ever Englishman rendered."[9]

Local Liberal member of Parliament John Gurdon-Rebow was also clearly impressed when, on 17 December 1867, he wrote to an associate in government named Adderley from Gurdon-Rebow's state at Wivenhoe Park in Colchester:

> You will remember my speaking to you, just before the adjournment of the House the other day, respecting the son of a person living at Colchester who is in the United States Military Service; owing to the reduction working in the U.S. army he is reduced & is over here for a few weeks to see his father & mother. I have just had some conversation with him on Fenian matters & I write to inquire whether you or the D. of Buckingham would like to have some conversation with him; He only remains here a fortnight having to return to the U. States. . . . If you or any confidential person, would like to see him I could arrange with him a meeting. He seems however to be a little afraid of being identified by the Fenians here in London. To many of them he is personally known . . . so that if you would name any other rendezvous. . . I believe there are no Fenians at Colchester. . .[10]

Le Caron was invited to a meeting at a townhouse at 50 Harley Street in a posh London neighbourhood, about five minutes' walk from Regent's Park. He wasn't surprised when the offer was made for him to enter into direct contact with the Home Office and to become a British spy within Fenian ranks. Le Caron didn't need time to think about his reply: "My adventurous nature prompted me to sympathy with the idea; my British instincts made me a willing worker from a sense of right, and my past success promised good things for the future." And it certainly didn't hurt that his once-distant father now considered him a patriotic hero.

As they met in the townhouse, the city of London appeared to be under siege. Police and soldiers stood guard over the South Kensington Museum, British Museum, gas factories, and powder magazines. "By every post Ministers received letters from panic-stricken folk, or from lunatics or cranks, reporting suspicious incidents, or giving warning of plots upon public or private property," Anderson later recalled. He was unsettled to hear that government private secretaries were now carrying revolvers, amid reports that the Fenians were plotting assassinations and the torching of public buildings and private houses. Daily newspaper accounts warned of impending "Fenian Fire" or "Greek Fire," a burning-liquid weapon used by the Byzantine Greeks in naval battles, which blazed even on water like the fires of Hell. Readers were cautioned to keep a supply of sand on hand to quell fires just in case they were set ablaze by assassins.

Ironically, Robert Anderson later learned that the attack on the Clerkenwell Detention Centre was not the planning of the Fenian hierarchy, but rather the work of Irish residents of London, acting independently. However, Fenian leaders saw the panic the explosion generated and decided further attacks were a good idea. As Anderson later noted, ". . . when they discovered that, by exploding a cask of gunpowder, they could throw not only the public but the Government of this country into hysterics, they rallied from their fright, and set themselves to profit by the lesson."[11]

CHAPTER 5

CANADIAN SPY

1868

A man who will engage to do what he offers to do, that is to betray those with
whom he acts, is not to be trusted.

—Sir John A. Macdonald on spy Henri Le Caron

General John O'Neill was delighted when Le Caron volunteered
his military services to the Fenian cause shortly after his return
to North America, and immediately found him work as an
organiser within the Irish Republican Brotherhood.[1] The year 1868 was
an American election year, meaning, in the words of Canadian prime
minister John A. Macdonald, the "Republicans and Democrats will fish
for the Irish vote, and therefore will wink as much as possible at any
action of the Fenian body."[2]

Within months of enlisting with the Fenians, Le Caron was in the
Oval Office of the White House, grandly introduced to the president by
O'Neill as Major Henri Le Caron. Things were moving quickly now as
Le Caron was reporting to the Canadian prime minister and the British
Home Office under the code names Thomas, Dr. Howard, R.G., R.G.
Sayer, and Informant B.

As he sat in the Oval Office, Le Caron made a mental record of the
president's reaction to the latest plot to invade Canada. As Le Caron
later recalled, Johnson told O'Neill that he couldn't be blamed for the
failure of the similar scheme to seize Canada in 1866: "General, your
people unfairly blame me a good deal for the part I took in stopping
your first movement. Now I want you to understand that my sympathies

are entirely with you, and anything which lies in my power I am willing to do to assist you. But you must remember that I gave you five full days before issuing any proclamation stopping you. What, in God's name, more did you want? If you could not get there in five days, by God, you could never get there; and then, as President, I was compelled to enforce the Neutrality Laws, or be denounced on every side."

Le Caron was stunned. It was as if the president of the United States was apologising to an Irish revolutionary.[3] As he sat in President Johnson's White House office, Le Caron masked his deep fears that if the Fenians struck quickly and hard this time, tiny Canada would be easy pickings.

On 20 February 1868 Le Caron wrote a letter to his father in Colchester that described how he was burrowed deeply into the Irish revolutionary movement. Before this date, his letters didn't contain much that couldn't be gleaned by a careful reading of newspapers. Now, he was clearly a high-level insider, writing: "Canada is as I told you before their field of action this coming spring, and [American president] Andy Johnson's administration will not impede their progress a great deal. He said only a few days ago at an interview when the subject was mentioned, 'I have always sympathized with this movement but a man can't always do officially what he feels unofficially. . .'"[4]

Le Caron certainly caught the interest of top levels of the Canadian and British governments with a letter he wrote directly to Prime Minister Macdonald on 9 March 1868 from Chicago. He warned of an assassination plot against the Prince of Wales, and signed it Donald Mackay:

> I must tell you that I was one of a council of five who met ostensibly to contract for some fire arms, but the enclosed subject was very unwittingly broached and those congregeated [sic] believing [sic] each other bound by sacred ties enough to commit any crime it was freely aired. I for one care nothing for such friendship when it results in meditated assassination.
>
> And when I tell you that the subject was no less than the killing of the Princes [sic] of Wales by poison or the dagger, you may feel surprised as I was. And I give you details to prevent any innocent persons from being included in the disgrace which must follow.

The plan is a plausible one. Three men, hired assassins, who have no connection whatever with the Fenian order, leave the country supplied with money, recommendations etc for the entrée into any place which they will be called upon to enter, and under guise of business, pleasure of what may best suit, are to accomplish by any foul means they may see fit to use, the death of the Prince of Wales or any noble which will cread a panic in England, and amidst the confusion which may follow, use every advantage gained to carry their hellish plot further.

They receive, upon accomplishment $25,000 a piece and upon attempt and failure one half of that amount.[5]

It was almost too wild to consider. But so was an attack on the Clerkenwell Detention Centre until its walls and those of neighbouring houses were blasted open. Three days after Le Caron sent the letter to the Canadian prime minister, a gunman shot and badly injured Queen Victoria's son, Prince Alfred, at a picnic in Clontarf, near Sydney, Australia. Some members of the crowd fainted and sobbed, while others struggled to get at the gunman so they could beat him to death. Order prevailed and the attacker was rescued by police, so that he could be properly hanged.

On 16 March Le Caron wrote to Canada's governor general, Lord Monck, from Lockport, outside Chicago. The letter, signed Donald Mackay, warned again that three hired killers were on their way from America to England in an attempt to kill the Prince of Wales.[6]

Thomas D'Arcy McGee knew the only people that Irish revolutionaries loathed more than the British, politicians, and spies were former revolutionaries who loudly renounced their views. In 1868, McGee was a politician and a former revolutionary surrounded by men who would gladly end his life. Since fleeing to Canada, dressed as a priest, after the 1848 uprising, the poet and former darling of the independence movement had grown progressively more conservative until he was a Father of Confederation for Canada, and a friend of Canada's first prime minister, John A. Macdonald. McGee and Macdonald often differed on political matters, which might be expected, as McGee was a Roman Catholic and Macdonald a Protestant Orangeman. However, Macdonald cared for McGee enough as a friend and a colleague to once counsel him to watch his health and curb his drinking. "Look here,

McGee," the prime minister said, "this Government can't afford two drunkards and you've got to stop."[7]

The more McGee advocated education and political involvement over violence for the Irish, the more he feared for his own life. Despite his worries, he refused to back down or hide his contempt for the militaristic Fenians. "These men deserve death," McGee told a gathering in Ireland. "I repeat deliberately, these men deserve death."[8]

Perhaps McGee calmed his nerves with puffs on a cigar on the evening of 7 April 1868, as he walked from an evening debate in Parliament in Ottawa to his room in a downtown boarding house on Sparks Street. The cigar was half smoked by the time he reached his quarters, and he likely didn't hear the footsteps of the man who had followed him. There was a full moon that night, and if McGee turned in the direction of the footsteps, he certainly would have seen the stranger's face. McGee probably noticed the man by the time he was pulling open his apartment door, but by then it was too late as the bullet from Fenian sympathiser Patrick Whelan shot through his skull. Macdonald heard of the attack within minutes of the gunshots, and rushed to his friend's doorway. The prime minister cradled McGee's limp, bleeding head on his chest until a wagon carried the body away.[9]

There were rumours that Macdonald would be the next target for a Fenian assassin, and that perhaps the prime minister's own chauffeur was part of the conspiracy. The Fenian Brotherhood rushed to publicly distance itself from the assassination. Three days after the shooting, members of the Fenian Brotherhood packed Greenwood Hall in Cincinnati, where Le Caron's old friend, General John O'Neill said:

> I feel constrained, my friends, to refer to an incident which happened a few days ago. I refer to the assassination of Thomas D'Arcy McGee. It was a cowardly, atrocious act, and no man with a drop of Irish blood in his veins could be guilty of it. The man who would murder a fellow being in cold blood is a dastardly coward. [applause] It has been charged by some of the newspapers throughout the country, that the assassination was planned by, and carried out by the Fenian organization. I am proud to stand here as a representative of that organization, and pronounce these statements a base lie, a lie made out of whole cloth. . . We are not cowardly assassins, going about seeking plunder. We are

> *honourable men, making war for the liberation of our oppressed countrymen.*
> *We are Christians, and propose to make war as Christians.*[10]

Le Caron wrote to the Home Office and Canadian government that McGee's assassination didn't appear to be connected to the top levels of the Fenian organisation. O'Neill still held out hope that he might lead a successful invasion into Canada, and didn't fancy himself as heading a gang of midnight assassins. O'Neill also feared the Canadian government's attention as he attempted to regroup for his next offensive. "The Fenian party has been much injured by the murder of D'Arcy McGee being fastened upon it," Le Caron wrote. "O'Neill repudiates that outrage, and probably so sincerely."[11]

Macdonald wasn't taking any chances. That month he revived border security, setting up a twelve-member Dominion police force. He appointed his old political ally, McMicken, as commissioner and installed Judge Charles-Joseph Coursol to handle the force in Quebec. Their duties were Secret Service work, including the protection of Parliament and other government buildings, and they also had the responsibility of fighting federal crimes, like mail theft and counterfeiting. Small as the force was, McMicken seemed eager to go deeper into the world of espionage, and suggested to Macdonald that female agents might be able to entrap some of the Fenians: "One plan presents itself to me and that is this—that one or two clever women. . . be obtained who. . . could get some of the susceptible members of the [Fenian] Senate into their toils. . . I went to Baltimore to see a woman of this stamp. I failed in seeing her personally but ascertained she might be secured for such a purpose."[12] Exactly what became of the "clever" Baltimore woman remains a mystery. Meanwhile, McMicken's male agents keenly watched over Lockport, Rochester, Brooklyn, Chicago, Buffalo, and key Canadian border points. McMicken was particularly excited that his agents included Le Caron, who was now communicating to him under the code name of R.G. Sayer. They also devised a crude code for their communications. Le Caron's telegrams looked like a merchant's business correspondence, with "cheese" meaning "arms," "fulfil the contract" meaning "start fighting," and "Brady" meaning "O'Neill."

McMicken wrote to Macdonald from his home in Windsor, on the Michigan border, to tell him about the spy whom Macdonald already knew as Donald Mackay:

My Dear Sir John

The person who wrote from Lockport and Chicago, Illinois, pursuant to arrangement made came to Detroit to see me. I had a lengthy interview with him yesterday afternoon and another today. The facts he revealed to me abundantly [illegible] his being thoroughly up to all that is going on. He also produced the most satisfactory testimonial to warrant his being relied upon. He is an Englishman by birth, went to France, there adopted the name of Le Caron which he has borne during his residences in the United States, now about 8 years. He is married, has a wife and two children—has been in confidential correspondence with the British authority, only as late as last March he [illegible] a remittance of £60 sterling from Cap. Hozier. He was in the Am. Army during the war was much with O'Neill as they both served under Genl Rosencranzy. He holds a Captains commission the IRA but O'Neill + others urged him to go out. . . and seek an appointment on O'Neills staff when the movement began. To do this he would have to throw up his situation in which he hast at present and he has no other support for his family. They only pay $60 a month to their officials and this would not be certain or of any duration. . .

What he has stipulated for is this—that he will enter the service as an organizer. Will accept a position on O'Neill's staff. Will run the risk consequent upon any actual engagement on Canadian soil looking to his Opportunity to escape or taken as a prisoner in which case permission is to be made for his safety. He is to furnish me from time to time with correct information as they proceed in the work and in one season inform me of the actual points of attack with all particulars in order that we may be prepared for them. I am to pay him $100 Am per month for the two or three months. . . Providing his services are as valuable as he supposes they will be, he is to receive a suitable recommendation. . . to the Home Government as a means of obtaining from them some birth or employment as his life would no longer be safe in America. . . he and family are to be provided with passage to England. His father lives in Colchester in Essex England and is in some situation under the government.

There can be no doubt of this person's information. In him appears the best opportunity as afforded of correct and timely information being had of the contemplated movement and if he renders services he presumes he can I think his conditions are not at all extravagant. . .

I remain

My Dear sir John

Yours most faithfully
GM McMicken[13]

A week later, on 15 June 1868 Macdonald wrote back, saying he had no problem with paying Le Caron $150 a month (worth a little under two thousand dollars U.S. in early 21st Century terms), or in offering him a suitable recommendation for future employment if he lived up to his billing. However, the Canadian prime minister also cautioned: "A man who will engage to do what he offers to do, that is to betray those with whom he acts, is not to be trusted."[14]

Within days, McMicken wrote again to Macdonald, telling him of a report Le Caron had just filed from Chicago, which told how an IRA leader had said, "for God's sake do your best to make our people understand that we are prepared for an immediate campaign... we must make history for ourselves." McMicken added that Le Caron had been instructed by the British Home Office to also be in communication with Governor General Monck. "I think the arrangement I made with him is quite to his satisfaction and I fully believe he is the best 'Card' we have got yet," McMicken added optimistically.[15]

McMicken wrote to Macdonald again on 18 June reporting that Le Caron estimated the movement had about thirty-five thousand dollars (about four hundred and eighty thousand dollars today) on hand. Their security was getting tighter in anticipation of their next invasion attempt. "He says the meeting of Sunday evening last was one very carefully conducted, he says 'under advice from Head Quarters a countersign has been instituted without which no one can possibly gain admittance.'"[16]

Eleven days later, McMicken was able to send the prime minister a recent circular from O'Neill at Fenian headquarters in New York to its 524 "circles" or cells of members across the United States. Among other things, O'Neill warned members to be on the lookout for spies: "As British spies both male and female are very numerous and active at the present time especially in those States which border on Canadian Territory, I would caution the members of the Organization against speaking with any person except those they know to be members in good standing on matters relating to the Brotherhood. And as it is feared that some of these spies have joined circles in several places, and are very loud in their love of Ireland and denunciation of British rule, the true men of the Brotherhood cannot be too much on their guard."[17]

McMicken was clearly optimistic when he wrote to Macdonald on 7 July: "This month I verily believe will dissolve the O'Neill phase of Fenianism entirely. . . The day of their power of evil is I trust gone by. . . Chief informant [Le Caron] now occupies an excellent position and writes me daily."[18]

Le Caron followed up by including comments from a recent letter sent from Fenian headquarters to officers and members, again stressing how the movement was going underground. It warned "Be Reticent" and continued, "Silence is not only a virtue but in all matters pertaining to the objects intentions and workings of our organization is an absolute necessity. Every member of the Brotherhood should carefully guard against discussing or conversing on our affairs in public. . . The country is swarming with his spies and his agents, and the utmost caution is demanded. . ."[19]

Throughout that summer, Le Caron wrote to Ottawa about pistols and ammunition that were shipped to St. Albans in small schooners, and how O'Neill was thinking of sending him to lead a cavalry unit of 150 men from Chicago to somewhere in western Ontario. The purpose would be as a diversionary tactic, by "a system of rapid marching and depredations strike terror among the people creating a great consternation as possible." The Fenians had apparently scrapped an earlier plan for an attack on the west coast of British Columbia as well. "They were to seize and occupy Victoria, in British America, from which place privateers could be sent out to prey upon British commerce in the Pacific," Sweeny later wrote.[20]

On 29 August McMicken sent Macdonald a blunt, urgent message. He was about to meet with Le Caron in Massachusetts, and he urged the prime minister to be ready to act with dispatch and discretion: "military all over. . . rapidly. You must have everything ready to move at any minute. Yet at same time keep your preparations and information dark. They are earnest and bound to make a raid in a short time. . ."[21]

By this time, Le Caron was head of a Fenian circle in Lockport, Illinois, holding the position of "centre" or commander. He wasn't a doctor yet and supported himself with work at the Norton Flour Mill in the town.[22] His status within the circle meant he received all official reports and documents issued by O'Neill, which were immediately mailed to his political masters in Canada and Britain. Le Caron reasoned that the attack would come in the fall of 1868 before an American presidential election when both major parties were wooing the Irish vote. By October, the invasion still hadn't begun, and Le Caron was now hearing that O'Neill was planning to recruit some leading Confederate generals, including Pierre Gustave Toutant de Beauregard, who had opened fire on Fort Sumter in Charleston Harbor to start the Civil War; Wade Hampton III, who was wounded five times in the first Battle of Bull Run; and Nathan Bedford Forrest, a former slave trader and founder of the Ku Klux Klan, who fought opposite Le Caron at Murfreesboro, Chickamauga, and Nashville. Soon that scheme fizzled too, and Le Caron was writing McMicken to say that the Fenian invasion of Canada was postponed until the following spring.

Le Caron's chief British contact, Robert Anderson, was a naturally tidy and discreet man, and Le Caron grew to respect his marked ability to keep a secret. This extreme discretion wasn't just an admirable personality trait, but also a reason why Le Caron was still alive. Anderson's early days on the job only reinforced his natural inclination towards silence. He was shaken by the fate of an earlier informer, who had reported to Lord Mayo, then chief secretary for Ireland. The spy's name had been mentioned at an official dinner at the Viceregal Lodge in Phoenix Park in Dublin, and his name overheard by a servant. Soon afterwards, the agent was shot dead. From that point on, Anderson refused to speak the names of informers or pass on their letters, and at one point, a frustrated Sir William Harcourt, Britain's secretary of state, accurately remarked that "Anderson's idea of secrecy is not to tell the Secretary of State."[23]

Back in Illinois, things were improving financially for Le Caron, who now had two children to support: Henry and baby Ida. His former regimental surgeon helped him secure a position with steady pay at the Illinois State Penitentiary in Joliet as hospital steward or resident medical officer. An aggressively positive contemporary local history proudly noted that each Joliet inmate had the benefit of a Bible in his or her cell. It continued that "The prisoners are under good and kind discipline, and no efforts seemed to be spared, consistent with their safe-keeping and the ends of justice, to secure their physical, moral and religious comfort and improvement."[24] In reality, if prisoners didn't know much about graft and corruption when they were sentenced, they had every opportunity to learn these dark skills from fellow inmates and penitentiary staff. "Corruption was in every place," Le Caron later noted, ". . . money could accomplish everything, from the obtaining of luxuries in prison to the purchase of pardon and freedom itself. Everything connected with the prison administration was rotten to the core."[25]

For the right price, prisoners could eat at the governor's table, wear their own clothes, and strut about the facility like the lord of a manor. At the top of this pyramid of graft was a man known as the King of Forgers or, more properly, as Colonel Cross. The son of a prominent Episcopalian clergyman, Cross was well versed in theology, medicine, science, the law, and hypocrisy. He dressed fashionably, smoked the best cigars, dined at the governor's table, and loved to brag that he had never robbed a poor man, which made him sound like a midwestern Robin Hood. There's no record of anyone being so rude as to point out that there wasn't much gain in robbing poor men. Cross's time was spent helping fellow prisoners with their legal appeals, but he asked Le Caron if he could also be his assistant in the hospital. Le Caron consented, and soon was hearing stories of Cross's "tricks with the pen," including how he had forged his own release permit from Sing Sing Prison in Ossining, New York, on notepaper and an envelope bearing the seal of the state governor.[26]

The possibilities, both good and bad, seemed endless in Le Caron's adopted country for those with enough money and gall.

CHAPTER 6

IRA Organiser

April 1868

. . . transacting the duties of their various positions with all the pomp and ceremony usually associated with the representatives of the greatest nations on earth.

—Henri Le Caron describes Fenian headquarters in Manhattan

The telegram to Le Caron from General O'Neill in New York City was short and to the point: "Come at once, you are needed for work."[1] With those eight words, Le Caron was summoned to the Fenian headquarters in a townhouse mansion at 10 West 4th Street in Greenwich Village, near Washington Square.[2] The brownstone had the impressive look of an embassy, which was exactly the effect leaders like O'Neill desired. It was a far cry from the desperate lot of the Fenian supporters living in nearby Five Points and Hell's Kitchen, which was a jumble of high-rise squalor near Times Square west of 8th Avenue and between 34th and 59th streets, described by *Gangs of New York* author Herbert Asbury as "the most dangerous area on the American continent."

O'Neill's terse telegram was a call-to-arms for Le Caron, who was expected to immediately leave his pleasant, interesting prison job, with its steady pay cheque, halt his medical studies, and accept less security and safety for his family. There was also a personal price as Nannie had befriended the wife of the prison's chief physician. Nannie knew about her husband's secret life as a spy, but kept this a guarded secret from even her closest friends. Despite the costs, there was no question about Le Caron's answer. The telegram from O'Neill offered a chance to further impress his father, satisfy his need for adventure, and explode the world of the Fenian revolutionaries. It also gave him a fuzzy sense of righteousness, even though he never thought too deeply about political theory. He quickly offered his resignation to the prison warden, who listened with a mixture of disgust and disbelief.

Inside the grand Fenian Brotherhood headquarters, Le Caron found O'Neill, now the brotherhood president, surrounded by staff and underlings, "transacting the duties of their various positions with all the pomp and ceremony usually associated with the representatives of the greatest nations on earth." Le Caron was installed as a major and military organiser of the Irish Republican Army, which brought a salary of $60 per month, plus $7 a day expenses. His task was nothing less than organising the different Irish military bodies in the eastern states under the Fenian umbrella.

Le Caron loved the idea that he was now able to simultaneously collect payment from the Fenians and British while helping them plot against each other. His duties included addressing public meetings, and his first speaking engagement was with O'Neill, in the Brooklyn neighbourhood of Williamsburg. Le Caron knew precious little about Ireland's struggle for independence, and he wasn't particularly comfortable with public speaking either.

There seemed to be no safe way out of the speech, although he kept grasping for one as he entered Williamsburg. Wild enthusiasm greeted Le Caron and O'Neill when they arrived at the hall, and it didn't hurt that Le Caron's name was mispronounced by the meeting's chairman as "Major M'Caron." It was O'Neill's job to tell the chairman which speaker to call next, and each time O'Neill whispered a name, Le Caron felt a fresh surge of panic.

Speeches were long, speakers were plentiful, and the crowd kept interrupting with applause. Le Caron was buoyed by the possibility that he might not have to speak at all. Perhaps he would only have to feign disappointment that there wasn't time for him to take the podium. He was feeling the glow of this possibility when he heard O'Neill whisper to the chairman to call him as the next speaker. His heart pumped wildly and his head felt ready to explode. The crowd cheered enthusiastically and Le Caron somehow felt buoyed by the sheer magnitude of his fraud.[3]

Le Caron told the crowd of his pride at being among the Fenians at such a magnificent meeting, which was true in a sense. He promised he would not detain them for too long, which certainly was true again. The previous speakers had been so on point, and so inspiring, that he had little left to say. Now he was clearly lying, but the audience lapped up his gracious words. In these pre-television days, such speeches weren't just politics, they were entertainment as well, and Le Caron's platitudes filled some inner void for the crowd before him. He began to tell the audience that if what he had experienced that evening was indicative of the spirit of the Irish in America. . . He did not have to complete the thought, as his words were drowned out by the din of cheers.

When audience members finally quieted enough for him to resume speaking, Le Caron said he knew they were eager to hear from the "Hero of Ridgeway," General O'Neill himself. The applause was now absolutely out of control. The crowd had the chance to show their affection for a genuine, real-life, Irish-American hero. True, the Ridgeway operation in the Niagara region of Canada wasn't a great military success. True also, O'Neill spent roughly as much time retreating as he did occupying British soil around Ridgeway. But the fact remained that O'Neill had planted an Irish flag before his ungraceful flight, and Le Caron wasn't about to break the jubilant spell with depressing facts or qualifiers. He pressed on a little further at the podium, saying that, in conclusion, he could simply beg them as lovers of liberty and their shared motherland. . . Again, the thought didn't have to be finished as an eruption of cheering drowned him out yet again. Le Caron soldiered on at the podium, through the applause, entreating them to place at the disposal of General O'Neill the funds necessary to carry out their holy cause, the liberation of Ireland from 700 years of tyrant's rule.

As the applause climaxed yet again, Le Caron realised just how little it took to rouse these Irish zealots. He considered his audience poor and deluded, and felt he could hoodwink them as easily as those he considered "unprincipled, blatant, professional Irish patriots," who stood with him that evening.

In London, a far quieter, but nonetheless significant event took place, which was barely noticed, let alone applauded. By April 1868 the public panic over the Clerkenwell bloodshed had abated, and the British government's secret anti-terrorism office was quietly shut down. Robert Anderson remained in London as a liaison with Dublin Castle, but now his anti-terrorism duties were severely diluted and he worked virtually alone.[4] The wall between Britain and potential attackers was very thin indeed.

CHAPTER 7

DAILY DISPATCHES

Cleveland, 1868

. . . night after night [I] have to speak & associate with a pack of low dirty foul mouthed beings—worse than niggers.

—Henri Le Caron to British spymaster Robert Anderson

The deeper Le Caron slipped into the Fenian fold, the closer he grew to his Canadian spymaster, Gilbert McMicken. "I found him ever ready and willing to help me, meeting at a moment's notice, placing everything at my disposal, and watching over my safety and my interests with a fatherly care which I shall ever recall with thoughts of the keenest appreciation."[1]

Le Caron and his British spymaster, Robert Anderson, were like brothers. On 19 November 1868 Le Caron wrote to Anderson using his birth name, Thos. Beach, which was strangely incautious. The letter was from Cleveland, after Le Caron had toured Fenian troops there and in Michigan and Illinois. He reported that Fenian ranks had fallen off by about 25 per cent due to frustration that there still hadn't been another attack on Canada. "Everyone is disheartened & consider the only favourable opportunity lost," Le Caron reported. However, O'Neill hadn't given up, and optimistically told Le Caron: "Our final preparations are now so far on the road to completion that one more bold earnest and determined effort on the trail of the organization will place us in a position at an early day to unfurl once more the green flag of our fathers."

Le Caron's report made it clear that the strength of the Fenians was unbreakably bound to the mainstream American political system. The Americans won their freedom on the battlefield against the British less than a century before, and now, the Fenians felt, it was Ireland's turn to repeat the process and establish a republic of their own. The revolutionaries did have concerns that they might just be used for votes if they didn't assert themselves, as Le Caron wrote:

> James C. Downey of Providence will be made Senator. Dunne will be thrown out. The Republican local politicians of Cin gave the orga 100 uniforms for their votes. [Indiana Republican Congressman Schuyler] Colfax made three contributions at various places. Irish changed Chicago. To 5000 rep majority & everybody feels the Irish have done a good thing & gained power with the Rep Party & caused the Dem. Party to value them more in future. O'N was not wise in forbidding officials to take a hand in American politics for it has caused several of his best men to leave the org—all condemn him for it they consider that as the Rep & Dem. Parties only care for the Irish to use them for voting purposes, the Irish all when the opportunity presents itself use them in return.

Then, Le Caron signed off his letter with a paragraph that showed utter contempt for Irish nationalists, as well as for African-Americans, presumably including those whom he had led and helped free during the Civil War: "I am anxiously waiting to hear from you whether or not you wish me to continue in my present capacity or not. Tis a thankless office as it exists not certainty from either side & night after night have to speak & associate with a pack of low, dirty, foul mouthed beings—worse than niggers."[2]

It's a horribly racist comment, and he clearly wasn't worried about upsetting his spymaster. For context, but not justification, it's important to remember that just 35 years before, slavery was legal in the British Empire and that when America was founded, a sixth of its residents were slaves. Indeed, John and Quincy Adams were the only presidents between the founding of the nation and 1850 who didn't own slaves. Even Abraham Lincoln, "The Great Emancipator," is sadly lacking by modern standards. In his inaugural address on 4 March 1861, Lincoln wasn't prepared to challenge slavery, saying, "I have no purpose, directly or indirectly, to interfere with the institution of slavery in the States where it exists. I have no lawful right to do so, and I have no inclination to do so." Expediency, not altruism, pushed the president to alter this stance during the war, and write to Andrew Johnson, his military governor of Tennessee, that slaves represented a "great available and yet unavailed of, force for restoring the Union."

There was a Fenian council of war in upstate New York in Troy at the Troy House in November 1868 that brought Le Caron in contact with John Roche, considered a leading Fenian in the area. All of the Fenians now seemed particularly nervous about spies in their midst, but even in that environment, Roche stood out as hypercritical and suspicious. As Le Caron later recalled, "He had been, I discovered, originally a resident of Montreal, and as I had been instructed by O'Neill to visit and study the enemy's country, I indicated to Roche my desire of ascertaining the names of a few reliable brothers whom I could visit. The truth was that the Canadian Government were at this time particularly anxious to find out the extent of the organization which they knew existed in several of their large cities, notably Montreal, Kingston, and Toronto; and I thought this a good opportunity of getting some useful hints."[3]

Roche told him the names of several leading Canadian Fenians, then watched as Le Caron wrote them down in a book. A month later, Le Caron and Roche were together again at the Masonic Hall in Philadelphia, the site of the Fenians' annual convention. They were among some four hundred delegates, and their arrival was celebrated by no less than six thousand armed and uniformed Fenian soldiers parading the streets. When O'Neill talked once again of marching on Canada, the support was overwhelming. Discussion also included a report from the sister organization in Ireland about the Clerkenwell House of Detention explosion. That blast had jolted British Prime Minister Gladstone into more serious consideration of greater autonomy for Ireland. Now, Fenians at the convention wondered if even more explosions might shorten their path to independence.

The arrival of John Boyle O'Reilly at the convention created a frisson of excitement. O'Reilly was handsome and cheerful, "with good feelings running back from every pore of his nature, like refreshing water from a perennial spring," in the words of Irish revolutionary Michael Davitt. O'Reilly was editor of the *Boston Pilot*, the Catholic newspaper where Thomas D'Arcy McGee had been editor years before, back when McGee called for the American annexation of Canada. O'Reilly was also a poet and author of the novel *Moondyne*, which Le Caron considered "delightfully written." The romantic plot of *Moondyne* was based on O'Reilly's own life as Fenian Prisoner Number 9843 in Freemantle, Australia. He wrote that he had been helped to escape by his lover, the warden's daughter, who gave him boots and clothing even though she knew his freedom also meant their permanent separation.[4]

Any spell created by the arrival of O'Reilly was snapped when Le Caron heard his name mentioned loudly from the convention floor. Roche angrily told delegates how Le Caron had written down the names of Canadian Fenians just a month before in Troy. At best this was a careless, dangerous, suspicious act. At worst, Roche continued, it was proof that Le Caron was a British spy.

Le Caron shot back by playing the part of an injured innocent, and this seemed to work, at least for the time being. However, he feared that real damage had been done, which, if left to fester, would threaten his mission and his life. So he wrote a letter of resignation as an officer of the Irish Republican Army, indignantly stating that he couldn't be expected to do his duties when faced with such a disturbing lack of confidence in his loyalty. Soon afterwards, on 29 December 1868 Le Caron received a letter from J. Whitehead Byron of the War Department of the Fenian Brotherhood at 10 West Fourth Street in Greenwich Village, urging him to soldier on past the insults: "If the officers of the organizations who have been vilified and calumniated were to resign on that account, some of its best officers could not now be at their post. The 'Patriot's meed is bitter;' they must bear with much, even from those who should be the first to defend and sustain them."[5]

And so Le Caron retained his revolutionary title. He also stopped taking notes at meetings.

On 8 January 1869 Le Caron wrote to Anderson, pushing for a favour. He said that his parents had "about 10 children," and that his father was a true English patriot, who worked hard for the government during the day, and helped underprivileged boys at night. Could Anderson do something about getting him a promotion? "Father is one of the most worthy men going, honest, hardworking & intelligent. . . every man woman & child will testify to his good qualities from Rebow MP to the Ragged boys. . . I wish to God this country had a few like him to run the govt but he has England on the Brain—never been 50 miles from home in his life. Perhaps though because he was a darned sight too poor."[6] Despite the plea, there's no record that Anderson helped Le Caron's father advance in the government.

In America, Le Caron stabilised his position inside the revolutionary ranks, staying close to O'Neill. Le Caron informed McMicken that the Fenian Convention still overwhelmingly supported O'Neill, "the hero of Ridgeway." Despite the 1866 Campobello Island and Ridgeway debacles, plans for another Canadian invasion were endorsed without a dissenting voice.

In Ottawa, the Fenian threat remained highly personal for Thomas D'Arcy McGee's old friend Macdonald. In a highly unusual move, Macdonald sat beside the judge hearing the trial of Patrick Whelan, who was charged with McGee's murder. Once Whelan was convicted, Macdonald resisted pressures for a new trial or at least an appeal to the Privy Council, even though he was normally flexible and amenable to such displays of mercy.

Some five thousand people turned out in an Ottawa snowstorm on 11 February 1869, when Whelan took the final few steps of his life. Once a brash public supporter of the Fenians, Whelan now denied any connection to the movement, although he used his final breaths to say, "God save Ireland and God save my soul." It was Canada's last public execution.

In the autumn of 1868, Le Caron first met Alexander Sullivan, an ambitious Fenian in his mid-forties from Chicago. Smallish, invariably clean-shaven, polite, and well-dressed, Sullivan looked like a kindly priest, if one didn't study his eyes too carefully. "His face is a striking one, more perhaps for the eyes than for any other feature—a dark, piercing and magnetic pair they are," a contemporary journalist noted. "Nobody ever came into anything like close relations with Alexander Sullivan without liking him thoroughly or hating him thoroughly."[7] Irish member of Parliament T.P. O'Connor (known to friends as "Tay Pay" for his sing-song pronunciation of his initials) also wasn't impressed by Sullivan, calling him "one of the strangest figures I ever met, even among the crowded gallery of remarkable personalities in the movement both in Ireland and in America. He was a thin, pale man, with a tranquil, not to say impassive, face; willowy and almost feeble in physique, but, as was proved on more than one occasion in his life, with an iron nerve and a ruthless, and indeed even ferocious though cold, temper behind the delicate physique."[8]

Sullivan's parents were originally from Cork, Ireland, and his father, a sergeant in the British Army, had been posted in Amherstburg, near Windsor, in Ontario, Canada. Sullivan emigrated from Canada to America "under a cloud," as Le Caron later heard, a pattern he would repeat in future moves. He settled in Detroit in the Corktown district around Michigan Avenue. Corktown took its nickname from County Cork, and its residents would later include a man from a humble farming background named Henry Ford, who later founded the automaker that bears his name. Sullivan set up a boot-and-shoe store in the Bresler Block on Michigan Avenue, which he heavily, even excessively, insured. Suspicions were naturally aroused when it burned on the night of 12 May 1868. Sullivan evaded arson charges, partly because of an alibi offered up by teenaged schoolteacher Margaret Buchanan, the youngest of 13 children of an old Detroit family that had achieved some stature through their boiler works. Buchanan was apparently smitten by the ambitious arsonist, and the fire gave her a chance to show her feelings. Sullivan retained his freedom after she lied to authorities that they were together at a Catholic church at the time of the blaze.

Sullivan had the ability to speak eloquently about great causes. A member of the Republican Party, he was an early advocate of equal rights for African-Americans, and he later championed the eight-hour day for workers. He told those attending the funeral of New England abolitionist Wendell Phillips that he "was one of the first men whose utterances aroused in my blood hatred of human slavery, and gave to my tongue some of its little power to denounce bondage even before I reached manhood."

Sullivan was a Fenian "centre," or key member, for Michigan, and backed the Republican presidential ticket of General Ulysses S. Grant and Schyler Colfax, even though the Irish-American vote had been overwhelmingly Democratic. Le Caron was dispatched by his Fenian superiors to Detroit to investigate suspicions that Sullivan was brokering the Irish vote for his own personal gain. They spoke several times, with Sullivan maintaining that everything he did was in the best interests of Ireland. "The Irish vote, argued he, had been hitherto solidly cast for the Democratic Party," Le Caron later recalled. "Only a division of that vote would cause them to be a potent power in politics. With that position and influence to which they were entitled assured to them, they could make terms with the American Government for the cause of Ireland."

Sullivan eventually agreed to resign as state centre of the Brotherhood, but remained active in Irish and American politics. His reward for stumping for the Republicans in the 1868 election was an appointment as tax collector of internal revenue in Santa Fe, New Mexico. Not long afterwards, he was promoted to the post of secretary of the territory. He switched careers yet again, running a Republican newspaper in Santa Fe. Despite the ostensibly respectable promotions, Sullivan still moved under a dark and unsettling cloud. There were reports that a rival had shot at and missed him in Michigan, and now, in his new southwestern home, there were stories that he was shot at, and missed, yet again. He was a target, but an elusive, moving one.

CHAPTER 8

BLOWN COVER

I am in a little Hell on Earth.

—**Henri Le Caron, August 1870**

The 16 May 1869 message to Le Caron from John Byron of the Fenian War Department in Greenwich Village was easy to understand and chilling: "We are making preparation for a fight as quick as circumstances will permit—<u>a fight is certain</u> and you shall have due notice."[1] By now, Le Caron had been promoted in Fenian ranks to inspector-general, and given the task of supervising the placement of weapons along the Canadian border. He was expected to move fast in getting weapons into the hands of Fenian soldiers.

On 19 July 1869 when Gilbert McMicken wrote to John A. Macdonald, the invasion plans were again stalled. The Canadian spymaster reassured the Canadian prime minister that Le Caron would know of any change as quickly as possible:

> *My informant [Le Caron] was one of their most active and trusted auxiliary organizers and they can speak freely and truthfully with him. They would look for and expect him and whenever a move was actually ordered. He is not in Council now merely as they cannot pay him and they know he cannot give his time to them without pay. . .*
>
> *I have my agent (LeC) running about now in the West and may at any time be called to Head Quarters as he is much trusted by ONeil [sic]. . .*

I look for a letter from LeC today or tomorrow and may possible have to meet him somewhere west. . . I will keep you informed of all that I learn from any source. . .[2]

The false starts were preying upon Le Caron's nerves. Three months later, O'Neill sent Le Caron word that the attack on Canada was almost ready, writing, "We are likely to have work of a Congenial nature for you soon." Le Caron's handwriting was faint and shaky, as if he was under great stress, when he wrote to McMicken on 12 October. He noted that Fenian Colonel John W. Dunne had arrived on a secret mission the previous night from Fenian headquarters, and that the march on Canada was set to begin "in a few days."

Le Caron worried about his safety and his family's financial well-being. He pleaded with Ottawa for a promise of money for his family should something happen to him. He was 28 years old now, and feared that he couldn't support Nannie, Henry, and Ida while continuing to spy on the Fenians. If he was killed in battle during the invasion attempt, or discovered as a spy and executed, he feared they would be lost as well. "Just what I am going to do I don't know yet but think I am all right with everybody. I have not a cent to work with + must ask you to send me some funds by return. a *[sic]* few days will tell the tale doubtless." He signed the letter to McMicken, "faithfully, TB."[3]

The next day, Le Caron was frantic as he prepared to head to battle: "expect to start in day or two. . . I will write result of affairs from day to day + shall expect you to back me in money for I have not a cent. And have to borrow to start." His signature, again scrawled and crooked, was now in his father's initials, J.B.[4]

A day later, on 14 October Le Caron's nerves and finances weren't any better, and there was a trace of defiance in his tone as he wrote:

If you please send me money at once to Wilmington. I. . . wait to I came + must leave some with wife if you wish me to do my best don't delay for I must stall on receiving dispatch and from what I hear here I must be in NY very soon.

I have no personal desire in this matter but only want to serve the good cause.

faithfully yours,

TB
Address to W. where I shall wait on Telegraph. . . This is if you have not already sent.

By 19 October some money had arrived and invasion plans were apparently once again on hold. His nerves were soothed, at least for the time being, as he wrote Ottawa, under the initials T.B.:

Received with enclosed check for which accept my best thanks. Since writing last I have heard nothing from HdQrs., in reference to myself am really at a moments notice. . . I can assure you that still much is being done by the ON friends to induce him not to move. + really he's not quite certain that we will move before spring. O'N feels that he must move or die on account of so many promises being made by him + I suppose I may leave for the east at any moment."[5]

On 1 November McMicken wrote to Canadian Prime Minister Macdonald, saying that O'Neill's future in the revolutionary movement hinged upon his invasion plans:

LeC says he now feels confident that nothing short of a failure to obtain money will stop ON from attempting some sort of move. . . unless he [O'Neill] can create some sensational stir such as the Ridgeway affair his term ends in December and he must be President or nothing. . .

I will wait here to get communication from LeC. By which I will be better able to judge what course to take. If possible he will manage without any person being sent to communicate with;. . . ON keeps every one hard at work and he fears he will have little or no time to write. LeC is somewhat anxious about the measures to be taken to provide for his personal safety. He says if a [illegible] takes place he cannot possibly back out but must stick by ON and there fore trusts all that can be done will [be] done to secure him from harm in any case he will do his duty to the utmost of his ability in what he has undertaken for the first and should harm happen to him trusts the Govt will remember he has a wife and two children without him. . .[6]

On 3 November McMicken wrote again to the prime minister with more specifics on the invasion: "I hear from Beach that he was to leave Albany on Wednesday. They have 8000 Breech loaders ready for use, have a good deal of ammunition on hand and are busy about getting more. They are now busy making preparations for distributing arms etc. The movement is now considered certain beyond doubt, and will take place between 1st and 15th Prox."[7]

Three days later, Le Caron wrote to Ottawa himself, reminding the Canadians they would soon be faced with a serious decision. Would they make a move against the Fenian arsenals and ruin the invasion before it even began? Or would they plan to trounce them on the battlefield instead? And what were their plans for protecting Le Caron's safety?

> The general has decided to call a Council of War in the beginning of Dec. to decide what will be done and the best time. If the move can result in taking and keeping Montreal this winter, and 10,000 men are decided as necessary to do it, we will go, making that a foothold for our spring campaign. . . The thing to be decided is will you let the move take place and kill it or crush it for ever? Or will you prevent it for a few years by seizing all the arms and munitions of war? You can do either, if the latter you must look out for me that's all![8]

Macdonald was drinking hard now, even by his boozy standards. The prime minister's finances were shaky, and the elation he and his second wife, Agnes, felt over the birth of their daughter, Mary Theodora, in February had descended into fear and depression after the infant was diagnosed with hydrocephalus. The baby's head was unnaturally large, her legs were useless, and her future, if she survived at all, would likely be one of severe mental and physical handicaps.[9] McMicken was clearly worried about the prime minister's drinking binges, and cautioned him on 11 November that any indiscretion could cost Le Caron his life. "LeC is really in a delicate position and feels anxious about his information not being used in [illegible] to bring him under suspicion. I need not [illegible] this consideration upon you but in duty to him I mention it."[10]

Le Caron made yet another move up the revolutionary ranks that month as O'Neill wrote him: "I will appoint you Lieut Colonel and acting adjutant General I.R.A. for the present. Salary one hundred dollars per month." That raise meant he received more money now from the revolutionaries than the Canadian government, which paid him $84 monthly.[11]

Throughout November 1869 Le Caron and O'Neill visited border spots in upstate New York and Vermont, mapping out new locations to stash arms. A month later, O'Neill received a mixture of good and bad news when the Fenian Senate announced that it considered preparations for the invasion of Canada ready. On a more ominous note, they said they also planned a hard look at how O'Neill was handling Fenian funds.

O'Neill knew he was in trouble. He had been stealing money from Fenian coffers, and now a Fenian treasurer refused to massage the books to cover his thefts. Embarrassed and vulnerable, O'Neill privately approached Le Caron and admitted his wrongdoing. "The opportunity was too good a one to be lost," Le Caron later stated. "I advanced [O'Neill] the money, and took his note of hand, thus saving his reputation. . ." That note from O'Neill read: "$364,41/100. Received from Colonel H. le Caron, three hundred and sixty-four dollars and 41/100, borrowed money, to be returned whenever demanded," and signed JOHN O'NEILL. Pres. F.B.[12]

There were now about fifty Secret Service agents working for McMicken, including some who monitored the movements of Le Caron, not knowing he was a fellow spy.[13] They hung around bars where Fenians drank and attended Fenian rallies. Despite their growth in numbers, there was still no more important Canadian spy than Le Caron, who scrawled McMicken an eight-page letter on 21 January 1870 from Ogdensburg, New York. In that letter, Le Caron noted that men in high-level American government circles were considered Fenian friends. He told Ottawa he wanted an assistant, who could serve as a bodyguard, and also more money. The Fenians weren't paying his salary as promised, and O'Neill hadn't paid back his loan: ". . . the time is fast approaching when I must have someone with me. . . he [New York governor John T. Hoffman] wishes success to us and will do nothing to injure our progress—you won't be surprised at this I suppose—a promise upon the part of the Gov. to keep us posted—present information advice and promises prove to me we have a friend in Hoffman as he always was to the cause of Irish liberty. . . you must be careful to look out for my safety. . .[14]

Canadian and British officials were sharing correspondence, with Britain playing a senior role in shaping strategy against the revolutionaries. British officials felt it was best to let the Fenians invade Canada, and then thrash them on the battlefield. In a 10 February letter, Governor General Lord Lisgar, also known as Sir John Young, wrote to British foreign secretary Earl Granville that they were confident in the accuracy of Le Caron's intelligence reports:

> We know exactly the spots where the arms are stored but there are all sorts of difficulties in the way of the seizure. The arms are placed in small quantities, some buried, some in garrets, some in grocers stores and whiskey houses. . . I sent this morning for Mr. McMicken, the officer who is expecially charged by the Government with the duty of collecting all possible information on Fenian matters. He has a number of informers in his pay acting independently one of the other, and at different points along the frontier as well as at New York. Some of these men, one especially, is a man of some importance in the Fenian association, and fully aware of all that is going on. Mr. McMicken has no doubt whatever as to, the perfect accuracy of his information. . . Mr. McMicken is further of opinion, that, with the present perfect means of gaining information at his command, it is better to let the raid take place so as to give the raiders a lesson which will not be easily forgotten and will probably squash the Fenian organization altogether.[15]

The trap had been set. Now, they just needed the Fenians to step into it. In a 10 February letter to McMicken, Le Caron noted the presence now in the Fenian ranks of Michael Kirwin, a former lieutenant in the Thirteenth Pennsylvania Volunteers in the Civil War. Kirwin was competent and battle-hardened, and his presence gave the invasion plans more credibility. He had been arrested in Ireland in February 1866 after the Habeas Corpus Act was suspended, and imprisoned in Mountjoy Prison in Dublin until the American government intervened for his release on the grounds that he was an American citizen. Now, Le Caron sent McMicken a letter from O'Neill to Fenian military leaders in which Kirwin was referred to as the Fenian "Secretary of War." O'Neill's letter said preparation for war must be their only priority: "Brothers, if you be so situated that business or family duties will prevent you from getting your commands in readiness for active and immediate service, you will please forward your resignations to the Secretary of War at once, and at the same time send on the names of persons suitable to take your places. .. Preserve the utmost secrecy with regard to this circular, and reply at once. Delay, and you are guilty of neglect of duty!"[16]

McMicken wrote Macdonald on 12 February warning that the Fenians could be marching on Canada in a little more than a month:

> *I have returned from having an interview with "Beach." He is fully impressed with a conviction that the measures now in operation of O'Neill will result in an attempted movement and that sometime towards the end of March or by unforeseen causes of delay the beginning of april... He says O'Neill apprehends no difficulty whatever in putting the force reckoned upon over the line that's about 900 mounted men and 2500 infantry.*
>
> *I enclose two letters of recent date one of the 1st ... from Oneill to "Beach."*
> *.... The enclosures I shall have to return to Beach again and must therefore request you to return them to me in a few days as I am to put them in his hands at Prescott junction on Tuesday 22nd when he will be on his way back to his duty, having now gone west to visit his family, a member of which (a daughter) is ill.*[17]

Also that month, McMicken sent an agent, John C. Rose, to be close to Le Caron, so that he could relay important messages between them. One such dispatch was dated 24 February 1870 and sent to McMicken from Burlington, Vermont. The invaders planned to march north in just two weeks. The telegraph had been in existence for more than a quarter of a century now, but he was taking a serious gamble with security in sending such messages. Even with such instantaneous communications, the message would be arriving with precious little time for the government to act: "I am full of business. 48 cases of material arrived since I was here last and I now have 10 cases more. 80,000 rounds of B. Loading ammunition and more Carbines and B. Loaders, and 11 cases of them ordered tonight... 10th of March just think—2 weeks more."[18]

O'Neill was running hard to save his job and establish his place in history. The Fenian Senate, backed by the Irish American, Irish Republican, and United Irishman newspapers, now accused him of graft and corruption. O'Neill knew that a great victory would silence his critics and make him a hero for the ages in Ireland—the warrior who won the country's freedom. The glory for victory was dizzying. The penalty for inaction—or failure—was unthinkable. He would be remembered as a cheat, if he was remembered at all. The Fenians had already slipped behind two weeks in their scheduled date for invasion, and any more delays could be disastrous. On 21 March Le Caron wrote to McMicken, "Things are getting exciting."

In Ottawa, Macdonald continued to drink heavily, in liquid flight from his personal pressures. In Albany, New York governor John Hoffman updated the Fenians on any planned government actions against them. In the town of Malone in the northeastern tip of New York state, which Le Caron considered "the Gibraltar of Fenianism," McMicken's agent Rose watched over Le Caron as he gathered weapons. Le Caron considered Rose "one of the most faithful and trusted servants of the Canadian administration," and had no clue that the Fenians suspected Rose after a visitor from Ottawa thought he recognised him. The Fenians spying on Rose noted that he always seemed to be following Le Caron, and concluded that he must be a British spy who was monitoring Le Caron. One day, moments after Rose sent out another of Le Caron's dispatches from the local post office, he was, in Le Caron's words, "waylaid, robbed, and brutally beaten, and subsequently brought back to the hotel in as sorry a plight as I ever saw."[19]

It was hard enough for Le Caron to see Rose in such intense pain, but even worse to have to hide his concern. Flush with shock, Le Caron managed nonetheless to "applaud their cowardly assault, and to denounce my brave friend, who was bearing all his sufferings in silence and with a splendid spirit." It would be months before Rose was able to walk again.

By April 1870 the Fenian leaders still hadn't issued the order to march, although Kirwin and O'Neill sent out a dispatch from the Deckertown, Sussex County, New York headquarters of the Fenian War Department, which called upon "commanding officers of regiments, companies, and detachments" to be made ready "to move at a moment's notice." Such dispatches warning of imminent attacks on Canada were now sounding familiar and even foolish. "Officers and men must avoid the use of uniforms or any insignia that would distinguish them," the dispatch continued. "Officers must not be recognized by military titles, and officers or men must not speak of Fenian matters while en route. Take no man who is a loafer or a habitual drunkard. Take no man who has not seen service, or who has not sufficient character to ensure his good behaviour en route and in presence of the enemy."[20]

O'Neill ordered Le Caron to meet him in Buffalo, where he told him face to face that he had ordered an immediate march on Canada. His army was so strong, O'Neill boasted, that "no power on earth could stop it." Le Caron telegraphed his alarm to Ottawa. Le Caron and O'Neill left Buffalo for Milton, Vermont, on Saturday, 22 April with O'Neill buoyant in the belief that the invaders would take Canada by surprise this time. Le Caron was promoted to brigadier-general, and in fine spirits. "I [was] laughing to myself at his coming discomfiture," Le Caron later recalled.[21]

Some 1,300 Fenians were positioned along the border, and O'Neill planned to move them from Vermont into New Brunswick without delay. The Fenian invasion was set for 26 April. Meanwhile, Canadian authorities also struggled to assess rumours that Le Caron had forwarded of a plot to kidnap the Queen's son, Prince Edward, who was visiting Canada.

At dawn, troops gathered at Hubbard's Farm, a half mile from Franklin. O'Neill lined them up for a brief pep talk on duty and glory and history. "Soldiers, this is the advance-guard of the Irish-American army for the liberation of Ireland from the yoke of the oppressor. For your own country you enter that of the enemy. The eyes of your countrymen are upon you. Forward. March."[22]

Le Caron looked down from a hill onto a picturesque valley, where a gently flowing creek gently marked the border between Canadian and American soil. He couldn't help but contrast the sweetness of nature that morning with the almost out-of-control energy of the marching Fenians, so eager for battle.[23]

The troops marched with "a certain amount of military precision," in Le Caron's words. When they reached the tiny wooden bridge between the nations, they cheered wildly, with bayonets fixed on their rifles. "A few paces, and on their startled ears came the ringing ping, ping, of the ambushed rifles, as the Canadians poured a deadly volley straight into their ranks. Utterly taken aback, they stopped, broke rank, and fled. . . an ungovernable mob. . ."[24]

Le Caron surveyed the chaos from the middle of a public road when someone shouted at him, "Clear the road, clear the road!" As a covered wagon sped past, he barely caught a glimpse of O'Neill inside, his face a portrait of abject dejection.[25]

It was somehow even more humiliating than the earlier failed attack on Canada. This time, they didn't even get to plant an Irish flag on Canadian soil before dashing for safety. When O'Neill wrote his report to the Fenian Senate, he still didn't suspect his aide, Le Caron. "During the past winter months competent and reliable men, Colonels Henry Le Caron and William Clingen were employed in locating our arms. . . at convenient points along the border," he wrote, still blind to the betrayal.[26]

Henri Le Caron slipped away from the Fenians on Friday, 27 April saying he was going to Burlington, Vermont, to check into the condition of O'Neill, who was now in custody in an American jail. Instead, he snuck from Rouses Point, New York, to Montreal, eager to relay his stories to Canadian officials in Ottawa. That night, he visited McMicken's Quebec counterpart, Judge Coursol, and then set out by train the next morning to Ottawa.

The train paused at Cornwall for a half hour's dinner break, and Le Caron looked up from his dinner plate to see two men marching fast toward him.

"That is the man!"

A wandering preacher, who had seen Le Caron at a Fenian gathering near Malone, pointed an accusing finger toward him.

The second man, who was tall and had a military bearing, put his hand on Le Caron's shoulder and announced in a brusque, Scottish accent, "You are my prisoner."

Le Caron laughed and turned back toward his dinner, but the stranger's hand remained on his shoulder.

"You are my prisoner," the man repeated. "You must come with me at once."

"But won't you let me finish my dinner?"

"No."

"For what reason? Why am I arrested?"

The dining room was hushed as the man announced, "You are a Fenian."

The anger was almost palpable as other passengers glared at him. It was clearly safer for Le Caron to leave with the tall man, whom Le Caron later learned was the mayor of Cornwall, Dr. William C. Allen.

Le Caron was led to a room adjoining the ticket office, and ordered to hand over his luggage and keys. All he had with him was a handbag, but there were enough secret Fenian documents inside it to cost him his life.

The mayor was suspicious, but also curious when Le Caron asked him to step aside for a private chat. They went into the ticket office, where no one else could hear their words.

"It is true that I was a Fenian, but I am also a government agent. I was even then on my way to Ottawa to see Judge McMicken," Le Caron told him. Le Caron urged the mayor to send him on to Ottawa under guard, so that he could prove his statements true.

In the background, the mob called for blood, with shouts of "Hang him!" "Lynch him!"

The mayor relented, and Le Caron was sent on to Ottawa under the guard of a lieutenant who was on his way home from the Hubbard's Farm battlefield. Guards kept the mob from attacking Le Caron and Le Caron from bolting for safety. They also stood between the spy and one of his few visible vices. Le Caron was a chain smoker, but his captors would not let him open a window so that he could light a cigar and soothe his nerves, fearing the jockey-sized man might jump to freedom. "This was really a serious grievance with me, for they could not possibly have inflicted a greater deprivation than that in the matter of smoking," he later recalled. "All through my life, even down to the present time, I have been a great smoker, sometimes consuming as many as sixteen cigars in the day, a statement which will probably puzzle some people who hold that tobacco ruins the nerves."[27]

When Le Caron was delivered to the Ottawa police station, McMicken was uncharacteristically solemn. He listened to details of Le Caron's capture, and then signed a formal receipt for his custody. Once the guards were gone, McMicken became his usual genial self. They took a cab in the darkness to a private club, where they met other veterans of the Fenian campaign, who had served for Britain as soldiers and not spies. It was a party atmosphere now, with Le Caron the hero of the hour. McMicken dispatched a club porter to fetch $350 for Le Caron's expenses.[28] The porter couldn't keep the news to himself, and was the source for a newspaper report, which stated that an important Fenian was in Ottawa immediately after the raid. The report continued that this Fenian received a substantial sum of money from a government official. It was just a few words printed in the newspaper, but more than enough to endanger Le Caron's life.

There were now jokes among British and Canadian ranks that "IRA" stood for "I ran away," and Le Caron was awarded a $2,000 bonus for his role in preventing the invasion.[29] McMicken wrote to John A. Macdonald on Dominion Day, 1 July declaring the spy was full value for the money:

> Taking into account the sums at different times paid to him in cases of exigency he has received from me for the period of his service an average salary of $100 per month. . . He rendered the only gun the Fenians had unserviceable by removing the Breech piece and concealing it so that it could not be found for several hours after the repulse of the invading body under O'Neill. . . He also delayed or caused the delay of bringing up the reserve force of Fenians some 400 strong to the support of O'Neill for about 2 hours instead of some 20 minutes and thereby contributed to the complete discomfiture of O'Neill and the collapse of the movement. He is now bitterly denounced by the Fenian newspapers—not however as a traitor—but as a hired tool of O'Neill without heart in the cause and not an Irishman, chiefly blamed for his disregard of their war material and for inviting the country people around to help themselves to arms. . . If he ever encountered any risk or is subject to any now it is entirely owing to his own imprudence, which he will readily admit. He is very excitable and very fond of having it known that he was a great instrument of discomfiture to the Fenians,

that although unfaithful to them he was a true hearted Englishman. . . would
when there was no occasion whatever for it reveal his name and occupation to
parties who need not and should not have known anything of the kind.[30]

Clearly, Le Caron's nerves were raw, as McMicken wrote to Macdonald on 6 July 1870. The prime minister wasn't in any better condition than the spy, just returning to his duties after a collapse in the East Block of Parliament in Ottawa in May when he passed a particularly large gallstone.[31]

After his latest, most crushing humiliation, O'Neill languished in an American jail for six months for violating U.S. neutrality laws before he and other Fenians were pardoned by President Ulysses S. Grant. The Fenian army was now in tatters, and even their optimistic estimates placed the number of Americans involved in the movement at fifty thousand compared to between one hundred and fifty thousand and two hundred thousand immediately after the Civil War. Another attempt at a full invasion of Canada now seemed futile. They would use terror instead.[32]

CHAPTER 9

HEROES' WELCOME

White House, Washington, D.C.,
22 February 1871

Glad to see you.

—**American president Ulysses S. Grant**
greets freed Irish revolutionaries

Someone who did not know journalist Jenny Williams might dismiss her as shy and unfocused or too young, as a woman in her mid-twenties, to be taken seriously. However, those who did know her appreciated something big was happening when she latched on to the story of Jeremiah O'Donovan Rossa, the imprisoned editor of the *Irish People* newspaper in Dublin.

Rossa was convicted in 1866 of seditious writing after he called for foreigners to invade Britain to help Irish revolutionaries. Once behind bars, his days were spent in tiny, dark, solitary cells, his hands chained behind him. Williams was horrified to hear that the rare times when he was allowed to bathe, it was in filthy water. When he ate, it was with his hands bound behind his back, so that he had to lap up porridge while on all fours, like a dog. Often at night, in the dark, guards heard Rossa singing Gaelic songs, and thought he had gone mad. Those who knew Rossa well understood this was his way of staying sane.[1] Lest he become too comfortable anywhere, Rossa was moved from prison to prison, and not allowed pictures of his wife or baby as their images might give him joy or hope. For his part, Rossa was hardly a model inmate. At one point in his prison stint, when his hands were not bound, he responded to an order to salute the Dover prison governor by throwing a latrine bucket in his face.

Jenny Williams was the *nom de plume* for Jenny Marx, the eldest daughter of Communist theorist Karl Marx and his wife, Johanna (Jenny), the daughter of Prussian nobles in the von Westphalen family. Those who knew young Jenny Marx, like her father's friend and fellow revolutionary Frederick Engels, didn't doubt her powers. "Despite a reticence that could almost be taken for shyness, she displayed when necessary a presence of mind and energy which could be envied by many a man," Engels wrote.[2]

The Irish revolutionary movement was in many ways a cross-section of Ireland. Its ranks included Roman Catholics and Protestants, religious zealots and atheists, capitalists and socialists, deep thinkers and ragtag hooligans. They shared a hatred for British rule and a desire for independence. What should be done with that independence was open for debate.

Rossa embodied the fierce resistance to British control that united the movement. He was an adolescent during the horrors of the Great Famine of the 1840s, and like others of his generation, damned the English for sitting back and collecting taxes while letting his people starve. As he grew into adulthood, he added "Rossa" to his surname as an announcement (however questionable) that he was directly descended from the Irish princes of Rossa. Now, confined in a succession of cold, dark English cells, it appeared that British authorities were bent on breaking that pride, and Williams felt she had to do something to keep it alive.

Jenny Marx was raised on revolution, and wasn't a year old when her parents were expelled from Paris for their political views. The Marxes had already been kicked out of Belgium and Prussia for similar reasons, and wound up next in a three-room flat in London's downtown Soho district, amid tides of refugees from France, whose pain and dreams provided the inspiration for Dickens' *A Tale of Two Cities*.[3]

Writing under her pen name, Williams described Rossa's imprisonment on 1 March 1870 in the leading French newspaper, the *Marseillaise*. In the 9 March edition, she quoted from a letter from Rossa said to be smuggled out of prison. In it, Rossa told readers of the cruel treatment he had suffered behind bars that had killed some of his friends and made his life a daily hell.

As Engels later wrote, "This had an effect. The disclosures in a big Paris newspaper could not be endured."[4] Rossa was even more of an irritant to the English behind bars than he was as a free man. A few weeks later, on 5 January 1871 the government of British Prime Minister Gladstone announced a general amnesty, which freed Rossa from his life sentence on the condition that he and fellow freed revolutionaries not return to Britain until their sentences had expired.[5] Many of the 30 freed convicts sailed for Australia, but Rossa, John Devoy, John McClure, Henry Mulleda, and Charles Underwood O'Connell boarded the S.S. Cuba from Liverpool to America. By the time they reached New York harbour, they were known as the Cuba Five and greeted with a hero's welcome. An official greeting was issued from the United States House of Representatives, and they were met on 2 February on the steps of the White House by President Ulysses S. Grant. The president offered his best wishes and said, "Glad to see you."

Soon, Rossa and Devoy were moving in Le Caron's Fenian circles. The spy considered Rossa an agent of "dynamite and devilry," but could see nothing in his appearance to suggest any "undue ferocity." "His face, though determined, was yet not without its kindly aspect, while his love for the bottle betrayed a jovial rather than a fiendish instinct. His fierceness, indeed, lay altogether in speech. Voluble and sweeping in his language, he was never so happy as when pouring out the vials of his wrath on the British Government."[6]

Rossa had some money of his own, having published a book about his hellish prison days, and his tales of mistreatment in British prisons also rewarded him with a certain celebrity status. He opened up a saloon in the Five Points neighbourhood, where it was said the "atmosphere seethed with hatred of Britain," and was quickly recruited by the Republicans to run against Boss William M. Tweed, whose career was synonymous with Democrat corruption. Rossa lost, but popular belief in Five Points was that he actually tallied 350 more votes than his rival, losing out only in the counting process.

Le Caron considered Devoy to be a far less pleasant man than Rossa. Temperamental and egotistical, in Le Caron's view, Devoy had no tolerance for those whom he considered amateurs in the work of revolution. He was also deeply suspicious of potential spies, and let Le Caron know that his French name gave him an uneasy feeling. Le Caron noted that a Frenchman, the Marquis de Lafayette, was a general in George Washington's revolutionary army, and remained quick and loud in his denunciations of all things English. Le Caron realised that if anyone in the Fenian circle was likely to discover his true identity, it would be Devoy, a truly driven man. As a fellow Irish nationalist noted, "He never married. The cause was for him wife, family and home."[7]

When Swedish engineer Alfred Nobel developed U.S. patent 78,317 in 1867, he forever changed the face of modern building and destruction. Nobel was a singularly complex man—a pacifist and a misanthrope, a multi-millionaire and a socialist, demonized as a "merchant of death," and hailed as the creator of the enormously prestigious peace prize that bears his name. He became a force in history when he mixed extremely volatile nitroglycerin with silica to create a malleable paste. This paste could be placed into cylinders to create what seemed to be an enormous contradiction—a controlled explosion. His called his invention, "Dynamite or Nobel's Safety Powder," creating the word "dynamite" from the Greek word *dynamis*, meaning "power." It was the perfect tool for a time when engineers sought to move mountains and stone to build railways and harbours and mines in the name of progress.[8]

It's not surprising that Rossa's mind was soon bursting with the possibilities of U.S. patent 78,317. While Irish gangs once torched barns and haystacks of landlords, extreme Irish nationalists could now dream of quietly travelling to the heart of British power and blowing up English monuments like London Bridge or the Houses of Parliament in the Palace of Westminster. Le Caron noted that Rossa couldn't stop thinking of new ways to attack the English, including launching dynamite from pedal-powered submarines onto British ironclad ships. It was with considerable unease that Le Caron noted Rossa's new nickname, O'Dynamite, although some of his detractors in the nationalist movement still dismissed him as O'Donovan Assa.[9]

After a four-year break in his studies, Le Caron transferred from Rush Medical College in Chicago to the Detroit College of Medicine. He and Nannie now had three children (daughter Gertrude was born earlier in 1870), and medicine promised a secure career to provide for them. McMicken welcomed the move as he was curious about William Mackey (Michael) Lomasney, a newcomer to Detroit's Corktown district. Soft-spoken, with a trace of a lisp, and just in his mid-twenties, Lomasney was both popular and respected in nationalist circles, and known affectionately as The Little Captain. Born in Cincinnati, Lomasney's father was a Fenian and he carried on the family struggle, sailing to Ireland in 1865 to aid in an anticipated uprising. After briefly serving time in Britain on charges of stealing weapons for nationalists and shooting a police officer, he became a member of the Toronto circle of Fenians in 1866, along with Edward O'Meagher Condon and Reverend John Curley.

It was easy enough for Le Caron to find Lomasney in his Michigan Avenue bookshop, greeting customers. "I formed a very pleasant acquaintance with Mackay [sic] Lomasney, and found him a most entertaining man," Le Caron later noted. He was also amazed at Lomasney's chameleon-like quality, as he appeared an entirely different person when sporting a full, bushy beard than when he was clean-shaven. It was as if he could hide without going anywhere, with a few subtle changes to his appearance.

It was only a matter of months before Le Caron completed his medical studies, and was able to begin supporting himself and his family as a doctor.[10] He moved back to Illinois with Nannie and young Henry, Ida, and Gertrude, setting up a practice outside Chicago in Wilmington, near Braidwood, in his new residence on Water Street.

Any hopes of normalcy ended with a telegram he received that spring, shortly after his arrival in Wilmington. O'Neill informed him of yet another plot to attack Canada. On 16 June 1871 Le Caron wrote under the code name of R.G. Sager to McMicken about plans to invade what is now the province of Manitoba, noting that O'Neill was even more impoverished than usual. "I received a telegram from O'N wishing me to meet him in Chicago thinking perhaps he wanted to pay me the note I hold against him I ran to you," Le Caron wrote. "[H]e came here yesterday from Detroit I saw no money of course but I learned something of interest to you."[11] Le Caron told McMicken he would be willing to help Canada again—for a price. His words show he was motivated by more than idealism as he wrote, "Have no desire to leave my practice—but if it pays well I am in."[12]

CHAPTER 10

PRAIRIE RAID

Manitoba, October 1871

You must go back. You can do nothing to save yourself in this wild lone country—to proceed would be self murder.

—**Canadian spymaster Gilbert McMicken**
is warned to leave Manitoba

There was more than a little irony when, in the late spring of 1871, Fenian commander John O'Neill came calling on his old comrade Henri Le Caron in Illinois. O'Neill brought with him several letters from William Bernard O'Donoghue, who had served as a secretary for Manitoba Métis leader Louis Riel. O'Neill was now energised by a vision of fighting alongside Riel's Native forces against the British. Apparently he forgot that he and many others in his Fenian ranks had once served in the American cavalry, driving Natives out of their traditional homelands, creating many of the conditions that Riel was struggling to change.

Le Caron told O'Neill cheerfully that he could free up 400 breech-loaders and ammunition for the assault, taking O'Neill with him to a spot where he had stashed carbines and ammunition along the border. Privately, Le Caron was amazed and disgusted as he was sure that O'Donoghue had received permission from his archbishop, Alexandre-Antonin Taché, to push for the united attack on Canada.

McMicken was on a short stopover at his Windsor, Ontario, home when he got the news from Le Caron in late September 1871 that an attack on Manitoba was imminent. This would have been of particular interest to the Canadian spymaster as he was preparing to move west after having been recently appointed to take the post of agent of Dominion lands for Manitoba, in addition to his titles as commissioner of Dominion police and acting secretary of the Intercolonial Railway Commissioners.

McMicken knew the rebels were weak since O'Donoghue didn't even have the funds to pay his train fare from Chicago to St. Paul, Minnesota. He likely wasn't aware that O'Donoghue also didn't have the authority to speak for Riel or his governing counsel, the Union Nationale Métisse. Most likely, McMicken also didn't know that O'Donoghue had already been rebuffed by other Fenians, and that O'Neill was his last, desperate hope.[1] Long gone were the heady days when the Fenians dreamed of mustering a united force of more than sixteen thousand to storm across the Canadian border. Now, O'Neill could pull together only 41 volunteers for his invasion scheme for Manitoba. Sorely lacking funds as well as men, O'Neill schemed to raise money for the expedition by robbing Hudson's Bay Company posts a few miles from the Canadian border at Pembina, North Dakota, and Fort Garry en route to the Northwest.

McMicken's federal force was even tinier than that of the invaders—just eight Canadian government agents, including his son Ritchie. They stayed near St. Paul at a tiny hamlet called Morris, Minnesota, which consisted of nothing more than one rail station building. It was there, after supper, where the government men met with Taché, who arrived on a stage from Fort Garry. Even though Le Caron heard that the archbishop had encouraged the rebellion, McMicken found him "exceeding affable and quite willing to converse freely on the topic which at that moment interested me most, and engrossed my thoughts." McMicken later recalled that Taché was clearly worried about the prospect of upcoming violence as the Métis were, in McMicken's words, "intensely agitated over the unfulfilled promises of the Government and the harsh and insulting conduct of the more recently arrived Canadians from Ontario."

On the morning of 28 September Riel met with a dozen members of the Union Nationale Métisse, in his home in St. Vital near Winnipeg, where they mulled over the questions: "Does the Government fulfil sufficiently its pledges towards us? If it has not yet done so, have we reasons to believe that it will fulfil them honestly in the future? Are we sure that O'Donoghue is coming with the men?" and "If he [O'Neill] is coming, what conduct must we follow respecting him?" Clearly, Riel was more bewildered than inspired by O'Neill's ragged attack plans.[2]

McMicken later recalled that he urged Taché to come with him to Fort Garry to defuse things. As McMicken later recounted the conversation, Taché replied that he had an extremely important meeting in Quebec that he could not miss. McMicken countered that he would embarrass Taché in the press if he didn't help stifle the attack. While the Fenian force was laughably small, McMicken worried that it might still be enough of a spark to ignite a Métis uprising. His new Manitoba posting, which had promised such potential for personal financial gain, could quickly turn into a war zone.

Before they parted the next morning, McMicken tried yet again to convince Taché to come to Fort Garry with him. He later recalled that he even offered to pay his expenses. Taché again refused, but did agree to take a telegram for Ottawa, which he could send when he reached St. Paul. With that, McMicken later recalled, the two men shook hands and parted.

McMicken and his tiny party stopped at 1pm at a hamlet called Pomme de Terre, French for "potato," where the filth—even by frontier standards—disgusted McMicken: "It was not only forbidding, it was revolting—yet we all ate more or less, as shipwrecked mariners are compelled to eat."

At sundown, the stage stopped at Macaulayville, the site of the meeting between Taché and the rebels a few days before. The woman who ran the local inn impressed McMicken as "cleanly, good-looking, intelligent, and possessing a loving and a loyal Canadian heart." Before they parted, she warned him that she had heard that a Fenian named Bodkin and a small band of sympathisers were on their way to Fort Garry, armed for battle, with green ribbons pinned to their breasts.

McMicken and his tiny party travelled through the night, and when they finally stopped again to change horses in a hamlet named Georgetown, a man abruptly told them, "You must on no account go on any farther, but return the way you came. You will be robbed and killed to a certainty." The speaker had been at Grand Forks the previous day, and told them of overhearing a man there remark, in front of more than a dozen men, that his friend, Mr. McMicken, was on his way by stage to Fort Garry with $1m. It was a crude attempt by the Fenians to lay a trap for McMicken and his party. "You won't attempt to go on. No, no, no, you must go back," the man told McMicken again. "You can do nothing to save yourself in this wild lone country—to proceed would be self murder."

McMicken ignored the warning and pressed on behind a fresh team of four horses. At Grand Forks, home to about seventy residents, they found a good canoe to "escape the banditti by taking the river" and freeing their fellow stage passengers of the danger of attack. Before they went to sleep that night, McMicken's men agreed upon a code in case they stumbled upon the Fenians in the wilderness. If this happened, they would say, "Is that dog all right?"

Somewhere in the darkness that night, McMicken heard his son Ritchie ask, "Is that dog all right?" Then Ritchie said to strangers, "A cool night for travelling, boys."

"You bet," was the reply.

McMicken and his tiny group hurried past the strangers' canvas-covered wagons. It was now a sprint into the night and the wilderness to the Northwest and the Métis leader Louis Riel.

At the next coach house, McMicken picked up a new driver, an Americanised Irishman with Fenian sympathies, who spoke affectionately of an impending invasion of Canada. They pretended to be in full sympathy with his views before pressing on again, finally reaching Fort Garry on 2 October. It was a Monday night and the Fenian raid was likely coming on Wednesday afternoon or Thursday morning. An emergency public meeting brought some one thousand volunteers, many from the Hudson's Bay Company, into the dull, drizzling evening. The only problem now was finding rifles for all of them.

About twenty Fenians under O'Neill and O'Donoghue stormed the Hudson's Bay Fort at Pembina, looking to finance their invasion with robbery. Their enthusiastic charge wasn't necessary since the only person inside was a one-armed man, and he wasn't in a fighting mood. Shortly afterwards, O'Neill and his followers were captured by

American soldiers there as yet another attempt to seize Canada by force had ended in humiliation for the General. His only consolation was that his latest humiliation was private as the invasion—and defeat—went almost entirely unnoticed.

Riel clearly wanted no part of the frantic charge as he wrote on 7 October to Lieutenant-Governor Archibald from St. Vital:

> Our conduct, as several trustworthy persons have been prayed to inform you, has been worthy of faithful subjects. Several companies are already organized and others are being formed. Your Excellency has been able to convince yourself that we, without having been enthusiastic [Can anything be franker?], have been devoted. As long as our services shall continue to be required, you can rely on us. We have the honour to subscribe ourselves, of Your Excellency, the most humble servants.
>
> [Sgd.] Louis Riel[3]

For his part, Archbishop Taché was livid when he later heard McMicken's version of events, and published an open letter to McMicken in which he sharply denied meeting with O'Donoghue to plot anything: "I met him two days before I met you; I merely exchanged a few sentences with him and stopped my conversation short, as I perceived at once that he was endeavoring to deceive me. . ." Taché also made a point of distancing himself from any connection with O'Neill: "The stranger, whom I saw with O'Donoghue at Georgetown, was not O'Neill. I knew that much. . ."[4]

Wherever the truth lay, the Northwest adventure was over for O'Neill as he and his party were turned over to American authorities. Four days later, they were tried and acquitted on what Le Caron considered a ludicrous technicality—that the Pembina attack took place on Canadian and not American soil. This seemed doubly odd to Le Caron since ownership of that land was a matter of dispute between Canada and the U.S. Back in Manitoba, Lieutenant-Governor Archibald reflected on what might have happened had the Fenians succeeded in forging an alliance with the Métis, and concluded, "If the Métis had taken a different course, I do not believe the Province would now be in our possession."[5]

When O'Neill next saw Le Caron, the thrice-humiliated general didn't suspect him of the latest betrayal, just as he had never doubted his loyalty in the past. Now, in the words of Le Caron, it was clear that O'Neill was a broken man, and he "made my life a burden. Discredited and disheartened, he took to drink and went entirely to the dogs."

The only positive force left in O'Neill's life seemed to be the love of his wife. They had met years before, when he was a patient and she was a Sister of Mercy nurse charged with his care. They had fallen in love then, and these feelings were so inescapable that she abandoned her vows as a nun for marriage. Now, even her constant love could not stop O'Neill from sliding deeper into drink and isolation. He died of a paralytic stroke in Omaha, Nebraska, on 8 January 1878, near the tiny community of O'Neill, which bears his name and where he had struggled to establish Irish colonies on the American plains. He was just 44, but somehow he seemed much, much older.

CHAPTER 11

DR. MORTON

Braidwood, Illinois, 1870s

... never accused of any sort of dishonesty.
—Local newspaper describes resident Henri Le Caron

It wasn't the scenery that drew the people to Braidwood, Illinois, in the early 1870s when Henri and Nannie Le Caron decided to relocate from nearby Wilmington. Braidwood was a decidedly ugly place, sitting on flat, relatively featureless plain, with thin soil, an underlayer of quicksand, no streams, and nothing more scenic than vistas of tall grass in the summer and snowpiles in the winter.

Despite the bleak setting, people were arriving in droves in the post-Civil War years to the community about sixty miles southwest of Chicago, and at the foot of the road to California that would later become known as Route 66. In less than a decade, Braidwood lurched from being barely a speck on the map, and home to just 50 people, to boasting a population of 2,550 by 1873, when it was incorporated as a municipality. Among those who heard Braidwood's clarion call were Henri and Nannie Le Caron, who moved there with their children, Henry, Ida, and Gertrude and a woman known as Miss Lizzie Beach. Miss Lizzie, in the words of a contemporary account, "was understood by his neighbors to be his half-sister."[1]

Braidwood's sudden appeal could be explained in a word: coal. Coal was needed to fuel the Industrial Revolution, and rich veins of it lay under the dull, flat plains of Braidwood. Its influence was so overwhelming and life-altering that some residents called the boomtown Eureka to celebrate its discovery. The town's proper name honoured James Braidwood, a Scottish-born Republican and the son of a poor coal miner, who sank the community's first coal shaft, built the community's first house, lost the community's first house to fire, fathered the community's first White child, and lost the community's first White child to illness.

The first time Henri Le Caron rode into Braidwood with his young family, he must have noticed something a little odd. The thriving little town boasted seven churches, three schools, and a massive sprawl of mining machinery. It might have taken Le Caron a moment to notice that nowhere in this explosion of new construction was there anything but wooden buildings, with the exception of a small brick schoolhouse and a bakery. Both of these pioneer structures were built before the discovery of coal. Since that time, the coal companies that bought up the land kept a clause in all of their land title deeds, reserving the right to mine coal under the surface. That meant all new buildings, including the churches, were constructed of light wooden frames that could be torn down quickly and cheaply should a fresh vein of coal be discovered underneath.[2]

The main business street of Braidwood ran more than a mile, with stores, shops, and offices, ending at the gates of the Eureka Company. It was amid these tightly packed wooden buildings that Le Caron hung out his shingle as a doctor, advertising in a local business directory, "LeCaron, H. Dr., Drug Store, where may be found Drugs, Medicines and Chemicals, all the new Patent Medicines, Perfumery, Pure Wines and Liquors for Medical Purposes. Physicians' prescriptions carefully compounded and all orders correctly filled, day or night."[3] A contemporary local history described the young doctor as polite, hospitable, well dressed, with a "fine tenor voice," and as someone who was "never accused of any sort of dishonesty."[4]

After the Northwest invasion debacle and O'Neill's pitiful decline, Le Caron didn't expect much more excitement or income from Fenian affairs. He could now finally concentrate on providing for his young family. His Irish connections gave him almost more medical clientele than he could handle. He also moved into mainstream politics, running for the local school board on "the people's ticket" and failing to win a seat. He did gain an appointment on the board of health, which brought him an additional $100 a year.[5] There was also a far more lucrative appointment as supervisor of Braidwood, which brought a daily payment of $2.50, plus travelling allowances.

Compared to the incomes of other Braidwood residents, these were fairly valuable sidelights. Underground coal miners sacrificed their health and shortened their lives for no more than $12 to $15 weekly during the winter, when there was steady work. During the busy season between Thanksgiving and Easter, when demand was highest for coal, they could expect to see the sun only on Sundays and holidays. Coal miners made half that pittance during the slack summer months, while African-American strikebreakers, brought in from West Virginia, received no more than $1 per ten-hour day.

As one of Braidwood's half dozen company doctors, Le Caron was guaranteed as much work as he could handle if he was willing to look after miners for relatively low pay. Miners who didn't die young from black lung or falling rocks could expect to suffer from asthma due to the poor air quality in shafts, and it was cheaper to replace them with other poor workers than to improve safety in the mines. Le Caron was soon also spending time on the Illinois state medical society and assisting in establishing the Illinois Pharmaceutical Society. He lobbied successfully for state laws regulating the practice of medicine and pharmacy, and also managed to somehow find time to set up a drugstore in nearby Brace Hill, Illinois. He also took on a position as an agent for a large wholesale drug house, further expanding his travel opportunities.

A contemporary county history lists Nannie's maiden name as Melvin and not her real family name of Melville.[6] Perhaps it was simply an error, or perhaps the Le Carons were gently covering their tracks in case his identity as a spy should ever become known. In *The History of Will County*, Le Caron created the further fiction that he was born in France on 26 September 1839, the son of Francis v. Le Caron, "who was a speculator and money broker."[7]

Irish nationalists in America were now weary of the Fenians' self-destructive intrigues and humiliating invasion attempts. A new organisation called the Clan na nGael was formed for those who chose to carry on the struggle for a free Irish republic. The name literally means "family of the Gaels," and there was a hope that a new name and brotherhood would help refocus revolutionary energy on the English rather than the in-fighting of the past decade. The Clan na nGael was also born of the realisation that armed invasion against England was likely futile, and that revolutionaries could hurt their enemies more with terror.

Terrorism required surprise and surprise required secrecy, and so not just anyone who professed a love of Ireland was permitted to join the new organisation. While the Fenians had proudly marched in their green uniforms with gold trim on the downtown streets of American cities, the Clan na nGael was quietly constructed upon codes and deception and trust. The Clan na nGael was structured on what Le Caron called a "compact secret basis," with subordinate bodies or "camps" in all the leading centres of the United States. "Secrecy was the text preached in every direction," Le Caron noted.[8]

Le Caron was sponsored into Clan na nGael ranks by Alexander Sullivan, the ambitious former Detroit Fenian "centre," with the well-dressed appearance of a kindly priest and the dark, cutting eyes of an assassin. Le Caron's membership application could have been blackballed by negative ballots from three existing members, but he survived this stage of the entry process. Next, Le Caron was asked a series of questions testing his loyalty to Ireland, with several key words changed through a childish code, in which letters of the alphabet were shifted by one, so that "Irishmen" became "Jsjtinfo" and "Jsfmboe" meant "Ireland."

In the next stage of the initiation ritual, Le Caron was blindfolded and heard an earnest voice announce, "We have deemed you worthy of our confidence and our friendship. You are now within these secret walls. . . We are Jsjtinfo [Irishmen] banded together for the purpose of freeing Jsfmboe [Ireland] race. The lamp of the bitter past plainly points our path, and we believe that the first step on the road to freedom is secrecy."[9]

At this solemn juncture, Le Caron stepped before the president of the meeting to hear the words, "Destitute of secrecy, defeat will again cloud our brightest hopes; and, believing this, we shall hesitate at no sacrifice to maintain it. Be prepared, then, to cast aside with us every thought that may impede the growth of this holy feeling among Jsjtinfo [Irishmen]; for, once a member of this order, you must stand by its watchwords of secrecy, obedience, and love. With this explanation, I ask you are you willing to proceed?"

Le Caron answered affirmatively, and now heard the president say, "Every man here has taken a solemn and binding oath to be faithful to the truth we repose in him. This oath, I assure you, is one which does not conflict with any duty which you owe to God, to your country, your neighbours, or yourself. It must be taken before you can be admitted to light and fellowship in our order. With this assurance, and understanding, as you do, that the object of this organization is the freedom of Jsfmboe [Ireland], will you submit yourself to our rules and regulations and take our obligation without mental reservation?"

Finally, it was Le Caron's turn to pledge:

"I will foster a spirit of unity, nationality, and brotherly love among the people of Jsfmboe [Ireland]. I furthermore swear that I do not now belong to any other Jsjti sfwpmvujpobsz [Irish revolutionary] society antagonistic to this organisation, and that I will not become a member of such society while connected with the v.c. [United Brotherhood, another term for the Clan na nGael], and, finally, I swear that I take this obligation without mental reservation, and that any violation hereof is infamous and merits the severest punishment. So help me God."

With that, and just a few more reminders about the need for the strictest secrecy, and the holiness of the cause of Jsfmboe [Ireland], the chapter's president turned back to the assembly. With two raps of his gavel, he proclaimed, "Brothers! It affords me great pleasure to introduce to you your new brother."

The blindfold finally removed, Le Caron's eyes opened to a room full of fellow members of his branch of the Clan na nGael, which was known as the Knights of the Inner Circle. Le Caron was looking upon a society so secret that many of its members even shunned the rituals of the Roman Catholic Church in which they had been baptised. They felt that an Irish revolution couldn't truly flourish so long as they detailed their plots to clerics in the confessional. "A revolutionary movement must be secret and unscrupulous, and, to be successful, they could not enter on the contest for freedom with the yoke of the Church around their neck," Le Caron noted.

Le Caron learned earnest oaths in which he promised that all knowledge of the Clan's inner workings must be kept secret under penalty of death. There were also handgrips and passwords, much like those used by the Masons. Ironically, if Macdonald and McMicken had somehow appeared at a Clan na nGael meeting, they would have been oddly familiar with many of the secret rituals as the Canadian prime minister and police commissioner were Masons themselves.

The 1870s began in Braidwood with optimism and promise of wealth, but money was in short supply as the decade ended. Chicago was the hub of the nation's new railway industry, and tiny Braidwood existed to fuel those engines. By the late 1870s, however, the rail industry was sputtering and the economies of both communities were as sick as an underground miner's lungs. Once-optimistic workers became tramps as once-busy shops closed their doors, while the former boomtown's newly constructed streets became battlegrounds between workers, bosses, and strikebreakers.

Braidwood coal miners were asked to take a pay cut on 1 April 1877, slashing their winter rate from $0.90 to $0.65 per ton of coal they extracted, with the summer rate falling from $0.85 to $0.70. The workers balked, and 300 African-American strikebreakers arrived in trainloads from impoverished West Virginia. In June, the pro-union Braidwood *Daily Phoenix* newspaper reported that the company was hanging tough on its call for wage cuts: "The men are, without a doubt, willing to accede to any honorable compromise, but at the companies offer they think it is just as well to starve outside as to starve inside the mines working as slaves." By late July, the strikers were threatening to kill all of the strikebreakers, starting with the African-Americans from the South, whom they called Black Crows. Strikebreakers fled, and the governor sent 1,300 soldiers to town to restore order and production.

The Braidwood marshall was now making regular patrols of the railway lines, watching the newly homeless, many of whom were reduced to living in boxcars. *The Wilmington Advocate* newspaper reported in its Braidwood section: "A well known young man of Braidwood, under the influence of the oppressive heat, fell asleep upon the porch of a certain store, and upon awakening, found himself minus two gold rings from his fingers. He is now hanging on to his eye teeth, fearing their departure next." Perhaps the ultimate low point in Braidwood's descent into poverty and crime came on the Sunday night when the local Catholic priest shot the town marshall dead in the priest's home, thinking the marshall was a tramp and a prowler, and not a friend and an unannounced visitor.[10]

As the Illinois economy gasped and sputtered, Le Caron found the prospect of working again for the British government as a spy more attractive. On 27 May 1875 he wrote to Robert Anderson in London, on drugstore stationery, marked "Miner's Drug Store, Books, Stationery, Etc." Le Caron told of his love for the land of his birth, and said he was still willing to once again serve England:

"I begun to assure you that if anything does occur, I shall do my utmost to take a part... I will not bother you with false rumors and I am not writing this with a view to get money, but I occupy and can and will retain a certain position with a crowd that will always be looked after in the event of any assistance being required and we do not know what may turn up in the next few years here."

He signed the letter, "I am faithfully yours, B."[1] Le Caron would later state that he feigned fights during this time with Nannie to give him an excuse to leave his home and travel as a spy. "In reality there never was the slightest trouble between us. By such devices as this I was able to move about rapidly from one place to another without exciting comment or suspicion."[12] He declined to say that not all of his trips out of town were for spying or the pharmaceutical business.

It wasn't considered odd, in January 1878, when a boy was seen loitering around a Toledo cemetery. A couple of days later, however, local police had a strong interest in asking him if he knew anything about the disappearance of the bodies of a 12-year-old boy and an 83-year-old man. Bizarre as it seems in modern times, the trade of bodysnatching had an old, if not honourable, history, both in America and England. After William Shakespeare's death in April 1616, a stone was placed over his tomb, inscribed with the curse:

> Good friend for Jesus sake forbear
> To dig the dust enclosed here!
> Blest be the man that spares these stones,
> And curst be he that moves my bones.

On 28 January 1829 William Burke of County Tyrone, Ireland, was executed after confessing to murdering 16 people with William Hare, his landlord at a boarding house in the neighbourhood of West Port in Edinburgh, Scotland. Their victims included elderly pensioners, prostitutes, a mentally challenged man, and a deaf boy. Their main customer was Dr Robert Knox, a leading anatomist, who taught at Edinburgh Medical College.

Their technique for murder is still known by forensic pathologists as "burking." Burke, a heavyset man, would sit on a victim while Hare blocked his or her mouth and nose. This gave Knox's students fresh, largely undamaged corpses for dissection.

Knox and Hare were spared the gallows, but all three men were remembered in a popular skipping and hopscotch song by Edinburgh children, which went:

> Up the close and down the stair,
> In the house with Burke and Hare.
> Burke's the butcher, Hare's the thief,
> Knox, the boy who buys the beef.

In New York City, bodysnatching drew nasty headlines at least as far back as 1788 during what became known as the Doctors' Riot. The violence began when a medical student held an arm of a corpse out of a window, and told a boy walking past that it belonged to the boy's mother. By a horrible coincidence, the boy's mother had died shortly before this, and by a further cruel twist of fate, a search of her grave showed that her body had been removed. The boy's enraged father led a mob to the New York Hospital, and two ugly days passed before the rioting stopped.[13]

In post-Civil War years, bodysnatching flourished in an America that was numb to violence and desperate for scientific progress and medical relief. There were now a dozen medical schools in the Cincinnati area alone, including the Ohio Medical College, which trained some three hundred students. The explosion in medical school admissions naturally was accompanied with a surge in demand for cadavers, as would-be doctors needed to sharpen their skills before cutting open live patients. Medical laboratories engaged the nighttime services of rings of "sack-em-up men," and J.F. Baldwin, a Columbus, Ohio, surgeon and medical historian, noted that the offence of grave-robbing was viewed as little more than a misdemeanour, which brought, at worst, a mild fine or short jail term. "There seemed to be little or no moral turpitude attached to it, and medical students quite generally were glad to accept the invitation of the [university] demonstrator of anatomy, or other procurer of bodies, to go with him and looked upon it as a mere lark."[14] There were more than five thousand graves robbed in Ohio alone between 1811 and 1881 as Ohio grave-robbers also stocked the medical schools of Fort Wayne and Ann Arbor. As Ambrose Bierce noted in *The Unabridged Devil's Dictionary*, a "grave" was "A place in which the dead are laid to await the coming of the medical student."[15]

When police questioned the teenager who had been loitering around the Toledo graveyard in January 1878, he became nervous. He told them that his name was Henry Morton, and then broke down and said that he belonged to a grave-robbing ring led by his brother, Dr. Charles Morton. The confession was only partially true. It was correct that he was part of a grave-robbing ring, but Dr. Charles Morton was really Dr. Henri Le Caron of Braidwood, Illinois. Soon, Le Caron was in custody, although his captors didn't know his true identity or that of his accomplice, Nannie. She was described in the press as an attractive blonde, and offered an investigator a hundred dollars and a promise: "I will not only give $100, but I will see that the bodies are returned within twenty-four hours."[16]

Nannie's mood abruptly changed when the detective refused to take the bribe. Her next move was to threaten to shoot whoever had implicated her husband, not realising that it was their son. Police searched their quarters and found the standard kit of a grave-robber: boxes of sawdust, a bloodstained canvas sack, an augur bit, and rope. As police pressed him for answers, Le Caron said that he was 35 years old, and driven to grave-robbing by poverty. He definitely wasn't the poorest man in Braidwood, but he was far from rich. There was far more money in digging up graves than there ever had been in digging up coal, or in keeping coal miners alive.

As Le Caron sat in the local jail, two letters from Ann Arbor, Michigan, arrived in the local post office for Dr Morton. Shown the letters, Le Caron tossed them into a fire, then stomped on them for good measure. Officers managed to retrieve some of the charred correspondence, which admonished Morton for sending a young boy's body, and told him he shouldn't deliver any corpses younger than 14 years old. The letter referred to some sixty corpses that had been dispatched by Morton from the Columbus area, and noted that his current contract with a firm identified as A.H. Jones and Company from Ann Arbor was for another 70 bodies.[17]

Le Caron likely made his first foray into the nasty business of grave-robbing shortly after the Civil War while a medical student at the Detroit Medical College. Grave-robbers in the Detroit area worked the rural cemeteries near Ann Arbor, Michigan, and outside Sandwich, Ontario, right under the nose of his spymaster, McMicken, who had lived in nearby Windsor before moving west to Manitoba. There were 525 medical students enrolled in the Ann Arbor medical school in the 1874–1875 academic year, and they all needed bodies upon which to practise.

Long before Le Caron arrived in Ann Arbor, there were rumours around the medical school there about the activities of a faculty member, Dr. Moses Gunn. The professor arrived on campus in 1846 with an innocent-looking collection of trunks, at least one of which contained the body of an African-American man. Gunn left the university for the battlefields of the Civil War, serving as a surgeon for the Army of the Potomac, Fifth Michigan Regiment. Not long after Gunn returned to the campus in 1867, he became tangled in a dispute with the institution's regents, and quit to teach in Chicago. The loss of the professor was troubling enough, but a story that circulated around campus was that he had bound and gagged the janitor of the medical building and locked him in a room before fleeing with his collection of some forty corpses. Worse yet, Gunn dared the regents to do anything about it since he could go public with his account of how their respected medical school was the headquarters of a far-flung body-snatching ring.[18]

Le Caron apparently filled the void left by Gunn's departure, running a body-snatching network that reached into Indiana and Ohio. Nannie did much of the paperwork, taking orders and coordinating deliveries. They could expect to make between eight and fifteen dollars for the body of someone between 12 and 18 years old, more than double a coal miner's wages for a week of hard labour. The bodies of children under that age weren't wanted as they were too small, while fat men were considered too hard to transport and dissect. There was also the belief that plump corpses spoiled too quickly. Body-theft rings tried to keep prices of adult corpses around the forty to fifty dollar range, but often settled for about thirty-five dollars a body, which they reasoned was worth the risk of six months in jail or a $1,000 fine.

The easiest targets for Le Caron and other bodysnatchers were the potter's fields, which held graves of the poorest members of society. Such modest burial sites were not protected by cement or heavy stones, like the graves of the well-to-do, and there were no armed Pinkerton's security guards to stand guard. Coffins holding paupers also didn't have locking lids, or the "torpedo" design pioneered by a Columbus firm, which would, its maker promised, explode if anyone disturbed the body. Compared with the bodies of the rich, the poor were relatively easy pickings, and all social classes looked basically the same, once dead, shaved, naked, and laid out on a slab. Perhaps the easiest target for Le Caron was the graveyard at the Ohio Penitentiary. A letter to the editor of the *Ohio State Journal* (Columbus), dated 17 February 1871, casually noted that "there bodies are buried by day, to be dug up at night by unforbidden resurrectionists."

It was the sign of a raw amateur to dig up an entire grave to reach a body. True professionals, and Le Caron was certainly in their ranks, burrowed a small hole, on a sixty-degree angle, toward the head of the coffin. They used an augur to pop open the head of the casket, hooked the body under the chin and dragged it out slightly so that the clothing could be cut away with a knife. A rope was fastened to the corpse's head and shoulders, so that it could be dragged out and placed in a sack. Done properly, the gravesite was undisturbed, and mourners could go on mourning, unaware that they were crying and praying over an empty box. Bodies sent on long-haul trips were injected with embalming fluids, and sometimes salt peter-and-water solutions, then packed in sawdust to reduce the stink and leakage. Le Caron chose to send bodies to Ann Arbor in pickle barrels under the dummy company name, Quimby and Co.[19]

The most efficient body-snatching rings employed observers to attend funerals, so that they could see the direction in which the head was pointing, and note if heavy stones were placed around the casket. This explained the police officer's interest in the youth who had been hanging around the Toledo cemetery.

Even for professionals like Le Caron, the unsavoury trade posed definite risks, and not just to his reputation. Back in 1876, in Newport, Ohio, Le Caron and a man named Henry Godar were fired upon while attempting to steal the body of a prominent Mason. Both men were apparently injured, but Le Caron managed to escape, while Godar was captured and convicted. The near brush with death didn't keep Le Caron out of the graveyards. Ohio bodysnatchers had a boom year in 1878 when the medical school changed its curriculum, increasing the emphasis on practical anatomy. This translated into a higher demand for corpses for the laboratory tables.

Le Caron's skin broke out in sores, similar to smallpox, as he awaited trial from his Toledo jail cell in early 1878. A doctor who looked at him concluded he would likely be dead within a day, and transferred him to the local pesthouse, where security was less stringent and the most common form of escape was death. Shortly afterwards, the prisoner Le Caron vanished. Jail authorities later concluded that he had managed to splotch his skin with croton oil, used in traditional Chinese medicine as a liniment, which gave him the appearance of smallpox-like symptoms to dupe the doctor.[20]

Six weeks after his escape from the Toledo pesthouse, Le Caron, Nannie, and his two assistants checked into a Cincinnati boarding house. Their landlord quickly became curious about their habit of leaving their rooms at 8pm and returning at 4am Nannie, who dressed like a man during the nighttime forays, lamely explained that her husband had a fondness for nighttime fishing. Meanwhile, Le Caron introduced himself as Dr. Gabriel at the Miami (County) Medical College on Tuft Street between Elm and Plum in Cincinnati, and said he needed somewhere to store "stiffs" that he was shipping to the medical school in Ann Arbor.

It was while the Le Carons were in Cincinnati in May 1878 that a funeral was held in Congress Green Cemetery for Congressman John Scott Harrison, the youngest son of former American president William Henry Harrison, and the father of future American president Benjamin Harrison. Mourners at the Harrison funeral noticed that the earth was disturbed a few feet from the headstone of a family friend, 23-year-old William Devin, who had died a few days before. The ground might have been disturbed by hogs, rooting for food, but it also might be the work of less pleasant creatures: professional grave-robbers.[21]

A check of Devin's casket revealed that his body had been stolen. Accompanied by a police officer, John Scott Harrison's son, John, and nephew, George Eaton, set out to find Devin's body. They heard a story about a cart quietly arriving at the medical college in the early morning hours. Those who understood grave-robbing knew that real professionals sometimes put burlap around wagon wheels to muffle the vehicle's sounds for pre-dawn runs to medical schools. That way, they could dump their corpses into a chute like an order of coal, and then speed away, almost unheard.

Accompanied by police, the Harrison party searched the college, and were ready to leave when an officer decided to check behind a dumbwaiter door. He swung it open and saw a taut rope, supporting a nude male body. There was a sheet over the dead man's head and shoulders. The sheet was pulled back and John Harrison screamed, "That's my father!"[22]

Someone had sheared off the congressman's long white beard, and severed his carotid artery, but there was no doubt that the body hanging in the chute was that of the president's son. An inspection of the congressman's gravesite revealed that, although the grave had been covered with stone, cement, and earth, the grave-robbers had still managed to burrow into his casket.

The Harrisons were a family who knew how to get things done, and who were used to being taken seriously. They wanted answers as well as the body of young Devin. They wrote letters to the press to generate tips and inflame public opinion. Soon the public was reading about the bizarre findings of an inspection of the Ohio Medical College. It revealed that a chute, ramp, and hoist, much like a residential dumbwaiter, were built into the architecture of the morgue, so that bodies could be discreetly delivered, and then hidden until needed for dissection.

The publicity was enormous and the investigation intense. The body of young Devin was tracked to the medical school in Ann Arbor, when the janitor, a four foot ten inch man named Nagler, caved under the pressure of interrogation. He revealed that doctors Morton, Gabriel, Gordon, and Christian were all the same man, not realising that those were all pseudonyms for Le Caron, which in turn was a pseudonym for Beach.

Authorities moved to charge Dr. Morton/Gabriel/Gordon/ Christian on 29 May 1878, but by the time the charges were drawn up Henri and Nannie Le Caron and their two assistants were long gone. Before they fled back to Braidwood, Le Caron quickly buried a stolen woman's corpse under the floor of the basement of the Miami (County) Medical

College. It was not an attempt to give her a decent resting place, but rather an unsuccessful effort to conceal evidence.

News of their sordid escape didn't reach back to Braidwood, where, in August 1878, Le Caron was still very much a respectable man. Rather than face justice for his crimes against the dead, he instead faced live voters as a Democratic candidate for the House of Representatives. He later reasoned that his close connection with Irish nationalism cost him the election, as he wrote, "It was the cry of 'The Fenian General' that lost me the seat with the English voters."[23]

There's no record of Le Caron ever publicly mentioning his grave-robbing arrest. However, in June 1880, Professor W.J. Herdman was called to account for the horrendous publicity of the Harrison case by the Ann Arbor University's Board of Regents. Anyone expecting him to be humiliated or repentant was in for a rude surprise. The doctor was defiant and patronising as he told them that he faithfully tried to follow all legal channels before resorting to bodysnatching. Ultimately, however, Herdman stressed that he needed between ninety and one hundred bodies a year for the University of Michigan's schools of homeopathy and medicine, and he intended to get them, one way or another.[24] "When necessary to try other sources, to draw from the pauper and friendless dead at our county-houses and asylums with the consent of the proper authorities if such consent could be obtained."

The professor made it clear that Le Caron acted outside his wishes when he turned his shovels on the graves of the rich and powerful. The professor continued, with a certain amount of indignation, that he was doing the poor a favour when he directed grave-robbers to dig up their remains. He was giving them a chance to pay back society:

> Now, I do not, as has been frequently charged against me, lack in sympathy for the pauper class in our community. Neither do I regard the body of a pauper any better suited for anatomical study than that of the millionaire. But the pauper has been the ward of the State or County, he is maintained at public expense, he is attended in his last illness by medical skill at public expense, and his funeral unattended by mourning friends and relatives is a charge that the public has to meet. Is it therefore asking too much that his body, unclaimed by friends, cared for by none, useless to himself, be made to contribute to the

welfare of his fellows who have given freely of their substance to provide for him in comfort and health during his natural life?

The problem, as Professor Herdman saw it, was not so much the practice of robbing graves, but rather the class of victims whose bodies were stolen. He didn't consider himself and the bodysnatchers in his employ to be criminals, or bodysnatching to be a real crime, "though not strictly legal."

Geography helps explain the quantum growth in Chicago's population in the post-Civil War years, as canals were built to link the Great Lakes and Mississippi waterways and the city's central location made it a natural railway hub. The city's population shot up from about thirty inhabitants in 1829 to almost three hundred thousand in 1870 and half a million by 1880. There was a distinctly Irish flavour to this population explosion in Chicago in the late 19th Century, with about six thousand Irish natives in 1850, almost forty thousand in 1870, and approximately forty-four thousand by 1880.

Alexander Sullivan, the man who sponsored Le Caron into the Clan na nGael, was among the newcomers, moving to Chicago from New Mexico in 1873. He first took a job as a reporter at the *Chicago Times*, where Margaret Buchanan, the woman who once furnished him with an alibi for the Detroit arson of his failing business, now wrote editorials. By the time of Sullivan's arrival, Chicago was ripe for someone with more ambition than morals. Within a year of his arrival, Sullivan was appointed secretary of the board of local improvements by Mayor Harvey Doolittle Colvin, a suitably corrupt politician who was accused by opponents of using patronage to turn the city over to thugs and gamblers. Meanwhile, Sullivan studied law at night and was called to the bar in the mid-1870s, around the time he married Margaret.

Sullivan's law office was in an elegant, if not gaudy, building on North Clark Street, at Oak Street, in a mixed residential and professional neighbourhood that was far tamer than what one would find walking half an hour south. South Clark Street was unapologetically profane, like Chicago politics, with an incendiary mix of brothels and saloons.

Prostitutes like Black Susan, who weighed upwards of 400lbs, were impossible to miss, should authorities care to find her, and ground out a living in a neighbourhood of wide-open gambling and prostitution dens, lubricated by political payoffs and favouritism. While Chicago politicians showed no inclination to cleanse their city, they did have a certain sense of decency. The board of aldermen demonstrated this when they changed the name of vice-ridden Wells Street to Fifth Avenue out of respect to its namesake, Captain Billy Wells.[25]

Marriage didn't bring peace for the Sullivans, but there's no record that tranquillity was one of their goals. Francis Hanford, principal of the North Division High School in Chicago, accused Margaret of adultery, or something close to it, when he wrote in a letter that she employed her feminine charms to influence school board patronage. Hanford's letter of complaint was supposed to be confidential, but ended up being read aloud in city council, including a passage that stated: "The instigator and engineer-in-chief of all deviltry connected with the legislation of the board is Mrs. Sullivan, wife of the Secretary of the Board of Public Works. Her influence with Colvin [the mayor] was proven by her getting Bailey dismissed and her husband appointed instead."

Sullivan erupted, with what might have passed for indignation. He, Margaret, and his brother Florence T. Sullivan drove their carriage on 7 August 1876, to Hanford's house on Oak Street between Clark and La Salle. They saw Hanford watering his little front lawn as his wife and two young children sat on the front steps of their home and watched. Stepping out of the carriage and into this picture of family bliss, Sullivan demanded a retraction of the letter before smashing Hanford in the face with his fist. Hanford dropped, pulled himself up, and took a swing at Sullivan, but was stopped with a bullet as his wife and children watched in horror. Two hours later, he was dead.

Sullivan claimed he was acting in self-defence. That was enough for a hung jury in his first trial, and a second trial cleansed him further with a verdict of not guilty. Le Caron heard whispers that he was acquitted because Frank Agnew, the sheriff of Cook County, had control over picking the jury, and that he made a point of selecting Clan na nGael men.[26] While Sullivan escaped conviction, the scandal was embarrassing for Chicago Irish Catholics, and the cloud over the Sullivans grew thicker and more putrid.

Sullivan would never hold public office again, but this wasn't an enormous personal loss, and his political influence only grew. By early 1869, the first Clan na nGael centre in the Chicago area, Club 16, was set up in Bridgeport, followed over the next year by Camp 96 on the Near North Side, Camp 99 in Goose Island, and Camp 117 in the stockyards area. Sullivan sat at the centre of all Chicago Clan na nGael activity, allowing him to swap Irish support for patronage with local politicians, which only increased his popularity among job-hungry Irish voters. Much of the work he found was in the city's police department, while his brother Florence was appointed clerk in the Superior Court of Cook County, and his close crony, Timothy Crean, became secretary of the Board of Election Commissioners.

Not everyone in the Irish community was seduced by the dizzying leaps in Sullivan's power. Some strong Irish nationalists considered him a despot and an embarrassment, feeling he tainted the sacred cause of Irish independence with venal, corrupt machine politics. For his part, Le Caron considered Alexander Sullivan to be unscrupulous, clever, dangerous, and an important man to know.

CHAPTER 12

UNCROWNED KING

London, 1870s

An ounce of parliamentary fear is worth a ton of parliamentary love.
—Irish Party leader Charles Stewart Parnell

The Irish Rule Home League was founded in 1873 with the goal of achieving Irish independence by peaceful, constitutional means. Sir Winston Churchill once described its founder, Isaac Butt, as "able, courteous, an admirable House of Commons man, [who] put his faith in the persuasive processes of debate." Not surprisingly, Butt didn't stand a chance. "Mr. Butt," said Charles Stewart Parnell, the man who pushed to replace him, "is too much of a professor. The first thing you've got to do with an Englishman on the Irish question is to shock him. Then you can reason with him right enough."[1]

At first, second, or even third, glance, Parnell appeared an odd choice to take the leadership of what was known as the Irish Party. He was a Protestant landlord, considered middling gentry, with faint blood ties to the British royal family, a Cambridge education, and a pronounced upper-crust English accent. Those weren't the credentials one expected from someone seeking to lead what was in many respects an anti-English Irish Catholic tenant revolt. His family's land ownings extended into the counties of Wicklow, Carlow, Kildare, and Armagh, and included the rambling estate of Avondale near Rathdrum in County Wicklow. The Avondale estate alone contained more than 3,800 acres at a time when many of his followers could not dream of owning a hundred acres. On top of that, Parnell had been essentially apolitical for much of his life in a country where political passions were as commonplace and natural as respiration. As a Cambridge University student, Parnell gave no hint of political interest or academic gifts. One Cambridge contemporary described him as "keen about nothing," and his days at the alma mater of Newton, Milton, and Erasmus abruptly ended when he was expelled for a drunken brawl with a manure salesman, which he capped by unsuccessfully trying to bribe a police officer.

The Irish Party sought to change the balance of economic and social power in his homeland, but Parnell seemed oblivious to the importance of money. He routinely ignored bills and letters sent to him, and he once let a hotel meal tab slide for a quarter of a century before settling up. On another occasion, Parnell treated colleagues to a luxurious lunch, left a huge tip for the head waiter, and then omitted to pay for the food.[2]

Nervous, socially awkward, quick to anger, aloof, arrogant, and seemingly indifferent to the feelings of others, Parnell was a jumble of quirks and contradictions tightly wrapped in a cold shell. He was loathe to give speeches or to engage in social chit-chat, and could lose himself reading treatises on engineering and mining. Astronomy engrossed him so much that he had to drop this pastime altogether for fear it would take over his life. He also loved the science behind shoeing horses, cutting crystals, brick-making, and he once designed a boat that supposedly wouldn't rock in rough waves. While his family included poet Sir Thomas Parnell, whose friends included literary greats like Alexander Pope and Samuel Johnson, Parnell had scant interest in fiction, except for *Alice in Wonderland*. He also didn't spend time reading about Irish struggles or history. It seemed the only opinions he was interested in were his own, and he did not have to read a book or chat with someone to learn those.

His mood shifts—from bursts of enormous energy to abject laziness—were the stuff of legend and psychiatric speculation. He was capable of restructuring the Irish Party so that it evolved from being a minor pressure group into a political force that held the balance of power in Britain, but he could not organise his own files at his country estate well enough to keep mice from nibbling away at valued papers. He could not remember crying once as a child or a young man, but was prone to nightmares and bouts of nervous sleepwalking. The colour green mortified him, which was strange for anyone, let alone an Irishman. For him, red represented British oppression, purple was sorrow, and green was bad luck, to the point that he once hurled a lover's diary into a fireplace because of its green cover.[3]

Parnell felt it was bad luck to draft a bill or policy paper on a desk illuminated by three candles, or to produce a bill with 13 clauses. He didn't trust the public any more than the fates. When he consented to sign autographs, he would write his signature in the upper right-hand corner of a sheet of paper so that no statement could be inserted above his autograph and attributed to him. He often wrote in invisible ink, and was cautious about eating eggs, thinking they were too easily poisoned.[4]

Many who took on the daunting challenge of trying to understand Parnell looked for clues in the role of a couple of key women in his life. His American mother, Delia Stewart, was the daughter of Commodore Charles "Old Ironsides" Stewart, an American naval hero, and Parnell's namesake. The commodore's accomplishments included an American congressional medal for bravery fighting the British during the War of 1812, and Old Ironsides's stepfather once served as a bodyguard to the United States' first president, George Washington. Sir Winston Churchill certainly thought that the best hope for an explanation of Parnell's personality and politics could be found in his mother. "From his mother. . . he had acquired a hatred and contempt for English ways and institutions," Churchill wrote. However, Parnell's future wife, Katharine, dismissed such arguments, writing, "It is a mistake to say that his mother, 'planted his hatred of England' in him, as she so seldom saw him as a boy." Parnell's brother John thought that the fact that he was spurned in love by an American woman helped explain his move into politics: "His jilting undoubtedly helped to drive his energies into politics, for he was deeply hurt at the idea of being considered a country gentleman without any special abilities."

While he hated many things British, Parnell definitely kept a stereotypically English stiff upper lip and a tight lid on public emotions.

Some people who knew him well didn't look into his sphinx-like face to gauge his mood, but instead glanced behind his back to see how tightly his hands were clenched. Or they studied his eyes. Like Le Caron, his eyes burned with an unsettling, if not frightening, intensity. Poet Katharine Tynan remarked on his "eagle glance," his brother John called them "flashing eyes," and Irish member of Parliament T.P. O'Connor later wrote that:

". . . there was a strange power in those eyes of his when he turned their full blaze on you; I have seen many a man quail before their look. . . There was always an undercurrent of anxiety about Parnell; some of us, at least, knew the tragic history of his family, with its record of maniacs and suicide. There was enough in the appearance of Parnell himself, and especially in those blazing, enigmatic, red-flint eyes of his, to suggest that he had not escaped the hereditary taint, and many of us thought him quite capable at any moment of finding a refuge from his troubles in suicide.[5]"

There was something about Parnell that deeply impressed Irish revolutionary Michael Davitt when they first met in 1877. Davitt, a gaunt, "black Irishman" of the west, with deep, dark eyes and a swarthy complexion, took revolution as seriously as anyone. Born in 1846 during the Great Potato Famine, Davitt's background was as impoverished as Parnell's was privileged. Davitt was just four years old when his family was evicted from their home in County Mayo, and at age 11 his right arm was so badly mutilated when it was caught in factory machinery in Lancashire, England, that it had to be amputated. Even though he couldn't physically shoulder a rifle, Davitt took the Fenian oath for battle in 1865, James Stephens's "Year of Action." With his remaining arm, he carried powder and lead balls during a raid on Chester Castle in 1867, and soon found himself promoted to head of arms procurement for Fenian arms in England. Davitt well knew the danger of informers inside the Irish ranks as his freedom ended when John J. Corydon, who had been a Fenian envoy to Paris, sold out Davitt and fellow comrades for liberty and money.

The day he first met Parnell, Davitt had just been released from seven years in the dank cells of Dartmoor, one of the worst of Britain's harsh prisons. His newfound freedom undoubtedly put him in a good mood, but there still seemed to be something special about Parnell:

> It is like coming into the sunshine and among the flowers after a lifetime in the depths of a coal-pit. Making due allowance for this exceptional state of mind, Mr. Parnell appeared to be much superior to his recommendations. He struck me at once with the power and directness of his personality. There was the proud, resolute bearing of a man of conscious strength, with a mission, wearing no affectation, but without a hint of Celtic character or a trait of its racial enthusiasm.
>
> "An Englishman of the strongest type, moulded for an Irish purpose," was my thought, as he spoke of imprisonment, of the prevailing state of affairs in the Home Rule Movement, and of the work which "a few of us" were carrying on in the House of Commons.[6]

Davitt asked Parnell if he would like to join a secret organisation devoted to revolution. As Davitt later recalled, "He then said, slowly but clearly; 'No, I will never join any political secret society, oath-bound or otherwise. It would hinder and not assist me in my work for Ireland. Others can act as seems best for themselves.'"

Did Parnell's refusal to join a secret society mean he was not really a revolutionary? Or was this a shrewd tactical move? Or did he just hate taking direction from anyone? Certainly, Parnell often talked like a revolutionary, delivering his rhetoric with a dangerous spin with comments like: "In politics, as in war, there are no men, only weapons," and "An ounce of parliamentary fear is worth a ton of parliamentary love."

No matter how tough Parnell talked in Parliament, Clan na nGael leaders in America like John Devoy weren't particularly impressed by debates in Westminster. For them, sitting in the British Parliament was equivalent to recognising the legitimacy of the existing balance of power. Instead, Devoy thought that nationalist MPs could serve the cause better by quitting their seats at Westminster and establishing their own Parliament in Dublin.

In the autumn of 1876, on the 100th anniversary of American independence, Parnell and Fenian John O'Connor Power planned a tour of the United States. They envisioned a grand public ceremony in which they would present American president Ulysses S. Grant with a congratulatory address on behalf of "the Irish people." However, when they reached America, Grant flatly declined to accept their address or to publicly recognise the Fenians as spokespeople for the Irish people, citing an absence of proper protocols. America might have been founded on revolution, but a century had passed since those heady days of doing battle with the British. Now, the Americans were careful about publicly embarrassing a fellow nation. Parnell left Washington for Philadelphia and its Centenary Exhibition, grumbling, "Vulgar old dog." Despite his complaint, this gave Parnell the chance to study some American stone-cutting machinery that he might use in his Avondale quarries, where he dreamt of discovering gold. He also managed to pay a quick visit to study Virginia coal mines and attempted to rekindle a flame with a woman he fancied from Ireland, who had since moved to America.

Then, it was back to Washington to try once again to present their congratulatory message to President Grant. Again they were rebuffed and told that it could only be presented through the British ambassador. Parnell and Power departed once again in a huff after reiterating that they spoke for the Irish people. Grant, who was popular with many in the "Know Nothing" anti-immigrant movement, didn't budge. Power salvaged some pride by giving an address to the American people at Congress, while Parnell sailed home alone.

Behind the scenes in 1876, the Irish revolutionaries felt it was time to begin secret talks with the Russian government. Le Caron reasoned that it was a case of them thinking, "We must be friends because we share a common enemy." Perhaps Irish-American privateers could sail under letters of marque from Russia while attacking English vessels. Some millionaires with Clan na nGael sympathies seemed prepared to bankroll the scheme and outfit the privateers' ships. Chairman of the Executive Body of the Clan na nGael, Dr. William Carroll of Philadelphia, sounded out Russian officials in Washington on the plan with the help of a Florida senator.

Once again, the Irish leaders felt the sting of a snub. The Russians weren't even mildly interested in the plan. Making the rebuff worse, they went on to dismiss the idea that the Irish people really wanted total separation from Britain, or that the Clan na nGael truly spoke for most Irish-Americans. Carroll was dispatched by the Russians in the humiliating fashion that had become all too familiar for Irish revolutionary envoys.

The Canadian prime minister also certainly knew about humiliation. There were rumours that Macdonald attempted suicide when he went missing for several days in August 1873, in the depths of "the Pacific Scandal," when a Royal Commission was appointed to probe how railway promoter Sir Hugh Allan bribed many in government connected to railway construction. That sad episode made Macdonald a target of ridicule in cartoons and editorials, and of sharp attacks in the House of Commons. Finally, he resigned as prime minister in November 1873.[7]

There was a second, lesser-known scandal involving Macdonald and $300,000 that had been quietly set aside for Gilbert McMicken's secret police force. There were rumblings that Macdonald had siphoned off some twenty-five thousand dollars of this money for his Conservative Party and for a free-trade lobbyist. However, when he was called before a board of inquiry, bank records were missing and the matter could be pursued no further.

Macdonald weathered the scandals, as well as the depression and heavy drinking that accompanied them. He was re-elected in September 1878, giving McMicken and Le Caron a supporter once again at the top level of Canada's government. By this time, however, there wasn't much call for Le Caron to work with Canada any longer. The series of failed invasion attempts into Canada destroyed the Fenians' credibility and that of the Clan na nGael among Irish immigrants in Canada, which had never been particularly fertile ground for revolution. The young nation was founded on compromise, and immigrants who settled within its borders had made a conscious decision to live under the British Crown. Nevertheless, Americans celebrated their revolution, and continued to inspire Irish nationals with dreams of a successful uprising of their own.

In Ireland, some ten thousand tenants were evicted from their farms for failure to pay rent in 1879 amid fears that another famine was imminent. Displaced peasants struck back at night, murdering landlords, torching houses, slaughtering cattle, and inflicting what they considered night justice.

Meanwhile in London, Robert Anderson was trying to wake civil servants in the Home Office from the deep slumber that passed as an average workday. Anderson's son, Arthur Ponsonby Moore-Anderson, later wrote that his father found the "hours were from 11am to 5pm, a nominal 11am and a punctual 5pm" and that "much of that time was given to luncheon, gossip and the newspapers; and there was plenty left for games and ragging."[8]

Parnell's fierce attacks on the English in Parliament made him loved, hated, and famous when he sailed back to America for a second visit on 21 December 1879. Travelling with him was John Dillon, who was part of the New Departure movement created the previous year, which attempted to fuse the revolutionary spirit of the Irish Republican Brotherhood and Irish-American Clan na nGael with parliamentary activism of men like Parnell in a united call for land rights. It was to be a whirlwind speaking tour, ostensibly to raise funds for the charitable Irish Land League and, less publicly, to consolidate the new alliance between revolutionaries and their political allies.

Despite his years in Parliament, Parnell still looked awkward, nervous, and aloof at speakers' platforms, but now he was very much in demand. Le Caron sensed there was a massive deception underway as Parnell gave talks on 4 January 1880 before 8,000 Irish-Americans at Madison Square Gardens in New York, followed by addresses before the New York Stock Exchange on 9 January and a train tour of speaking engagements in Newark, Philadelphia, Boston, Brooklyn, Providence, Buffalo, Cleveland, Albany, Rochester, Washington, Troy, New Haven, Richmond, Wilkesbarre, Toledo, Haxle Green, Pittsburgh, Baltimore, Louisville, Chicago, Cincinnati, and St. Louis, and dozens of other stops. While Parnell talked of famine relief for the Irish, Le Caron felt his real message was a call for violent revolution.

Turnouts were large and boisterous, despite a series of mix-ups, like when Parnell was booked to speak at three communities named Springfield in three different states on the same day. Parnell now commanded far more respect than he did during his 1876 visit, and he was granted an audience with American president Rutherford Hayes and an address before Congress. He was introduced before the House of Representatives as the grandson of an American naval hero, and was greeted with applause when he described America as a beacon of the freedom the Irish wished to enjoy. "We do not ask to embroil your government with the government of England, but we claim that the public opinion and sentiment of a free country like America is entitled to find expression whenever it is seen that the laws of freedom are not observed," he told them. After pausing to let the applause die down, Parnell continued, "But many of us who are observing now the course of events believe that the time is fast approaching when the artificial and cruel system of land tenure prevailing in Ireland is bound to fail and be replaced by a more natural and a more just one." With that, the American congressmen applauded yet again.

At some points in the whistle-stop tour, Parnell was greeted onstage with artillery blasts, like a true head of state. Often local clergymen, judges, and officials of the Holy Order of the Knights of Labour went onstage to publicly welcome him. In Le Caron's home state of Illinois, Parnell was escorted to the podium by the Second Regiment of the Illinois National, who wore full dress uniforms and whose colonel was a member of the Fenians who took part in one of the raids on Canada. "At every point, under every circumstance, without a single exception, well-known and trusted men of the secret councils were by his side and at his elbow, pushing him forward into prominence here, bespeaking a welcome for him there, and answering for his thorough fealty to the grand old cause of all manner of times," Le Caron noted with disgust.[9] In Cleveland, as 50,000 supporters gathered in the streets, Parnell referred to the militiamen in his honour guard, saying each of them must wish that he was bearing their arms for Ireland. Then he added, "Well, it may come to that some day or other." In Cincinnati, he bluntly told supporters, "We shall kill the landlord system."

While the stage presentations were impressive, Parnell wasn't a success on a social level, and he once turned up two hours late for dinner with Catholic clergymen honouring him in New York. Rushed from city to city, and platform to platform, Parnell lost weight and energy as he endured rumours that ultra-militants planned to assassinate him and Davitt for being too soft. Davitt felt that they were also being shadowed by British secret agents, although he didn't suspect Le Caron, whom he met outside Chicago in Joliet, Illinois. While in Joliet, Le Caron treated Davitt for insomnia and excited him with talk of revolution. "No one suspected, at that time, the terrible secret of his [Le Caron's] life," Davitt wrote years later.

> He was introduced to me as one of General O'Neill's officers who had taken part in the Fenian invasion of Canada in 1867. He was a "Frenchman"—so his introducers represented him—and his manner and accent lent themselves to the disguise which was so vital to the successful concealment of his character and calling as a British spy. He was of small stature, slender build, gentlemanly manner, and good address. His face was a complete mask in its expression, owing doubtless, to years of habitual deception and to the practiced role of subservient complacency he had to assume in order to please his associates and offend no one by look or word that could excite suspicion the forehead broad, the eyes deep-set, dark, and strong, indicating a great self-confidence of extreme wariness. It was not in any sense a repulsive or disagreeable face, though it lacked regularity of features and was marked deeply with careworn lines. Although he struck one as a rather commonplace and by no means interesting personality, his chief passport to unsuspecting Irish good-nature being his well played pretense to French nationality and the fact that he had accompanied O'Neill...[10]

The tour brought Parnell to Toronto in March, and then he was on to Montreal, where he was hailed as a conquering hero. Back during the Potato Famine of the mid-1840s, Quebec was the first stopping point for many Irish immigrants who escaped to America in hellish two-month voyages below the decks of typhus-ridden ships designed to haul lumber. Some 7,553 of these immigrants never made it past the quarantine station on tiny Grosse "le, in the St. Lawrence River east of Quebec city.

Instead, they were buried in mass graves in long trenches in the soil of the young country that they hoped would offer them salvation.

Lit candles were placed in windows to greet Parnell as he arrived in Montreal by train at dusk. Almost a half century later, Timothy Healy, a radical journalist turned politician, still recalled the reception with awe. It was here that Healy called him "the uncrowned king of Ireland," a phrase previously used for Daniel "The Liberator" O'Connell, an Irish nationalist parliamentarian and lord mayor of Dublin who served three months in prison in 1844 for "creating discontent and disaffection."

Onstage in Montreal, Parnell sounded like a radical, but he did not bluntly call for bloodshed:

> We are engaged in trying to overthrow an ancient institution (laughter) the feudal system of land tenure in Ireland. In fact Lord Beaconsfield [also known as British prime minister Benjamin Disraeli] tells us or rather had just told the Imperial Parliament, that if we succeed in destroying the feudal land tenure in Ireland we should have dismembered the British Empire (applause). This had been the cry for 40 years and the Empire must have consisted of a great many limbs to bear such plentiful lopping off, but I, as an Irishman, speaking within the dominions of Her Majesty Queen Victoria (a storm of hisses) in perhaps one of the most loyal portions of that Dominion, and big in every way responsible, affirm my belief that if the British Empire can only be maintained as a consequence of the suffering misrule and degradation of Ireland, that the sooner it is demolished, the better (great applause). I don't believe, however, that the giving of justice to Ireland would entail the dismemberment of the Empire.

It wasn't quite a revolutionary speech, but it was enough to make revolutionaries applaud wildly. It was also Parnell's last speech of the tour, which raised some £60,000 for famine relief and another £12,000 for League general purposes in ten weeks, while winding more than ten thousand miles through 62 cities.[11] During his April stay in Montreal, Parnell received a cable that a British election had been called, after Conservative prime minister Benjamin Disraeli declared Ireland to be in a state of rebellion. Weathering a furious snowstorm, Parnell rushed back to the New York docks, escorted by the 69th Irish Regiment of the Army of the Potomac. "Parnell," recalled Healy, "stood on the bridge the whole time until the tender left, with head uncovered; and it was a fine sight to see the 69th salute as we sailed off, and Parnell wave his hand in response, looking like a king."

Parnell certainly didn't feel like one, and later wrote, sounding more than a little like Le Caron: "I cannot describe to you the disgust I always felt with those meetings, knowing as I did how hollow and wanting in solidarity everything connected with the movement was."

The first time Irish Party member of Parliament T.P. O'Connor saw Captain William Henry (Willie) O'Shea, he was singularly unimpressed. O'Shea was attempting to win a seat for the Irish Party, and O'Connor summed up the slim, sandy blonde 40-year-old as "Slightly overdressed, laughing, with the indescribable air of the man whom life had made somewhat cynical, he was in sharp contrast with the rugged, plainly dressed, serious figures round him."[12]

It shouldn't have been surprising that O'Shea came across to O'Connor as somewhat of a snob as he was a "castle Catholic," or a descendant of the old Norman aristocracy. O'Shea held the rank of captain in the Eighteenth Hussars only because his wealthy solicitor father had purchased it for him. O'Shea enjoyed strutting about in his finely tailored uniform, but didn't seek out combat, and his greatest drama with the Hussars was a nasty tumble from his horse during a steeplechase. When he predictably grew tired of military life, O'Shea sold his rank to another member of the upper crust.

His wife was the former Katharine Wood, from a well-placed, if not particularly wealthy, English family, and daughter of an Anglican clergyman. By the time O'Shea was launching his political career, he and Katharine shared affection, if not passion, and they certainly looked good together. Appearances were of prime importance to the captain, who loved to preen in velvet jackets, sealskin waistcoats, and diamond stick pins.

The captain could be kind to Katharine, and gave her a King Charles spaniel named Prince in 1866 before they were married to comfort her as her father lay dying. However, O'Shea could also be boorish, as at their wedding, when he was visibly unimpressed by a locket given to him by an unmonied in-law. He clipped the locket onto the spaniel Prince, saying curtly, "This will do for the dog."

After he left the military, Willie O'Shea dreamed of owning a horse farm, a venture with unhappy associations in his family. Katharine noted that his uncle Thaddeus "wasted his substance in gambling and in breeding unlikely horses to win impossible races." Willie carried on the family tradition, and lost considerable money with racehorses as well before moving on to fail badly in mining ventures. Politics seemed an easier bet than the military or business as Irish discontent certainly wasn't going away any time soon. Willie O'Shea was willing to praise babies and cattle in hopes of winning the votes of earnest, rough-hewn Irish peasants, although he wasn't particularly thrilled about it.

By 1880, the O'Sheas had been married 13 years, and Willie spent much of his time apart from Katharine, their son, Gerard, and daughters, Norah and Carmen, who lived in Wonersh Lodge, North Park, Eltham, a suburb with a rural feel about eight miles from central London. Across from their home, on the other side of a park, was the fine yellow-brick Georgian mansion where Katharine's aunt, Mrs. Benjamin Wood, known affectionately as Aunt Ben, aged in semi-seclusion. The octogenarian widow of Southwark member of Parliament Benjamin Wood paid for Captain O'Shea's family home, his Charles Street apartment in London, and his children's educations. The captain might have been a proud man, but he didn't let that interfere with living off of her money.

Perhaps Katharine and Willie O'Shea drifted apart because of his frequent and extended trips to Europe. A branch of his family had settled in Spain and France after the failed 1641 Irish rebellion, and they had done extremely well financially, to the point that they ran a bank. At one point, Willie was absent from England for 18 months, during which time Katharine grew bored tending to her children and riding her ponies. He shared her ennui with the union, and a friend thought he was speaking of Katharine when he said he wasn't thrilled by pretty women. "They were a very much over-rated pleasure," the captain sniffed.

It is impossible to talk of the O'Shea's tired marriage without factoring in the influence of Aunt Ben. She had strong, if singular, beliefs and practices, which included washing out her mouth and nose after kissing babies as she associated babies' mouths with milk, and the thought of milk repulsed her. Even more repugnant to Aunt Ben was the thought of divorce, and it was understood that this was not an option for Willie and Katharine (whom she called "Swan" for her beauty) as long as Aunt Ben was alive and paying their many bills.

And so the O'Sheas maintained appearances, if not passion. Willie would pay "flying visits" home to Eltham, when he would take his children to mass. Katharine would sometimes visit him in London, playing hostess at dinner parties for business connections in private rooms in the Georgian-style Thomas Hotel in Berkeley Square in the fashionable Mayfair district. She associated such affairs with numbing boredom, but she also realised that boosting her husband's career could only benefit them both.

Throughout the spring of 1880, the O'Sheas often invited Charles Stewart Parnell to their soirees, considering the elusive, controversial bachelor member of Parliament to be the ultimate trophy guest. Parnell hated mingling and social niceties, and had a particularly uneasy feeling about Willie O'Shea, who carried himself with the absolute confidence shared by geniuses and idiots. The O'Sheas fell into the habit of setting a place at their dinner table for Parnell, which Katharine would fill herself when he did not arrive. She was delivering yet another invitation for Parnell to ignore in July 1880 at the Palace yard in Westminster when she happened upon him. It was the first time they had met face to face and she would never forget it. "He came out, a tall, gaunt figure, thin and deadly pale," Katharine recalled years later. "He looked straight at me smiling and his curiously burning eyes looked into mine with a wondering intentness that threw into my brain the sudden thought: 'This man is wonderful—and different.'

"I asked him why he had not answered my last invitation to dinner, and if nothing would induce him to come. He answered that he had not opened his letters for days, but if I would let him, he would come to dinner directly (after) he returned from Paris, where he had to go for his sister's wedding.

"In leaning forward in the cab to say good-bye a rose I was wearing in my bodice fell out on to my skirt. He picked it up and, touching it lightly with his lips, placed it in his button-hole."

The invitation was for 17 July and this time, Parnell did attend. True to form, he arrived late, but, untrue to form, he was apologetic about his tardiness. He even joined dinner guests for a play at the Gaiety Theatre, though he normally shunned the theatre even more vigorously than dinner parties. Most of his conversation was with Katharine O'Shea's married sister, Anna Steele, and when he did talk with Katharine, it was mostly about the pretty, blue-eyed woman in the United States with whom he had a sporadic relationship years before.

Despite the awkward topic of conversation, it was love at first sight for Katharine, who was 35 years old and a married mother of three, and Parnell, who was 34. Katharine O'Shea's gentle face and soft, intelligent eyes must have been a major part of his attraction for her. She was certainly struck by the fiery brown eyes burning in his weary face. Later, she recalled, "as the light from the stage caught his eyes, they seemed like sudden flames."[13]

In Victorian Britain, there were precious few common bonds between Queen Victoria's Protestant England and Catholic, revolutionary Ireland. There was, however, the shared belief that marriage was a sacrosanct institution blessed by God. Parnell and Katharine knew this, but felt propelled by an even more powerful force. By September, Parnell was writing to her as "My dear Mrs. O'Shea." By mid-October, he called Katharine "My dearest love," and not long after that "My Queen" and "Queenie."[14]

CHAPTER 13

SKIRMISHING

Early 1880s

I was, of course, shaking hands with danger and discovery at every turn.

—**Henri Le Caron**

Captain Charles C. Boycott must have felt something odd when he began his workday on 24 September 1880 as land agent in charge of rent collection and evictions on the 500 acre estate of absentee landlord Lord Erne in County Mayo, Ireland. Not one of his workmen reported for work that morning, and when he went to town to make inquiries, no one would give him a word or even a glance. It was as if the captain suddenly didn't exist.

The snubbing came in the midst of an agricultural crisis that brought back horrific memories of the Great Potato Famine. Harvests were again poor, food prices were low and falling fast, and small-scale farmers couldn't pay their rents. Like countless other landlords, Boycott refused to lower rents and continued to evict tenants.

The captain took his tough stance just as Irish rebels John Devoy and Michael Davitt had joined forces with parliamentarian Charles Parnell to demand Irish Home Rule. Davitt had had plenty of time to think about landlords like Boycott during his seven years inside Dartmoor Prison when he felt the government was trying to break his will in his cold, damp cell, where the food was terrible, and medical care almost nonexistent.

Throughout his incarceration, Davitt reflected on what went wrong within the Fenian movement, and concluded that a combined military and parliamentary movement was needed. It should be a potent fusion of the passions behind old-school rural, anti-landlord violence, modern urban terrorism, and parliamentary obstructionism. Perhaps the most powerful tactic was also the simplest and safest. They could simply ignore anyone whom they considered an enemy. Parnell adopted the idea, which he explained in a speech to farmers in County Clare:

> When a man takes a farm from which another has been evicted, you must show him on the roadside when you meet him, you must show him in the streets of the town, you must show him at the shop-counter, you must show him at the fair and at the market-place and even in the house of worship, by leaving him severely alone... by isolating him... as if he were a leper of old, you must show him your detestation of the crime he has committed.[1]

Isolation extended even to the grave, with the families of the shunned being refused caskets for their burial. Some one thousand British troops were brought in to guard the 50 Protestant Orangemen who harvested Boycott's crops that autumn. This cost the government £10,000 or, Parnell scoffed, "one shilling for every turnip."[2] Once the turnips and other crops were safely harvested, Boycott moved back to England, his name now a verb and noun synonymous with a collective cold shoulder in English, French, Dutch, German, and Russian.

The boycotting strategy, named for its first target, excited Irish nationalists with its power, simplicity, and effectiveness. The English feared that urban violence would follow. Home Secretary Sir William Harcourt looked to Robert Anderson to energise the Secret Service, which had effectively been killed three months after the Clerkenwell dynamite attack of 1867. Anderson reluctantly answered the call to duty, writing later, "Such work was never to my taste, and I had definitely turned away from it. I was still in touch with le Caron [sic] and some prominent Fenians in America, but not with the leaders of the organisation at home."[3]

Anderson felt he knew the identities of the leading Irish revolutionaries in London, but didn't know how to contact them. He later wrote that the Fenians solved this problem for him as they were eager to learn who was now in charge of the renewed intelligence network at Whitehall. A leading Irish revolutionary in London whom Anderson considered dangerous wrote a letter to the government, clearly trying to draw out the intelligence head. "He wished to give information to the government—that was the bait—but he would deal only with 'the gentleman at the head of the Intelligence Department'; he would hold no communication with the police," Anderson later wrote.[4]

True to his discreet nature, Anderson gave no indication of the man's identity as he continued:

I met the fellow by appointment one night. He lied to me for an hour whilst I listened as though I believed all he was telling me. This as I expected led him to ask for money. I then pretended to lose my temper. I said I had come prepared to pay him handsomely for information, but I was not to be fooled by the yarns he had been telling me. Taking a handful of sovereigns from my pocket I jingled them before him. The greedy look on his face told its own tale. He pleaded that if I would give him time he would tell me all I wished to know, and meekly asked for his expenses. I saw that the bait had taken, so I gave him a couple of pounds. . . Within a few weeks I had two of the most influential London Fenians in my pay.

British Prime Minister Gladstone hoped to quell tensions by passing a bill in Parliament that would give the Irish more control over their land, and Irish Land League members met in early 1881 to plan their response. Parnell was supposed to play a key role in the meeting, but unexpectedly didn't show up. It wasn't uncommon for Parnell to drift away for weeks at a time, but this was a crucial meeting. A member of the League worried about Parnell's safety as he searched the leader's mail for hints as to his whereabouts. He was shocked when he found a letter from Katharine O'Shea, wife of Irish Party member Willie O'Shea. It was clearly a love letter between the married woman and their unmarried leader. As Davitt later recalled, "None of his most intimate associates had hitherto suspected the liaison in which he was found entangled. It was a painful discovery, for, it was the first cloud that had fallen menacingly over what had promised to be the most successful political career that had ever been carved out of brilliant. . . service to the cause of Ireland."[5]

On 14 January1881 there was an explosion in a British military barracks near Manchester, killing a seven-year-old and injuring three others. Another bomb failed to do much damage at Lord Mayor's residence in Dublin, the Mansion House, on 15 March. The attacks were violent and bumbling and clearly the work of O'Donovan Rossa, acting on his own.

There were corrosive rumours in nationalist circles that Rossa was pocketing funds from the movement's "skirmishing," or dynamite and weapons fund. Le Caron's old Detroit neighbour, William Mackey (Michael) Lomasney, sought to bring the attacks under some form of control. In February, Lomasney announced that he had met with Parnell, who had surfaced after his disappearance with Mrs. O'Shea. Lomasney didn't know about the love affair, and gushed to fellow revolutionaries that Parnell was "eminently deserving of our support, and that he means to go as far as we do in pushing the business."[6] Meanwhile, the British government enlisted Pinkerton's tough guards to infiltrate the Clan na nGael in North America, which was funding much of the revolutionary movement in Britain.

The upsurge in Irish revolutionary spirit meant Le Caron was now back on the British government payroll, feeding McMicken and Anderson with reports that American Clan na nGael members were smuggling arms to Parnell's associates in Britain. McMicken travelled to Illinois to confer with his top agent, then passed on his information to Canadian prime minister Macdonald, who now had stomach ulcers on his long list of painful physical complaints:

> B informs me the Organization is on a very different basis and system than of old and that it is vastly improved in regard to management and that a better class of persons are now in it. He said funds were being collected for transmission to Ireland in cash and arms to an extent much beyond the O'Neill time.
>
> As evidence of his statements he showed me documents of the organization which he dare not part with but promised to obtain copies if possible for me

when we should meet again. I made extracts from some of these documents which I reproduce for you [illegible] a book of probably 150 pages contained a complete statement of all the existing "Associations" called the "Directory" . . . In examining the Directory I found in District J the following Record— 463—Braidwood, Ill., Emmet Club. . . Name of S.G. Dr. H LeCaron. This shows conclusively that our friend is still maintaining his connection with the organization and although not occupying an important position as formerly is still in a circumstance to know almost all that goes on. . . I agreed to pay Beach $75 per month.[7]

Reports reached Canadian Prime Minister John A. Macdonald that Fenians were stockpiling weapons, and that Fenians across Canada might riot if Parnell were to be arrested for his increasingly bellicose public speeches. The prime minister personally dispatched a woman, referred to in government files as Mrs. E. Forest, to the U.S. to gauge Fenian strength. She filed a report on 8 February from Buffalo, where she had stayed with a former school chum:

I soon found that her husband was a leading man of the Fenians and talkative on the subject. . . He said their affairs were progressing splendidly. . . He said the charge against O'Donovan Rossa that he had put the "skirmishing fund" to his private use was all false, that he had applied all of it to purchasing arms, which were stored in safe places. He said they had now enrolled 40,000 men who were drilled and ready to march at a day's notice. . . I got from him that they would not move until the insurrection would actually take place in Ireland. He said the rising would not take place there until they had everything ready. A hundred thousand men with arms in their hands would then appear in different parts simultaneously. . . As soon as a fair stand was made in Ireland, the forces in the U.S. would be put in motion to invade Canada. . . They would strike at two or three different points. . . New York is the head place. . . I am acquainted with Mrs. O'Donovan Rossa. . . I can easily renew the acquaintance and put it to profit as she is very communicative.[8]

On 5 April Mrs. Forest filed another report to Macdonald. She was now his chief spy in the east, while Le Caron covered the midwest. She noted that she had heard in Watertown, New York, that Parnell could do nothing for Ireland until someone shot British Prime Minister William Gladstone. There were also rumours that if Parnell was locked up, Canada's governor general, Sir John Douglas Sutherland Campbell, would be kidnapped within forty-eight hours. A parish priest in Watertown reportedly said that all Irishmen everywhere had to be ready "to buckle on their armor in defence of their beloved country." She also described a trip she made to Brooklyn, New York, where she found the Irish women were as militant as the men:

> I find myself in the midst of a Fenian neighborhood of course they don't go by that name. Mrs. Parnell mother of the Irish Agitator who boards quite near here has organized over sixty Ladies Leagues in Brooklyn not to speak of New York and Jersey City. These are the names of some of her Lodges, "Star of the Sea," "Spread the Light," "Central League." The ladies are very much excited, new Leagues are starting up every night. I was introduced to Mrs. Parnell, she asked me to join the League, saying that women had more influence than men. An extract from a speech by Rossa¹is... "I can assure you my brothers that the expenditure of $1000 and the work of less than a dozen men at home, have already cost John Bull [England] over $60,000,000..." My nephew overheard a conversation between two Fenians today they said there were over 18,000 men in Brooklyn under arms, and drilling every night—not to speak of New York. They said they could take Canada in 24 hours.⁹

Le Caron told fellow Clan na nGael members that he was going to Europe for his health. As soon as he landed in Queenston, he sent a letter to Anderson, telling him he was travelling on to Colchester, and that he could be reached through an address in the American Exchange on the Strand in London, near Charing Cross Station.

Meanwhile, the Clan na nGael in America became even more secretive, revising its constitution in 1881 to include a clause that read: "All persons of Irish birth or descent, or of partial Irish descent, shall be eligible to membership; but in cases of persons of partial Irish descent, the camps are directed to make special inquiries in regard to the history, character, and sentiments of the person proposed."¹⁰ This obviously was unwelcome news for Le Caron, who put out the word that his Irish mother would be mortified to learn that he was considered French. Hopefully, the mild joke would be enough to steer away suspicious eyes.

Le Caron knew there were those in the movement who already had a low opinion of him, like Fenian major William M'Williams, who despised Le Caron's old associate General John O'Neill. M'Williams publicly dismissed Le Caron as nothing more than an adventurer. Their ill will toward each other was so poisonous it found its way into one of the New York newspapers in a story that read:

> THE FENIAN CONGRESS AND A FENIAN ROW
>
> The Fenian Congress was in session yesterday. A quorum of the Executive Committee appointed in Chicago was in session all day. They say they intend to commence work as soon as they obtain possession of the munitions of war. Major M'Williams and Major Le Caron, two of the delegates, had a little onset in front of the Whitney House last eve, and blood might have flowed had it not been for the interference of several delegates.[11]

It was accepted wisdom that the next time Le Caron and M'Williams clashed, there would quickly be gunpowder in the air and a body on the ground. It was with some relief that Le Caron heard that M'Williams got into an altercation with an even fiercer antagonist, and was shot dead in Columbia, South Carolina. Soon afterwards, Le Caron was appointed to the Clan na nGael's Military Board.

The Clan na nGael was gaining strength. More Roman Catholics were joining, despite their Church's opposition to membership in secret societies. Le Caron found himself spending more time now with John Devoy, foreign editor of the *New York Herald*. Le Caron never felt comfortable around him, unable to shake the feeling that the taciturn ex-convict-turned-journalist suspected him of being a spy. Devoy spent much of his time trying to manage Rossa, who was becoming more and more of a liability to the revolutionary movement, siphoning off funds and launching unapproved attacks in England. Devoy tried to bring Rossa's drinking under control by sending him for treatments in a New Jersey detoxification centre, but few people around him expected miracles.

Others in the eastern seaboard Clan na nGael group whom Le Caron considered dangerous included Dr. William Carroll, a Donegal-born Presbyterian and one of the foremost physicians in Philadelphia;

James Reynolds of New Haven, Connecticut, who made his living as a gas and brass fitter; Michael Boland, a Louisville, Kentucky, lawyer and former lieutenant in the United States Army; lawyer Denis C. Feeley of Rochester, a former member of the Royal Irish Constabulary, and, in Le Caron's view, "one of the most prominent and bloodthirsty of rebels in the States." There was also Michael Kirwin, the Fenian secretary of war during the Canadian raid of 1870 and the charming J.J. Breslin, who helped James Stephens escape from Richmond Prison in Ireland in 1866 by becoming a prison guard.

None of Le Caron's Clan na nGael associates were more notable, however, or harder to define than General Francis Frederick Millen, who wrote for the *New York Herald*. Millen was Clan na nGael's chairman of the Military Board after a long career as a mercenary, which included fighting in Guatemala alongside rebels, in the Crimean War for Britain against Russia, and in Mexico, alongside many other Irishmen, in the overthrow of Emperor Maximilian. It was in Mexico that Millen was promoted to the rank of general. He was also notable for his amorous adventures. While in Ireland on a Fenian fact-finding mission in 1866, Millen courted and then wed a Tipperary County beauty named Mary Power, who had been the fiancée of imprisoned Fenian journalist Dennis Dowling Mulcahy.

However florid, these adventures in Millen's past paled in comparison to his deepest secret. That carefully guarded chapter of his life began in 1866, when John O'Mahony of the Fenians' American wing encouraged him to start an uprising on Irish soil using American Civil War veterans and financing. Millen sailed to Ireland, where he quickly became frustrated with Stephens and his inaction, dismissing him as a "numbskull" who only wanted to pocket money for his retirement. For his part, Stephens wrote Millen off as ambitious young man who sought to steal his job.

Millen was so frustrated with Stephens that on 10 March 1866, he quietly appeared at 161 West 4th Street in New York's Greenwich Village, around the corner from Washington Square Park. The building housed the office of Edward Mortimer Archibald, the British consul in New York. Archibald had little patience for "rads," or radicals, but plenty of time for Millen's message—that he had decided to inform on his Fenian brothers. As Millen left the Greenwich Village apartment, he suggested that Archibald refer to him in the future as Frank Martin.[12]

Back in Braidwood, Le Caron's status as senior guardian of the local Clan na nGael camp meant that a stream of top-level secret documents went through his hands. A strict rule required that all files that weren't returned to headquarters must be burned in full view of camp members. A sleight of hand, however, allowed Le Caron to substitute other papers for the documents that should have been burned, so that he could send the originals on to London. "I was, of course, shaking hands with danger and discovery at every turn," he later recalled.[13]

At the same time, O'Donovan Rossa was using his platform at the *Irish World* newspaper to push for donations to the Skirmishing—or Dynamite—Fund, writing: "Five thousand dollars will have to be collected before the campaign can be started. England will not know how or where she is to be struck." Its editor, Patrick Ford, also argued:

> *What will this irregular warfare of our Irish Skirmishers effect? It will do this much. It will harass and annoy England. It will help to create her difficulty and hasten our opportunity. It will not only annoy England, but it will hush her too. This is what we look for from the Skirmishes. One hundred dollars expended on skirmishing may cause to England a loss of 100,000,000 dollars. That would be a damaging blow to the enemy; and what is to prevent the dealing one of three or four such blows every year?*

Despite his warlike words, Ford didn't strike Le Caron as the type of man who would be calling for the slaughter of innocent people through dynamite attacks. Instead, he appeared of "medium height, spare of build and spare of feature, without any ferocity whatever marking the outer man, he gives the observer the idea of being a quiet, sedate, and rather retiring business person."

Rossa was now energised with a scheme to build a submarine torpedo-boat to attack the British navy under water, and construction began on a vessel at a New Jersey shipyard at a cost of some thirty-seven thousand dollars. Nothing became of this plot, however, except the expenditure of large sums of money, followed by rust. The submarine was eventually towed to New Haven, Le Caron noted. "Its principal use, as far as I could make out, was in supplying a certain number of patriots, charged with the control of its construction, some five dollars a day each as recognition for their invaluable services."

There seemed no end to the wild plots, which included ones to assassinate Queen Victoria, kidnap the Prince of Wales or Prince Arthur, and to employ "soldiers of fortune or discontent" from around the world to attack on Portland Prison and free political prisoners. In the background, Le Caron thought that humourless John Devoy had clearly emerged as the foremost Irish-American revolutionary, and that he was growing tired of working with Davitt, a socialist whom Devoy considered too soft.

The landscape for politics and terror was to change immeasurably when, in the words of Sir Winston Churchill, Britain's future prime minister, "The [British] Government then decided both to strike at terrorism and to reform the land laws" with land reform coupled with a sweeping coercion, or forced obedience, act which gave the Irish Viceroy "the power, in [Viscount John] Morley's phrase, 'to lock up anybody he pleased and to detain him for as long as he pleased.'"[14]

Parnell responded with seemingly interminable speeches on the floor of the House of Commons, which were so long and tedious that some listeners might have preferred a blast of dynamite to his continued hectoring. His aim was to grind Westminster to a standstill by exploiting the fact that Parliament had no strict mechanism for calling closure to a debate. In one particularly deadly filibuster, a half-dozen Irish Party members kept Parliament sitting continuously by talking 26 hours nonstop.

Parliament pressed on with the Land Reform Act, which Churchill described as "far more generous than anything the Irish had expected, but Parnell, driven by Irish-American extremists and his belief that even greater concessions could be extracted from Gladstone, set out to obstruct the working of the new land courts."[15]

The extremists were now so geared for action that any other course was simply too dangerous for Parnell.

Back in Braidwood, Henri and Nannie Le Caron remained respected fixtures of town life, with their neighbours totally unaware of his grave-robbing or spying sidelines. They didn't live ostentatiously, and their house was flanked by coal miners' homes, with a schoolteacher living a couple of doors away. The 8 June 1880 census listed Henri Le Caron as forty years old, living in an unnumbered house on County Road, with his wife, Nannie, 37, and their brood: 15-year-old Henry, 11-year-old Ida, 9-year-old Gertrude, 7-year-old William, 2-year-old May, and three-month-old Arthur Balfour, presumably named after the Conservative MP and future Irish secretary. Canada's top spy was sliding into middle age with roots and family responsibilities, making flight more difficult should his deadly secret ever become known.

CHAPTER 14

BOMBSHELL

Early 1880s

. . . he was the last person in the world you would take for a deep conspirator, and a constructor of murder.
—Henri Le Caron describes a future American ambassador

The very sight of John Devoy gave Henri Le Caron a cold, fearful shiver. Devoy clearly didn't like or trust him, but, if Le Caron paused to think about it, Devoy didn't seem to like or trust many people. Devoy was convinced that there were spies in his midst, and was capable of acting quickly and decisively if he discovered them. Devoy was also impatient for action in early 1881 or, in his words, "warfare, characterised by all the rigours of Nihilism."[1]

Le Caron also still felt uneasy about Alexander Sullivan even though the Chicago lawyer had sponsored him into the Clan na nGael. Vain, ambitious, and thoroughly dangerous, Sullivan was rumoured to have shot a political rival in New Mexico, and years after he moved to Chicago, he still played the part of a Western gunman, with his cowboy boots and ever-present pistol. Sullivan told him that, "a new plan of campaign was coming into force, nothing more or less . . . than one of cold-blooded murder and destruction." Le Caron hid his horror and disgust as the lawyer then told of how a supporter named Wheeler had invented a new hand grenade that could easily be carried in a satchel.[2]

Le Caron had warmer feelings for Colonel William Clingen, now commander of the Clan na nGael guards in Chicago, and he told Clingen that he planned a private holiday in Europe. The colonel responded by saying the organisation would take advantage of this trip by sending documents from Devoy that were too secret for the mails. Clingen arranged a meeting in March between Le Caron and Devoy at the luxurious Palmer House Hotel, a gold-walled, French Empire-style monument to ambition in downtown Chicago, where Devoy handed him sealed packets addressed to John O'Leary and Patrick Egan in Paris. O'Leary, the former financial agent of the Irish Republican Brotherhood and editor of *The Irish People*, had served nine years in English prisons for conspiracy. Egan, the treasurer and accredited representative of the Irish Land League, had escaped to France with record books from the League when Britain enforced its new anti-coercion laws. Paris was an attractive spot for Land League banking as it kept revolutionary funds at a safe distance from British hands.

On 31 March 1881, Devoy wrote a note for Le Caron on Palmer House stationery to serve as a passport of sorts for Le Caron as he travelled among Irish revolutionaries in Europe. It read: "This will introduce you to a friend of mine, Dr. Le Caron of Braidwood, Ill., who is going to spend a few months in Europe. Although a Frenchman he is a member of the Land League and had always been a good Irishman, barring the bull. I want him to make your acquaintance and, as he treated Davitt well when in his town, I know you will show him any kindness in your power. Remembrances to all friends."[3]

Le Caron left behind Nannie and their family of now six children, whom he supported with his three drugstores, medical practice, and spying. When his ocean liner docked at Liverpool on 12 April he immediately went to London to see his British handler, Robert Anderson, at his townhome at 39 Linden Gardens, in a tree-lined enclave in Bayswater near Notting Hill Gate. There, he showed him the packets from Egan. Then, after receiving instructions, Le Caron crossed the English Channel to Paris, arriving in the evening at Egan's luxurious quarters in the Hotel Brighton at 218 Rue Rivoli. The hotel faced the magnificent Tuilleries Gardens, a five minute walk from the Louvre. It was also less than ten minutes' walk from the Faubourg St. Honoré district, where Le Caron had lived as a youth under the name Thomas Billis Beach.[4]

The cheerful, red-haired Egan was wholly at home in his lavish surroundings, having become accustomed to luxury while serving as a director of the North City Milling Company, Ireland's largest such enterprise, as well as running his own business, the North City Bakery. Egan was clearly a capitalist in full bloom, with rich tastes in food, lodging, and entertainment. Egan had been expecting Le Caron's arrival, and had plans to take him to the nearby Opera Garnier with Mrs. A.M. Sullivan, the widow of a member of Parliament. Le Caron later described Egan as "a man of bright cheery presence, stout build, and jovial look and voice, the latter was marked in its Irish accent, with bright laughing eyes and warm handshake and a closely cut head of tawny hair, he was the last person in the world you would take for a deep conspirator, and a constructor of murder."[5]

The opera was a joy, and the next day, Le Caron delivered his packet to John O'Leary at his quarters in the Hotel de la Couronne, at 8 Rue de la Couronne in Paris's Latin Quarter.[6] O'Leary was living in far less luxury than Egan, but seemed comfortable in his surroundings. "I found the old man surrounded by his books and manuscripts, and from his appearance more fit for the patient secluded life of the student rather than the troublous career of the rebel." At first suspicious and uncertain, O'Leary gradually became more trusting until, by the end of the visit, he was gossiping freely.[7]

It was quickly clear that O'Leary was staunchly opposed to the "active"—or terrorist—policy. O'Leary pulled out a copy of the *Dublin Irishman* newspaper from the previous month, with his signed letter denouncing all secret warfare. He made it clear he also felt many in the nationalist ranks were dishonest, and Le Caron left their meeting feeling impressed with the grey-haired, stooped, thoughtful ex-convict.

"There was little about him then to remind one of the bright-eyed daring prisoner who, fifteen years before, had, from the dock of a Dublin court-house, hurled defiance at judge, jury, and Government alike; but there still remained with him the same fearlessness of tone and honesty and conviction which marked him out then, as now, a prince amongst his fellows of the Irish conspiracy."

In Paris, Le Caron also met for the first time with James Stephens, the leader of the Fenian Brotherhood in Ireland in 1865, and bitter rival of Irish revolutionary-turned-British-spy Francis Millen. Stephens had escaped from Richmond Bridewell prison in Dublin disguised as a woman, having, in Le Caron's words, "ended his inglorious public career by an unromantic exit in petticoats."

Stephens's home in exile was a boarding house near Jardin-des-Plantes in a rundown Bohemian area of the Latin Quarter, a longtime home away from home for Irish refugees. He made his living as a journalist and translator, preparing French language editions of Charles Dickens's works. He often wandered the galleries of the Louvre, gardens of Versailles, and classrooms of the Sorbonne, soaking in great art, greenery, and lectures on logic, metaphysics, ethics, and philosophy. He clearly didn't mind a good walk, having trekked some three thousand miles through Ireland under an alias in 1856 to gauge if the Irish were ready for yet another uprising.

Stephens's spirits lifted as he told Le Caron, in his Kilkenny accent, about how a sympathetic guard at Richmond Prison managed to sneak the key to Stephens's cell from a nail in the governor's safe, made an impression so that it could be duplicated, and then returned it to the nail. The ladder his associates provided was too short, and so he leapt from the prison wall in the dead of night. "It was no joke to jump twenty feet into the darkness," Stephens told Le Caron, in case this was ever an issue.[8] It was a rousing story, but Le Caron couldn't help feeling that Stephens was still trapped, as he sat puffing his black pipe in his modest room, in forced exile from his true home.

During his Paris visit, Le Caron maintained constant contact with Egan, who didn't know his way around Paris and couldn't speak French. Egan seemed happy for Le Caron's company and guidance, and wouldn't allow Le Caron to touch a bill, instead drawing upon the Clan na nGael's donated funds. As Le Caron later recalled, "He frequented the most expensive cafés, had the choicest of dishes, would only be content with the best boxes at places of entertainment, and, in a word, spent his money right royally."

Le Caron was particularly anxious to be with Egan at mail time at the Hotel Brighton so that he could hear him frankly discuss his correspondence. Le Caron learned that Egan enthusiastically backed Devoy's stance on "active" policy of violence, and he assured Le Caron that Parnell was onside with it as well. Egan boasted to Le Caron that he had been the backbone of the Fenian movement in Dublin for years, and that he was a member of the Supreme Council or executive body there. Egan also wasn't shy talking about finances, which was an increasingly touchy topic, with some members of the movement calling for an audit of Land League accounts. He said a three-member committee from the League had already gone through his books, and that a public audit would be just the thing Dublin Castle—meaning the British government—wanted. Le Caron successfully fought off a smirk as he thought of their extravagant evenings in Paris, paid for with Land League funds. Egan continued his monologue, saying that League funds had covered the expenses of Dutch officers assisting the Boer revolt against the British in South Africa, and for several groups connected to the Irish Republican Brotherhood in Ireland.

Le Caron and Egan travelled together across the English Channel to the House of Commons in London, where Egan introduced him to several Irish members of Parliament as "one of our friends from America." One of the first MPs they met was Parnell himself, who greeted him warmly. He was a tall, dark man who was handsome if not warm, and Le Caron found that his simmering eyes made his presence particularly forceful. That encounter lasted for only a couple of minutes, but it was considered important enough for the trip by train and ferry, which took the better part of two days, round trip. The contact made, Egan and Le Caron returned to Paris by different routes in case they were followed by spies.

They met back at the Hotel Brighton, and shortly afterwards, Egan told Le Caron that he had just received a fresh dispatch from Parnell, saying that he would like very much to visit with Le Caron again before he returned to America. Le Caron obliged, and boarded the train to repeat the day-long, 213-mile trip between Paris and London. The Irish Party leader evidently had something to say that was so confidential that he didn't want to entrust it to an intermediary or paper. A little inconvenience on the train was clearly worth the price of the face-to-face meeting for Le Caron.

In the lobby of the Houses of Parliament, Le Caron first met James J. O'Kelly, the former envoy of the Clan na nGael, who had enraged American members by sneaking money from the Clan na nGael's Skirmishing Fund to finance his re-election. If O'Kelly was embarrassed by his theft, he clearly didn't show it to his American visitor. Instead of appearing sheepish about the misappropriated funds, O'Kelly denounced O'Leary as an "old fossil." Le Caron had already heard O'Leary dismiss him as a turncoat, and so the animosity wasn't unexpected.[9]

When Parnell arrived, he tapped Le Caron on the shoulder and said, "I want to see you." He beckoned for the American and O'Leary to follow him into a corridor outside the library of the House of Commons, where they paced and spoke in hushed tones. "I was told detectives were watching us, and that spies had a place in every corner," Le Caron later recalled. (He later learned that this was correct, as other government agents quickly reported on his meeting back to the government.) Le Caron recalled his conversation with Parnell in this way: "The whole matter, said Mr. Parnell, following up O'Kelly's remarks in a hushed voice, rested in our hands in America. We had the money, he said, and if we stopped the supplies the home organisation would act as desired."[10]

Parnell continued that he believed that Devoy could do more than anyone else to bring about a clear understanding and alliance between disparate factions in America and Ireland. He went on to press Le Caron to arrange for Devoy to travel to Paris as soon as possible, with Parnell paying all of Devoy's expenses. He also mentioned that it would help pull the movement together if Alexander Sullivan and fellow Chicago lawyer and Clan na nGael member William J. Hynes were able to also travel to Europe for meetings with their Irish counterparts. Hynes, who often worked under the name Clifton, had travelled to Europe in an attempt to establish a working relationship between Irish revolutionaries and the Russian government. That attempt at détente failed. Even in the world of underclass revolutionaries, the Irish were having trouble finding respect and Hynes resigned shortly afterwards.

Parnell now shifted the conversation to what Le Caron considered a "veritable bombshell".

"There need be no misunderstanding," Parnell told him. "We are working for a common purpose—for the independence of Ireland, just as you are doing; for I have long since ceased to believe that anything but force of arms will ever bring about the redemption of Ireland."

Later describing the meeting, Le Caron said that Parnell explained that Ireland looked to America for finances to fuel the revolution: "He told me that he did not see any reason why an insurrectionary movement, when we were prepared to send money and men who were armed and organised—why a successful insurrectionary movement should not be inaugurated in Ireland. . . He went carefully into the question of resources and necessaries. He stated what the League could furnish in the way of men and money, and informed me as to the assistance which he looked for from the American organisation."

Parnell said the League Treasury could have £100,000 available by the end of that year. He directed Le Caron to make his views clear to Devoy, Sullivan, Hynes, and Dr. William Carroll of Philadelphia.

"You furnish the sinews of war," Parnell told Le Caron. "You have the power. If they do not do as you tell them, stop the supplies. The whole matter rests in your hands."

"I parted with him with the assurance that I would do all he wished." Then Le Caron took a seat in the gallery of the House of Commons, mulling over what he had just heard. His conversation with Parnell didn't seem real, but it had clearly just happened. The leader of the Irish Party had just outlined, in a businesslike, impassive manner, his plans for mass bloodshed.[11]

When the sitting of Parliament ended, Le Caron hailed a hansom cab, and rushed to Anderson's house near Notting Hill Gate, where he stayed until early the next morning, detailing Parnell's words.

Parnell was in a particularly pleasant mood the next day as Le Caron said goodbye to him in the tearoom of the House of Commons. Before they parted company, he gave Le Caron a photograph of himself, which he signed, "Yours very truly, Charles S. Parnell."

Next for Le Caron was a trip to Dublin, as Egan had provided him with letters of introduction to Dr. Joseph Kenny, MP, and Egan's brother-in-law, a man named O'Rourke. Soon after his arrival in Ireland, Le Caron and Kenny were visiting members of the movement inside Kilmainham Gaol, including Michael J. Boyton, a brother of Paul Boyton. Paul Boyton achieved some fame when he was congratulated by Queen Victoria and the Prince of Wales after he swam from France to England in a uniquely Victorian stunt, with a sail attached to a wetsuit he had designed.

The convict Boyton clearly didn't seek praise from English royalty. Devoy had described him as someone involved in carrying out the arrangements for "active"—or violent—policy. As they met in Kilmainham, guards obligingly gave them their privacy as Boyton pressed Le Caron to help him establish that he was a naturalised American citizen since this would likely secure his release. As Le Caron left the prison, he felt no doubt that Boyton was a violent man who wanted to be freed up to do violent things.[12]

Le Caron stopped briefly again in London, submitting a report dated 23 May 1881 for Anderson, which included Egan's prediction that there would be a viable revolutionary movement in Ireland within 12 months. Then he sailed home to America. He was a revolutionary envoy now, with fewer places to hide on either side of the ocean.[13]

The greatest source of political tension for Charles Stewart Parnell in the fall of 1881 wasn't the British government or Scotland Yard. It was the radicals within his own ranks, who never seemed satisfied by his efforts in Parliament. The demands of trying to hold together the revolutionary movement was tearing at Parnell. Ironically, the safest place for him was a British jail cell. Such accommodations would maintain his revolutionary status with those who called themselves "extreme nationalists," while removing him from the dangers of the fray. The British would have to ensure his safety as his torture or death in their custody would only inflame passions and create yet another Irish martyr. Perhaps that explains why Parnell's speeches became increasingly inflammatory, culminating with one in Wexford, Ireland, in October that all but begged British Prime Minister Gladstone to lock him up for coercion. Exactly what Parnell said isn't exactly clear, but the effects of the words were undeniable, as fellow Irish Party member Timothy Healy recalled: "Wexford folk are not easy to move, being largely of Norman or Welsh blood, but Parnell stirred them to their entrails."[14]

Not long afterwards, a police superintendent led Parnell from his quarters in Morrison's Hotel in Dublin to Kilmainham Gaol in the city's north end, which housed Boyton and scores of others in the revolutionary movement. The officer first allowed Parnell to drop a letter in the mail to Katharine O'Shea. Katharine was still married to Willie O'Shea, but was now pregnant with Parnell's child and very much in love with the Irish leader. His letter to her was an attempt to put a bright face on his imprisonment, and it also showed that Parnell clearly considered Katharine to be his wife, despite what the law, Church, society in England or Ireland, or her husband might say:

> *My own Queenie,—I have just been arrested [for coercion] by two fine-looking detectives, and write these words to wifie to tell her that she must be a brave little woman and not fret after her husband. The only thing that makes me worried and unhappy is that it may hurt you or our child.*
>
> *You know, darling, that on this account it will be wicked of you to grieve, as I can never have any other wife but you, and if anything happens to you I must die childless. Be good and brave, dear little wifie. . . Politically it is a fortunate thing for me that I have been arrested, as the movement is breaking fast, and all will be quiet in a few months, when I shall be released.*[15]

When someone asked who would take his place on the Irish political scene, Parnell defiantly replied, "Captain Moonlight," the Irish slang term for night vigilantism. Soon afterwards, his words rang true, with rioting and the closing of shops across Ireland.

As he was led inside Kilmainham, Parnell passed under a carving on the front door of writhing, serpent-like monsters. The carving was like a scene from hell, which seemed wholly appropriate, considering the fates of many of the Irish men, women, and children imprisoned there before him. Earlier inmates included nine-year-old Wilfred Carroll, who did a week's hard labour in 1847 for begging, and William Byrne, who, at the same age, was imprisoned for a week in 1855 and lashed a dozen times for possessing a stolen pig's ear. Kilmainham was damp and cold with its six-foot-thick walls. It was also a preferred address for many in the Great Potato Famine of the 1840s, since prisoners could at least expect some form of food on a regular basis.

Parnell was led to the east wing, across a hall from a cell where rebel leader Robert Emmet had been held in 1803 after a failed uprising. Emmet didn't realise his lawyer was a British spy working against him, and, not surprisingly, he lost his court case. Emmet was hanged until almost dead, cut down, disembowelled, and beheaded. His remains were left on a stake outside the prison door in a futile attempt to lure out his friends so that they might suffer similar fates.[16]

The east wing had been dramatically upgraded since Emmet's day. Rebuilt in 1862, it was now awash in light from overhead windows, meant to symbolise God's love and hope for sinners. One of Parnell's visitors, Irish Party member of Parliament F.H. O'Donnell, called his new accommodations a "genial parody of a bastille," while one reporter called it "the best room in the place." It faced the sun, was a relatively spacious fourteen by eight feet, with a twelve foot high ceiling and, for his added comfort, there were curtains and books from the Ladies Land League.

Parnell's prison days began with a 6.30am wake-up call, followed by a half hour's exercise; breakfast of porridge, bread, tea, or coffee in his cell; and more exercise from 10.30am to noon. If he wished, he could spend his exercise periods playing handball or taking target practice with an airgun. Next was a half hour's free association with other inmates in the glass-roofed central hall, where they could play chess, read newspapers, or receive guests. Visitors were supposed to stay only for a half hour, and they were cautioned not to discuss politics. These weren't strict rules, however, and even more relaxed for Parnell, who chatted with guests in a sitting room with armchairs and a hearth. Lunch and supper involved frequent servings of soup, boiled beef or mutton, potatoes, bread, and tea, cocoa, and coffee. Parnell was spared manual labour, and allowed to read until midnight. The revolutionary leader was largely a model prisoner. He did create a scene when guards tried to measure and weigh him until his captors reconsidered and decided to spare him the indignity.

Parnell was allowed to send Katharine numerous letters, and sometimes fused his passions for secrecy and popular science by using invisible inks. He described his new accommodations to Katharine in rosy terms, partly to reassure her, and partly because it was the truth. In one letter, he told her he "got all his food from the governor's kitchen, had two chops smuggled in daily, kept a cold ham in reserve, fell ill from over-eating of roast turkey, and was looked after and thoroughly spoiled by one of the suspects who allocated to himself the job of personal manservant, preparing frequent drinks, soda and lemon, coffee, and hot whisky." He joked to her that the food was so good that he was putting on weight.

Supporters sent him knitted green cardigans, scarves, and caps, but he refused to touch them as he despised the colour green and also somehow feared the gifts might be contaminated with arsenic. His biggest hardship was separation from Katharine, and in one letter, Parnell complained his imprisonment was "surely killing her." He mused to her about how nice it would be to quit his seat in Parliament and leave politics and go somewhere far away, with just themselves and their love.[17]

Their daughter, Claude Sophie, was born on 16 February 1882, and her sickly health sank Katharine further into melancholy. Katharine looked for traces of her husband's visage as she gazed into Baby Claude's brown eyes, and wrote him: "This child of tragedy rarely cried, but lay watching me with eyes thoughtful and searching beyond the possibility of her little life. I used to seek in hers for the fires always smouldering in the depths of her father's eyes, but could not get beyond that curious gravity and understanding in them, lightened only by the little smile she gave when I came near."[18]

Parnell begged for a snip of Baby Claude's hair, which he received and placed in a locket in his cell, by Katharine's picture. He was allowed to leave prison under guard in April to attend a nephew's funeral in Paris, and stopped over for a few hours in Eltham to see Katharine and hold his baby daughter. True to form, he also found time for work. In a bizarre scene, Parnell and Katharine's legal husband, Willie O'Shea, worked out details of a compromise plan for Parnell's release, with the captain acting as a go-between for Parnell and the British government. Meanwhile, Katharine sat downstairs, holding their sickly child. His work completed, Parnell caught the midnight train for Paris.

Parnell was back in his Dublin cell when he received the news that Baby Claude was dead. Soon afterwards, he was told that he was free.

It was a good career move for Willie O'Shea to negotiate Parnell's release from prison, even if it meant that Parnell would soon be back in his wife's bed. O'Shea was clearly more comfortable negotiating with English Liberals than associating with members of his own Irish Party, and enjoyed his meetings at the Thomas Hotel in Berkeley Square with powerful men like former Birmingham mayor Joseph Chamberlain, then a Liberal British member of Parliament. As Michael Davitt noted, "Mr. Parnell knew, of course, that O'Shea was, in reality, more of an emissary of the government than a Home Rule member, and the suggested ploy of compromise, in being imported to him, amounted to an indirect proposal to Mr. Gladstone."[19]

Others around Parnell also didn't trust Willie O'Shea, Davitt noted: "He was looked upon as a dangerous intriguer who was capable of working some harm to a party and a movement in which he had no standing of any kind, but over the fortunes of which, through his close association with their leader, he had a power of injury out of all proportion to the value of his public services and the capacity of the man."[20]

Parnell's sister Anna was repelled by any moves to compromise with the British government, even if it meant his freedom. She demonstrated her disgust by refusing to speak with her brother, adopting a boycott policy of her own.

During times of extreme stress, Parnell had been prone to waves of nightmares and sleepwalking. The troubling behaviour started up again upon his return to Katharine and Eltham. She altered his diet and held him in her arms when he woke up in his night panics, but she couldn't totally calm him. Even though Parnell had served only a few months in a soft prison setting, Davitt found the Irish Party leader clearly a changed man now, and no longer a danger to the British state. Instead, Davitt concluded, Parnell left Kilmainham "resolved to have no more semi-revolutionary Land Leagues and no more relations with men or movements which could involve him or his party in any conflict, open or secret, with law and order in Ireland. . . and this resolve he never deviated from afterwards for a single hour."[21]

This didn't mean that Parnell was free from danger as his Fenian associate Joseph Biggar warned: "The O'Sheas will be your ruin."[22] The warning was useless. Parnell was too deep into the intrigues of revolution and adultery for a tidy, safe retreat.

CHAPTER 15

THE GREAT DYNAMITE CONVENTION OF 1881

Palmer House Hotel, Chicago, 3-10 August 1881

... although the word "dynamite" finds no single place in the official records of the assembly, it was in the air and the speeches from start to finish.

—Henri Le Caron

> *Braidwood, Ills.,*
> *18 June 1881*
> *Mr Dear Devoy,*
>
> *Your telegram received—I have just time by this mail to write you but one item that I have been requested to convey to you. Your friend, Mr. E. [Egan], desires, though the request comes through me to you direct from Mr. P. [Parnell], that you at the earliest practicable moment meet them in Paris.*
>
> *Mr. P. [Parnell] desired me to assure you that there would be no trouble upon the head of your personal expense. He would see that you would be properly reimbursed. Doubting the prudence of writing you full details, I will by next mail send you general outlines of what they desire.*
>
> *Doubtless you have heard ere this from Mr. E. [Egan] upon this subject. The night before leaving I had a long interview with Mr. P. [Parnell] upon this subject and permit me to say that knowing the reliance and confidence placed in you by him I think that by acceding to his wishes you would accomplish much good.*
>
> *Fraternally yours,*
> *H. Le Caron[1]*

The next day, Le Caron sent another letter to Devoy in New Haven, Connecticut, urging him again to go to Europe as Parnell had requested.

In it, Le Caron called Egan "a noble hearted jolly good companion," and said Egan and Parnell sought "an understanding and a determination to if possible bring about a unity of purpose." He said that both men also shared "a firm expressed belief that the direct communication with you the leader and brains of the org. on this side would bring about what they believe to be the only inevitable [sic] that can possible inaugurate a bright future."

Trying to sound like a revolutionary, Le Caron added, "Armed force alone, can only accomplish anything and is the only reliance for the future." He concluded the letter with a joke: "I had a very enjoyable time and came back well, with a gain of twenty-two pounds of adipose tissue."

Devoy balked. He still didn't trust Le Caron. As for Parnell, the Irish Party leader needed his support as Parnell was feeling increasing heat from the revolutionaries in the Irish Revolutionary Brotherhood. A show of support from Devoy, a hardened revolutionary with respect on both sides of the Atlantic, would do wonders for Parnell's image in extreme nationalist ranks. Naturally, he wanted to make nice with Devoy. But what could Devoy gain from a meeting with him? Further prodding from Le Caron softened his stance. On 24 June Devoy telegraphed Le Caron, saying that he had just received a "note from E. [Egan] urging me strongly to go over. . . I should like to go very much if I could spare the time, and if I thought my visit would produce the effect anticipated, but I am afraid it would not. I have no authority to speak for anybody. . ." Devoy also balked at the suggestion that anyone on the European side of the Atlantic should cover his expenses, should he decide to travel: ". . . I would not, on any consideration, have them pay my expenses; that would place me in a false position at once."

Le Caron now moved on to Philadelphia and Dr. William Carroll to pass on Parnell's call for tighter ties between parliamentarians and armed revolutionaries. Carroll was openly frustrated with the socialist Michael Davitt and his talk of peaceful reform. Carroll was impatient for Davitt's complex and refined sense of humanity. "When Davitt ceases to be a Revolutionist," Carroll told Le Caron, "I have no further use for him." Carroll was also against the idea that any two or three people should make the decision regarding any practical alliance between the revolutionary and political forces. Instead, a decision of that importance should be brought up before the coming Clan na nGael convention in Chicago.[2] The convention was planned for the Palmer House Hotel, and if Carroll found any irony in a secret society holding a convention in the city's grandest, gaudiest hotel, he didn't let on.

Le Caron was now on to Chicago to meet with Alexander Sullivan and William J. Hynes, who were far more receptive to Parnell's message. Finally, Le Caron returned home to Braidwood, and wrote a full report for his British spymaster, Robert Anderson, and two long letters to Egan. He didn't write to Parnell as Egan cautioned that any direct communications with him were vulnerable to interception by British agents.

Henri Le Caron warned Gilbert McMicken that he should be ready for things to heat up again, and his Canadian spymaster was impressed enough to boost his salary from $75 to $100 monthly. The pot suitably stirred, Le Caron sat back and waited for whatever bubbled to the surface.

On the other side of the Atlantic, Captain Willie O'Shea noticed unfamiliar luggage in his closet when he paid one of his sporadic visits to the family home at Eltham. Upon further examination, he saw it belonged to Parnell. It shouldn't have alarmed him, but there was something brazen and undeniable about the portmanteau sitting there in his closet. It was bad enough that Parnell had impregnated his wife for the second time, but brazenly encroaching on the dandy's closet space was simply pushing things too far. A duel seemed the only way to repair his offended dignity, but Parnell coldly sloughed off the challenge, replying with words to the effect, "What did you do with my luggage?" O'Shea exacted a small measure of revenge as he heaved Parnell's portmanteau from a commuter train. Parnell couldn't have been too fazed, as the next year he built a cricket pitch on O'Shea's lawn.

The original Palmer House in downtown was destroyed in the Great Chicago Fire of 1871, and its replacement rose from its ashes in a defiant fusion of power and pretension, with silver dollars in the tiles of the barber shop, and a menu that featured buffalo, antelope, bear, mountain sheep, and blackbirds.[3] The aggressive attempt at grandeur clearly didn't impress British writer Rudyard Kipling, who scornfully wrote, "They told me to go to the Palmer House, which is a gilded and mirrored rabbit-warren, and there I found a huge hall of tessellated marble, crammed with people talking about money and spitting about everywhere. Other barbarians charged in and out of this inferno with letters and telegrams in their hands, and yet others shouted at each other. A man who had drunk quite as much as was good for him told me that this was 'the finest hotel in the finest city on God Almighty's earth.'"

The new, rebuilt, better-than-ever Palmer House was defiantly billed as the first fireproof hotel ever constructed, which made it a wholly suitable venue for the incendiary Clan na nGael convention that summer, which Le Caron would dub the "Great Dynamite Convention of 1881." To gain entry, the 160 delegates had to pass by two powerfully built guards at the heavy club-room doors, who made sure everyone passing could show proper credentials and utter the correct password.[4] Yet another password was required by another set of equally burly guards before delegates finally stepped into the inner sanctum, a ballroom thick with cigar smoke and debate, which was much like a boisterous gathering at a private men's club.

The mood of the gathering had been ramped up with the recent news that Gladstone's Liberal government had been defeated. Change, either for good or bad, was in the air. Presiding over the crush of waistcoats and black jackets was William J. Hynes, who Le Caron heard got his start in politics by rigging juries for Alexander Sullivan. Hynes had a loud voice, which was a necessary thing as he often had to shout down delegates when they jumped to their feet, ready to brawl.

No one was more full of talk and enthusiasm than "O'Dynamite" Rossa, freshly out of a detoxification centre and fully in his glory. He sought credit from anyone who would listen for real and imagined attacks on Britain, bragging that he was making books that detonated when opened and music boxes that exploded before completing a tune. No attack was too big, small, or bizarre for him, and he claimed that his agents, disguised as Windsor Castle cleaning ladies, had waxed the royal stairway, causing Queen Victoria to slip and take a nasty tumble in her home.

Sounding much like a government in exile, other ballroom delegates talked grandly of forging a treaty with Russia, despite the unqualified humiliations of previous attempts. The Irish revolutionaries had failed on all fronts regarding Russia as they were snubbed when they attempted to strike lasting bonds both with the Russian government and members of the Russian socialist movement. There were also pronouncements about supplying officers to the Boers, constructing a futuristic torpedo-boat, and buying and shipping guns and hand grenades. Delegates heard how 200 6lb cannons could be bought for $25 each, and sadder talk of foiled attempts to spring Irish prisoners from British prisons.

For his part, Le Caron was a member of the convention's Committee of Foreign Relations, where he outlined the views of Parnell and Patrick Egan. Of particular interest to Le Caron was Dr. Thomas Gallagher, a natty, 31-year-old physician from Green Point, Long Island, who sported a neatly trimmed beard and a gold cane. Normally self-controlled, Gallagher showed a boyish enthusiasm when he spoke of his experiments in the manufacture of explosives. Just a few months before the convention, Russian revolutionaries had used a dynamite-filled bomb to kill Czar Alexander II as he rode his carriage through St. Petersburg. Gallagher was so confident about his mastery of Nobel's new invention that he said he would personally transport it into the heart of England.

Le Caron also spoke with William Mackey (Michael) Lomasney, his former neighbour from Michigan Avenue in Detroit, who had just returned from England. Le Caron also had a chance to chat with Edward O'Meagher-Condon, who was truly fortunate his neck had not been stretched and snapped by a British noose. O'Meagher-Condon, who was born in County Cork and who fought on the Union side in the American Civil War, had helped spring two Irish prisoners from custody in 1867, killing a police sergeant in the process. During his trial, O'Meagher-

Condon boldly stated, "I have nothing to regret, to retract, or to take home. I can only say 'God save Ireland.'" Three of his associates were hanged for the attack, and O'Meagher-Condon was spared the gallows only because he was an American citizen. In 1878, he was freed from a life sentence in Portland Prison on the condition that he not set foot in Britain for at least twenty years.

Le Caron also noted the fiery words of a pioneer of the American labour movement, Terence Powderly, who for years ran the largest working-men's organisation in America, the Holy Order of the Knights of Labour, and who had decidedly strong views against England's leaders. Le Caron reported that he overheard the labour leader declare to fellow delegates that he was "in favour of the torch for their cities and the knife for their tyrants till they agree to let Ireland severely alone."

Alexander Sullivan didn't take sides in the bickering and in-fighting, managing to appear above such pettiness. When the debating died down, Sullivan had been elected Clan na nGael president, rewarded with more power in the organisation than had been at the disposal of any past president. The will of the members at the Palmer House was clear and dynamite offered a means for its expression.[5] Le Caron noted: ". . . although the word dynamite finds no single place in the official records of the assembly, it was in the air and the speeches from start to finish."[6]

Le Caron couldn't escape the feeling that John Devoy was onto him and his deadly secret that he was a spy. As the convention wound down, Devoy asked Le Caron what the English had done to him to make him so eager to blow them all up. His words had a sarcastic edge, as if Devoy didn't accept for a second the premise of his inquiry. Devoy didn't seem to really expect or need an answer. It seemed as though Devoy had somehow divined Le Caron's deadly secret. Was he just toying with him while waiting for the opportune time to go public with the knowledge that he knew Le Caron was a spy? Whatever the intention, the words certainly had an effect. As Devoy later recalled, Le Caron "was exceedingly nervous and hurried away from me as quickly as he could."

Devoy later wrote that he felt the Chicago convention was infiltrated by the British, and "that there was clear and incontrovertible evidence that there was at least one spy in the general convention held in the Palmer House in 1881; that its proceedings had been fully reported to the British consul in New York. . . that he was an officer in the organization after the convention, and was probably a delegate listening to me in that convention."[7] In fact, there were at least two high-level spies who were delegates and officers in the organisation, as the meeting was also attended by General Francis Millen.

In his report to Anderson, Le Caron estimated that there were now some fourteen thousand Irish revolutionaries in America, a faint echo of the one hundred and fifty thousand to two hundred thousand Fenians in the U.S. immediately after the Civil War. However small were their numbers, the revolutionaries who remained were true believers. Le Caron noted that the delegates at the Palmer House included at least forty lawyers, eight doctors, two judges, Protestant and Roman Catholic clergymen, merchants, manufacturers, as well as numerous working men. They shared the belief that dynamite allowed a small group of educated, serious men to inflict far more damage than an army had in the past. They left the fine hotel united in plans to reduce English grandeur to rubble.

Chapter 16

MURDER IN THE PARK

Dublin, 6 May 1882

I am stabbed in the back.

—**Charles Parnell, Irish Party leader,
on hearing news of murders in Dublin's Phoenix Park**

Now that it was clear that Clan na nGael affairs were going to consume more of his time, Le Caron politely pressed his friend Anderson for money. He noted to the spymaster in a 29 January 1882, letter that he had already received some £240 from the Home Office for his work, which had begun a decade and a half earlier. He wrote that it was a modest request to seek £50 every four months to continue his dangerous work.[1]

Things were on a financial upswing now for the Le Carons. His sister Lizzie, who had lived with his family in Braidwood, married a wealthy New York lawyer. Le Caron himself had left the grave-robbing business. Demand for pilfered corpses was waning now as the publicity surrounding the Harrison case prompted changes in the law, making it easier for bodies to be donated for medical purposes. Unkind wags joked that John Scott Harrison was responsible for as much legislation as a dead senator as when he was a living one. Few people outside Le Caron's home knew of his role in killing the dead trade.

Le Caron was now making a healthy income from medicine and his drugstores. Increased spying meant losing time at work and having to bear the costs of hiring a medical doctor to maintain his practice for him. If Le Caron was going to risk his life for England, he felt he should not also have to risk his family's financial health as well.

A slight haze lingered after the spring rain as Lord Frederick Cavendish and Thomas Henry Burke began their walk through Dublin's Phoenix Park shortly after 7pm on Saturday, 6 May 1882. The park's 1,700 rolling acres of grass and trees took its name from the Irish "fionn uisce" meaning "clear water," and its anglicisation into "Phoenix" could be taken as a lack of respect, if one was looking to take offence. Once the private deer and partridge preserve of the viceroy, the parklands were now home to a zoo featuring lions and drew Irish cyclists, families, and lovers, as well as a handful of English government workers.[2] Cricket and polo matches were in their final stages as the two unelected public officials approached the white-pillared Viceregal Lodge, where they were to dine.

Cavendish, aged 45, and 55-year-old Burke must have been the best-dressed men in the park, wearing their formal attire. Cavendish was a gangly, lanky gentleman of noble birth with a mild speech impediment, dark hair, and just a touch of grey in his beard. His wife's uncle was none other than Prime Minister Gladstone, and his new posting, which he just assumed that day, was to execute the wishes of the English government regarding Irish policy. It was a hopeful time as the new policies were marked by compromise and limited self-rule, much like what young Canada exercised inside the British Commonwealth.

Just a few hours earlier, Cavendish had first set foot in his office in Upper Castle Yard, at Dublin Castle, in the dingy maze of poorly lit offices where the governing classes had ruled since even before Cromwell's day. To those who knew him personally, Cavendish was easily likeable, but to those who chose to see him only as a figurehead, he was a contemptible symbol.

Burke was greyer, leaner, and far more hated by others in the park. An Irishman serving the English, he had just been appointed permanent under-secretary to Ireland, meaning he was Cavendish's right-hand man. To many of his fellow Irish, he was a "castle rat," or "castle hack," derogatory terms for an Irishman who scurried about the winding halls of Dublin Castle, carrying out the wishes of hated foreign oppressors. In truth, Burke cared deeply about his country, but his stiff, proper carriage and inexpressive face made him appear cold, foreign, and thoroughly English. For many years, he had lived apart from his fellow Irishmen, sharing a home with his sister. He didn't have to be told that his latest promotion meant he would be even more mistrusted in Dublin's Irish community, and have even more lonely work inside the dark castle.

Still, the prospect of implementing limited Home Rule meant the possibility for optimism that evening as the two formally attired men strolled across the park, deep in conversation. Perhaps—was it too wild to say?—the Irish and English could begin working together. Didn't everything feel possible that fresh spring evening? Weren't the bunting and flags under the city's triumphal arches signals of victory for both the Irish and the English?

Cavendish and Burke likely didn't notice when the black hansom cab pulled up close to them. Perhaps they also didn't see the men dressed in black who leapt out from it. Certainly none of the loungers or lovers or pedestrians or cyclists near them reacted either, even after the assailants drew long surgical knives. Seconds later, Cavendish and Burke lay bleeding on the grass, cut down from behind within sight, through a gap in the trees, of the Viceregal Lodge. Burke's death came almost immediately, while Cavendish gasped for life a few moments longer. Lord Spencer heard screaming from bystanders as he read papers from a nearby window of the lodge. His aides cautioned him to stay inside, lest he also be carved from ear to ear.

Later that evening, men dropped off cards bordered in black at local newspaper offices, announcing the bloody work was that of a newly formed Irish terror group, the Invincibles.

Telegraph stations opened the next day, even though it was a Sunday, in hopes a flow of information would help close the net on the killers. All ships and trains leaving Dublin were now under watch. Some witnesses to the murders were sure there was something in the killers' clothing that suggested they were Americans, while police wondered if the sword-like blades they wielded were in fact U.S. made Bowie knives. Back at the park, souvenir hunters carved up the ground where Cavendish and

Burke had fallen, eager to take home handfuls of bloody soil. Years later, Dubliners would say they could remember exactly where they stood when news reached them of the double murders.

Queen Victoria was dining at Windsor Castle in Berkshire when her private secretary, Sir Henry Ponsonby, handed her a telegram from Dublin, telling her of the attacks. Later that evening, another telegram arrived at Windsor Castle, this time informing Her Majesty that both men were dead.

There easily could have been a third victim left on the grass of Phoenix Park that evening. Robert Anderson's older brother, Samuel, a Crown solicitor, was also walking there on his usual route, which was known to anyone who cared to watch him. He was close to where the killers made their deadly attack when he remembered that he had promised to run some errands for his wife. He changed his course, satisfying his spouse and perhaps frustrating his would-be assassins.[3]

These should have been happy times for both revolutionaries and government officials. Just four days before the murders, Parnell had walked to freedom with three like-minded Irish members of Parliament under the writhing serpents carved above the front door of Kilmainham Gaol. Hours before the killings, Michael Davitt was freed from Portland Prison, where he had been confined for yet another sedition arrest. Gladstone had argued that their pardons "would tend to peace and security in Ireland." The Queen realised that such generosity would also bring Gladstone much-needed support from the Irish Party in Parliament. She viewed Gladstone's actions as dangerously lenient, and now drew a direct connection between the pardons and the horrific murders in the Dublin park. The Queen must have been thinking of how Gladstone's niece was Cavendish's widow when she wrote of Gladstone that night in her journal: "Surely, his eyes must be opened now."[4]

Davitt's first night out of prison was spent at the Westminster Palace Hotel on Victoria Street in London, an engineering marvel of its time, with elevators and in-house telegraph service. It was the same hotel near Parliament where the British North America Act granting nationhood to Canada was finalised, and where Canadian Prime Minister John A. Macdonald had celebrated his wedding breakfast. It was also here, opposite Westminster's clock tower and its famous Big Ben bell, where Robert Anderson lived shortly after he had moved from Dublin. Despite his tony new surroundings, Davitt found it hard to break his prisoner's routine, and he awoke at dawn, as prisoners do. He took a long walk in the great city, buying a newspaper at Notting Hill Gate. It was there, near Anderson's townhouse, that he learned of the Phoenix Park murders. He had been free for less than a day and suddenly there was no time to relax or celebrate.[5]

That Sunday morning, Parnell was accompanied by Katharine O'Shea as he left her home at Eltham for the Westminster Palace Hotel, where he was going to meet Davitt and celebrate their newfound freedom. His back stiffened at the train station as he picked up a copy of the *Sunday Telegraph*, as Katharine later recalled: "He stood so absolutely still that I was suddenly frightened, horribly, sickeningly afraid—of I knew not what, and, leaning forward, called out, 'King, what is it?'"[6]

Parnell was so dazed that Katharine had to push to get him on the train. It was as if the murderers were attempting to rip up his new policy of co-operation with the Liberals. He visited Willie O'Shea at Albert Mansions in London, who was then dispatched to see Prime Minister Gladstone with a letter offering Parnell's immediate resignation from Parliament. The Irish Party leader needed to make some strong public gesture that he was mortified by the murders, and he hoped that his resignation would make that clear. Then Parnell continued on to the hotel, where, with a total unappreciation for how self-absorbed he sounded, he told Davitt, "I am stabbed in the back."

The Invincibles saw themselves as extreme, pure nationalists, who could not live with any compromise with England. To many others, including devoted members of the Irish Party, they were no better than out-of-control street criminals who were driven more by hatred of England than love of Ireland.

Parnell, Davitt, and John Dillon, who had also just been freed from prison, quickly drafted a public denunciation of the murders for immediate publication, stating: "We feel that no act has ever been perpetrated in our country during the exciting struggles for social and political rights, of the past 50 years, that has so stained the name of hospitable Ireland as this cowardly and unprovoked assassination of a friendly stranger, and that until the murderers of Lord Frederick Cavendish and Mr. Burke are brought to justice, that stain will sully our country's name."

Later that day, O'Shea arrived with Gladstone's refusal to even consider Parnell's resignation. Privately, the prime minister worried that "if Parnell goes no restraining influence will remain; the scale of outrages will be again enlarged."[7]

Parnell's bitter enemy, Liberal home secretary Sir William Harcourt, relished reports that Parnell now asked for English government protection from fellow Irish revolutionaries. Harcourt and fellow hard-liners within the British government seized the opportunity to strike back by passing the tough new Coercion Act, and appointed an under-secretaryship for police and crime in Dublin to enforce it. Under pressure from Harcourt, Robert Anderson also joined the new department as its London representative. He was already responsible to the secretary of state regarding political crime, and had maintained his contacts with Le Caron and other informants, including Millen. As his son later noted, "never a week passed without his having to meet informants in London at his own home or sometimes in out-of-the-way places, for they never went to Whitehall."[8]

Unlike Parnell, the American John Devoy didn't rush to distance himself from the murders. Instead, he exhorted readers of the Irish Nation to shun any attempts to help catch the killers by offering reward money, and reprinted a telegram from Paris by Egan under the headline, "PATRICK EGAN ON BLOOD-MONEY," in which Egan slammed the suggestion that Land League money should be used as a reward to help catch the killers. Egan threatened his immediate resignation if this suggestion had any success whatsoever.

One of the first names whispered as a possible suspect in the Phoenix Park murders was James Carey's, a newly elected Dublin municipal councillor and a secret member of the Invincibles. A search of Carey's house on South Cumberland Street revealed bloody surgical knives, and police immediately locked him up in Kilmainham Gaol. Detectives ensured that he had a clear sight-line as official-looking men brought pens, ink, and paper to the cell next to his, where he believed fellow Invincible Dan Curley was being held. Was Curley now informing on him? What other reason could there be for the writing apparatus?

Not long afterwards, Carey asked if his wife and children would be placed under police protection if he began talking too. The British quickly agreed, and Carey told them of the bloody plot. Soon afterwards, tenants refused to pay their rents in the slum housing complex he owned, and Carey was dropped from Dublin Town Council. Carey would protest that while he did co-operate with authorities, his information did not lead to any fresh arrests. However, his co-operation and that of fellow Invincible Michael Kavanagh was enough to bring five members of the gang into court on charges of murder or of murder conspiracy. The Manhattan-based *Irish World* newspaper roared in defence of the arrested men: "Assassins! No; they were heroes. . ."

The *Irish World* championed a fund to support their families, although Le Caron observed that this excluded "from its benefits all connected with those who had had the good sense, though bad patriotism, to plead 'guilty' to their part in the fell transaction." Invincibles Joe Brady, Daniel Curley, Tim Kelly, Thomas Caffrey, and Michael Fagan went to the gallows in Kilmainham Gaol between 14 May and 4 June 1883. In America, the *Irish World* declared that 6 May the day of the Phoenix Park murders, must be set aside to honour them.

Meanwhile, Carey, his wife, and six children were quietly transferred, under police guard, out of Ireland as payment for his testimony. There were reports that the Careys travelled through Paris, southern France, Monaco, and back to London before they sailed for the Cape of Good Hope aboard the Kinfauns Castle. Carey's picture had been widely circulated in the press, but now his distinctive beard was shaved and he answered to the name Mr. Power.

By chance, Patrick O'Donnell, a middle-aged Donegal County, Ireland, man, was on board the Kinfauns Castle too. Tall, quiet, and poorly educated, O'Donnell was a veteran of the 1867 Fenian uprising in Ireland, and since then, he had lived in the United States. Somewhere around Cape Town, O'Donnell read that Carey might also be aboard the same ship. A picture of Carey in the *Weekly Freeman* looked just like the passenger identified as Mr. Power, except for the beard. O'Donnell studied the picture and the face of his clean-shaven fellow passenger, and concluded that Mr. Power must be the fugitive. To men like O'Donnell, a betrayer like James Carey was worse than a spy, and the thought of killing him under the ship's British Union Jack flag was only fitting. As O'Donnell later said, "When I learned who he was, I resolved to pick a quarrel with him, to give him a chance of defending himself, and to shoot him if I could. I did so, and I don't regret it." O'Donnell pumped three bullets from his revolver into Carey while he was on the high seas, fully aware that there was no chance of escape.

As O'Donnell awaited trial, *Irish World* editor Patrick Ford roared about the need for a massive rescue operation to free him, while raising $50,000 for his legal defence.[9] Heading O'Donnell's legal team was Charles Russell, one of the best lawyers in Britain, who would later be knighted and named lord chief justice. The defence first argued in London's central criminal court, the Old Bailey, that Carey's death took place in international waters, giving England no jurisdiction. Losing that argument, O'Donnell's counsel next argued that the shooting was in self-defence. When that tactic failed also, and O'Donnell heard his sentence of death, he defiantly shouted, "Three cheers for Old Ireland!"

The American Congress and White House pleaded for leniency for O'Donnell, an American citizen, but to no avail. His life ended on the gallows outside London's Old Bailey courts on 17 December 1883, where patrons at the Magpie and Stump pub across the street could pay for a "hanging breakfast," which combined a hearty repast with a clear view of his drop to eternity. The *Irish World* now paid for a monument at Glasnevin cemetery in Dublin, so that it could be chiselled in marble that O'Donnell "heroically gave up his life for Ireland."

For years afterwards, James Carey's name was infamous in Irish quarters everywhere, including Le Caron's American haunts. The *Chicago Citizen* newspaper noted on 13 February 1886 that it was a slur to even suggest that someone was related to Carey:

> *Mr. John Devlin, who has a large grocery business at Nos. 22, 24 and 26 East Randolph street, city, has been greatly annoyed by the circulation of a*

malignant report to the effect that he had in his employ a daughter of the late informer, James Carey, of Dublin. On the contrary, Mr. Devlin has in his store the sister of Mrs. Curley, widow of Daniel Curley, one of Carey's victims. Mr. Devlin is at a loss to know what malevolent motive was at the bottom of the false statement. He very naturally thinks that the rumor originated with some mean enemy who desired to injure him in his business.[10]

Le Caron needed no reminders of how time and distance did not blunt the revolutionaries' desire to extinguish their betrayers, like himself.

CHAPTER 17

BOMB SCHOOL GRADUATES

1882-1885

Let us meet our enemies with smiling faces, and with a warm grasp of the hand, having daggers up our sleeves ready to stab them to the heart.

—**Irish revolutionary Patrick Egan**

Patrick Sullivan wasn't impressed in the springtime of 1882 when Patrick Egan pledged at a meeting in Paris to deliver him $50,000 of Land League funds. Le Caron's Chicago neighbour wanted double that amount, plus half of all future funds sent from America or, he threatened, he would sever ties between the Clan na nGael in America and the Irish Land League. Faced with the possible loss of future American funding and the crippling of his movement, Egan buckled.[1]

On 15 May 1882 immediately after his return from Paris, Sullivan sent $100,000 to his Chicago law firm, and shortly after that, the sum appeared in his bank account. It was then withdrawn to pay a stockbroker to finance his personal speculation on the Chicago Board of Trade. None of those funds found their way into the Clan na nGael treasury or the revolutionary movement.

It was also in 1882 that O'Donovan "O'Dynamite" Rossa was finally expelled from the Clan na nGael. He was simply too unmanageable, and dipped his hand too often into the Skirmishing Fund. This splitting of the revolutionary ranks made them harder to monitor for Le Caron and even more dangerous for the English public.

On 4 September Le Caron wrote to Robert Anderson, once again complaining about finances. He repeated that his spying duties meant that he had to leave his businesses to others, which cost him money. He was now visiting Chicago at least once a week for Clan na nGael business, and now had some one thousand dollars in debts, he sadly noted. "I am not as prosperous in business matters as I should be and I think through no fault of mine." He continued in his letter that the Clan na nGael was actively fundraising, and he was expected to give donations, or lose face: "I have fourteen letters in my desk at this moment from Clare to New Mexico, containing Lottery tickets and appeals for money for convents, colleges, orphans, sick brothers, military companies and 'dead beats.'"

Le Caron continued that Braidwood was "one of the worst Irish Holes in the country," but said Braidwood "is not [the] Headquarters Chicago is, and will continue to be." Perhaps it was time for a move out of the ailing coal town. "There is no doubt I could advance your interests more in Chicago or even N.Y. than here." Meanwhile, he said he wanted a deal of $1,200 a year for five years for his continued efforts.[2]

The Clan na nGael's dynamite campaign was to swing into full gear in the winter of 1882 to 1883 under the guidance of Dr. Thomas Gallagher, who appeared so professional and enthusiastic to Le Caron at the Palmer House convention in Chicago, with his fine manners, gold-headed cane, and grand plans for carrying dynamite into the heart of English power. A secret message sent out by the FC (code for "governing body") told members "that it had no delicacy or sentimentality about how it would strike the enemy, or when or where... so that the suffering, bitterness, and desolation which followed active measures should be felt in every place."

Gallagher announced that he was taking a voyage to Europe on the steamship Alaska on 15 October for health reasons. Saying he wanted to visit relatives, he travelled from Liverpool to Glasgow, where there was a pocket of extreme Irish nationalists. Gallagher's next stop was London and the London Wall Hotel, where, for the next month, he laid the groundwork for anticipated horrors to come. Next was Dublin, where he stayed in the elegant Gresham Hotel downtown, about a twenty-minute walk from the seat of British power in Dublin Castle. From there, it was on to Donegal, ostensibly to visit more relatives, and then the port of Queenstown. The dapper doctor sailed home on the Bosnia on 10 December his plans apparently completed for future bloodshed. Throughout the trip, he identified himself as Fletcher.

Back in America, Gallagher met with Sullivan and Le Caron in Chicago in January 1883. "He soon wearied me, however," Le Caron later recalled, "for I found he could talk of nothing but dynamite, its production, its effectiveness, and the great weapon it was soon to prove against the British Government."

Gallagher outlined his plans for carnage to other key Americans in the revolutionary movement over the next few months. Then in mid-March, eight men sailed out of New York harbour, led by Gallagher, on the steamer Parthia I, bound for England. To avoid suspicion, they carried themselves as gentlemen, and fanned out upon reaching Liverpool. Gallagher found quarters at the grand Charing Cross Hotel opposite Covent Garden at the top of the Strand in London. Others in his team quickly set up a nitroglycerine factory in Birmingham, and soon the volatile liquid was in London, transported in rubber bags and stockings.

Gallagher had orders to keep to himself, but he remained a chatty man, particularly when the topic was dynamite. He consorted with nationalists who were friendly with Rossa, and word passed from them to "Red Jim" McDermott, whose handsome face had been a familiar sight in Fenian and Irish revolutionary circles since Civil War days. McDermott had tried "to organize dynamite clubs" in Montreal in 1882, according to Michael Davitt, who had an uneasy feeling about the man. James Stephens had similar qualms about him as far back as 1864. The instincts of Davitt and Stephens were true, as Red Jim was a spy, who had sold information to the British on the Fenian invasion plots of Canada. From Red Jim, it was a straight line for details of the dynamite plot to the desks of British government officials.[3]

Not long afterwards, Gallagher and his associates were arrested and their explosives seized. If the physician had maintained his freedom for just a few more days, Egan later complained, some of the proudest buildings in England would have been reduced to rubble.[4] Instead, in May 1883, Gallagher and three others were convicted. Once so comfortable in fine restaurants and hotels, with his gold cane and elegant manners,

Gallagher quickly became unhinged inside British prisons. By the time he was released on humanitarian grounds from Portland Prison in August 1896, he was insane.[5]

On 30 April 1883 Le Caron received US$150, as he agreed to a five-year contract, with payments retroactive to 1 January 1883, to continue spying for Britain. He signed the deal with Edward Archibald, the British consul who operated out of 161 West 4th Street in New York City's Greenwich Village, and who was Francis Millen's contact in 1866. For at least 17 years, Archibald had known Le Caron was a spy, and he had his own impressive cadre of informers as well, sharing intelligence freely with Gilbert McMicken, Canada's governor general, Lord Monck, Scotland Yard's Robert Anderson, and the British Home Office. In reaching the long-term deal, Archibald noted that Le Caron would continue to share information with his principal handler, Anderson:

> [I]nformation of the proceedings and movements of the v.c. organization, or other associations or persons connected in plots or projects for subverting the authority of the British Government in Ireland. That, for the better fulfillment of this engagement, the said Beach shall, in the course of the present year, remove to and settle in Chicago, not later than October next. In consideration of the diligent and faithful performance of the services in question, the said Beach is to receive a salary of Twelve Hundred dollars ($1200) a year, payable quarterly; and shall also be paid when he shall have removed to and established himself in Chicago, the further sum of seven hundred & fifty ($750) toward defraying the expenses of such removal.[6]

Back in Illinois in early February 1883, particularly heavy rains worried coal miners who ventured deep under Diamond Mine of the Wilmington Coal Mining and Manufacturing Company, on the Grundy-Will County line. The easy-to-reach veins of coal were exhausted now, and the deeper the miners tunnelled, the more dangerous their work became. Land above the shaft was marshy, with no drainage, and the weight of the rain waters and melting snow and ice strained the wood supporting the shafts that the men travelled through on their dark, damp, extended trips underground.

On 16 February 1883 the east side of the mine caved in, and the main entrance—and the escape route—from the shaft quickly became a pool of frigid water. A few men and boys near the surface who heard the sound of the emergency siren were able to scramble to safety. Search parties were sent down to seek out the remaining miners. One rescue team got trapped themselves, and when they finally crawled to the surface, vowed never again to go underground. It took 38 days to pump the near-freezing water from the mine, so that the bodies of the 15 men and boys who died underground could be given proper burials. The bodies of another 46 trapped miners were never recovered, entombed in the explosion of fallen rock and debris.

Dr. Henri Le Caron sat on a local relief committee, which decided that fellow miners, and not mine companies, should pay the cost of helping out the widows and orphans of those who died. Instead of approaching the companies for financial aid or a commitment to shore up existing mines, Le Caron's committee resolved "to ask every miner on the prairies to have his company withhold one day's wages to apply it to the relief fund. There are over two thousand miners on the prairies, whose average daily wage is $2.50, and the aggregate sum will make a very handsome contribution."[7]

The Braidwood economy, like Diamond Mine, had collapsed. Within a few months, the Le Carons moved to Chicago, closer to the core of Clan na nGael power. They lived in a succession of houses before settling in an apartment in a house at 177 La Salle Avenue, in a mix of residential and commercial townhouses and apartments near Sullivan's law office.

The new urban living quarters gave Le Caron a front-row seat for watching Sullivan interact with a newcomer to Chicago, Dr. Patrick Henry Cronin. Powerfully built and almost six feet tall, with a full head of hair and a luxuriant moustache, Cronin turned the eyes of ladies when he arrived in Chicago in November 1882. Others must have been impressed when they heard his tenor voice in local gatherings, singing "Hymn to Washington." Cronin never married, caustically suggesting that he was not long for this world and had no desire to make someone a widow. Instead, he was consumed with his studies and Irish politics, joining the Royal League, Legion of Honor, Ancient Order of Hibernians,

Independent Order of Foresters, Catholic Order of the Foresters, Celto-American Club, among other Irish organisations.

Born in 1846 near Mallow in County Cork, Cronin was raised in New York City, Baltimore, and St. Catharines, Ontario, Canada, where he was educated by Christian Brothers. Two of his sisters were nuns in Canada, while a married sister settled in St. Catharines and a brother farmed near Fort Smith, Arkansas. He studied chemistry in St. Louis, Missouri, before teaching school and working in a drugstore in Petroleum City, Pennsylvania. Then it was back to more studies, as Cronin earned a degree in medicine from the University of Missouri and Master of Arts at St. Louis University. There was a brief trip to Europe, where he was a commissioner at the Paris Exhibition, followed by study in European hospitals before he returned to St. Louis for even more medical training. His grades were exceptional, and not long after graduation he was professor of Materia Medica and Therapeutics in the college in St. Louis.

None of Cronin's many passions were stronger than his feelings for Irish nationalist politics, and he was a member of the Clan na nGael and Land League, and friends with John Devoy. His most notable gifts were his strong mind and soft heart. Friends smiled as they recounted how he had found a cat with a broken leg on the street in St. Louis, and was preparing to kill it with a drug when the animal stroked his hand with its paw. Cronin relented and nursed the cat back to health, and it became a fixture in his medical office. The doctor's chief weakness was, ironically, an overappreciation of his many strengths. He knew he had leadership potential, and wasn't shy in his ambitions, often preferring to drown out voices rather than listen to them. "In fact, so pronounced were his ideas in favour of his supremacy, that where he could not rule he was quite prepared to ruin," Le Caron concluded.[8]

Alexander Sullivan quickly befriended the formidable newcomer when he moved to Chicago, recognising a potentially valuable ally and dangerous rival. True to his form as a power broker, Sullivan helped Cronin secure a position at the Cook County Hospital. It seemed only convenient when Cronin moved into a suite of well-furnished rooms directly above the Windsor Theatre at 351 Clark Street North, at Oak Street, just a few doors down from Sullivan's law office.

It seemed to Le Caron that Cronin was better known and respected in six months in Chicago than an ordinary resident could hope to be after ten years. Cronin was elected president of the Eighteenth Ward Land League, then known as the Banner League or chief league of Chicago. He also was a guiding spring of Camp No. 96 of the Clan na nGael in Chicago, publicly known as the Columbia Literary Association. Behind the doors of this closed society, Cronin loudly called for bombing English government buildings and, Le Caron noted, "owing to his scientific attainments, he was appointed as chief instructor in the use and handling of explosives. . ." In other words, the soft-hearted former professor of medicine now ran an underground bomb school, with the goal of mass destruction.

It's perhaps not surprising that Cronin and Sullivan soon grated on each other's nerves. Both considered themselves natural leaders. There can only be one alpha male in a pack of dogs, and men's organisations aren't much different. Cronin noted that many Irish nationalists blamed Alexander Sullivan for Chicago's machine politics, and felt that he had allowed a sacred cause to be fouled by base, opportunistic saloon schemers. These critics included Democrats like William J. Hynes, who was said to have once fixed juries for Sullivan, and Patrick W. Dunne, the father of a future governor of Illinois. Others who considered Sullivan somewhat of a corrupt dictator included Republicans John F. Scanlan and Patrick McGarry and labour leaders Richard Powers and Daniel Gleason. By early 1883, Cronin was more comfortable with these men than with Sullivan as tensions between himself and Sullivan smouldered dangerously. It only got worse when a call went out for delegates for the Philadelphia Convention of 25-27 April 1883. Alexander Sullivan, his brother Florence, and other loyalists, were parachuted into Cronin's branch of the League and then elected as its delegates, to Cronin's disgust.

Soon Cronin was loudly accusing his former friend Sullivan of corruption. Sullivan struck back by calling Cronin a liar and a traitor. The Clan na nGael ruptured into two wings: the Devoy (or Vera Cruz) wing, which included Dr. Cronin and Luke Dillon of Philadelphia, and the Unlimited Security wing, which was made up of Alexander Sullivan and his supporters. Le Caron considered Sullivan's Unlimited Security faction to be the strongest, and pretended to give it his support.[9]

Toward the end of May 1883, Le Caron began hearing details of the Dynamite Campaign. Many nationalists opposed it, fearing it would only thwart the progress that Parnell appeared to be making in Parliament. Among those who rejected the Dynamite Campaign was Davitt, the one-armed man who had once gone to prison for running weapons for revolutionaries. Davitt hadn't softened in his desire for Irish independence, but he felt Parnell was making definite progress, which the terrorism threatened. Davitt later wrote: "Nothing at the time could well be more of a political antithesis to the means by which we sought to make landlordism impossible in Ireland, and no Englishman fearing for his life in London during the dynamite scare hated these outrages more than Mr. Parnell."[10]

Clan na nGael members planned to honour Patrick Egan in Milwaukee, shortly after Egan escaped to America in the spring of 1883, fleeing prosecution for his role in organising the Phoenix Park murders.[11] Le Caron accompanied Sullivan to the reception for Egan, and they chatted freely along the way, with Sullivan noting that the Clan na nGael was particularly nervous now about spies. There were fresh rumours that the British had dispatched scores of police to infiltrate their ranks and the Clan na nGael was not accepting volunteers as it sought to recruit unmarried men in the handling of explosives.

Sullivan volunteered that Dr. Gallagher, the genteel man with the gold-headed cane, had actually managed to secure a meeting with British Liberal leader Gladstone before the doctor's arrest and imprisonment. The words hung in the air, with no explanation offered. Sullivan moved on in conversation, saying he didn't apologise because his Unlimited Security wing had burned their books. Of course there were no records of meetings. Fewer records meant less evidence for British spies, who could be anywhere.

Back in London, Anderson understandably felt undervalued at Scotland Yard. His boss, Edward Jenkinson, had taken a profound dislike to him in the mid-1880s after the spymaster made it clear he wasn't going to share his contacts, like Le Caron. This grated against Jenkinson, an intensely private man himself, who had a mania for intelligence gathering. Sometimes, Jenkinson snuck about in wigs and false beards to escape detection, and sometimes he employed female agents, who used sex to entrap targets. Jenkinson could outwit criminals and terrorists, but he couldn't win over his own employee, so he decided to get rid of him. Jenkinson cut Anderson's pay, in hopes this might humiliate him into resigning. Anderson soldiered on. Finally, in March 1884, Jenkinson fired him, frustrated that he would never take the hint and quit.

Anderson was now shuffled to a post as secretary of Prison Commissioners. Even though he no longer worked at Scotland Yard, he stayed in contact with Le Caron, and maintained secrecy about their association. Once again, he proved that he was a man who could be trusted with Le Caron's secrets and his life.[12]

As Scotland Yard leaders wasted energy on infighting, bombers landed on England's shores from America with deadly plans. In the first half of 1884, dynamite was discovered at Paddington, Charing Cross, and Ludgate Hill subway stations in London. In February, dynamite rocked the city's main train and underground terminal, Victoria Station. Shortly before 9pm on 30 May a bomb went off near an archway between Trafalgar Square and Westminster Abbey on what journalist John McEnnis called "the street that governs England."[13] Hidden in a cast-iron urinal outside the Rising Sun public drinking house, it tore apart the neighbouring office of Scotland Yard's detectives' office, Special (Irish) branch. The urinal attack was humiliating for the police force, made worse when news leaked out that the terrorists had warned of the bomb in an anonymous letter. Also that night, a bomb exploded in the basement of the Junior Carleton Club, a posh gentlemen's club in the back of St. James Square, with signs announcing "Quiet" on its walls. It was likely meant for the Carlton Club, the neighbouring Georgian edifice where Britain's Tory establishment liked to unwind after a day of governing. Another bomb, discovered at the foot of Nelson's column in Trafalgar Square, was dismantled before it could explode.

The wave of bombers on England's shores included Luke Dillon of Philadelphia, who told confederates that he carried his dynamite in a belt, hooked to a button of his vest, which he could ignite if he felt threatened. For Dillon, Ireland was an abstraction, but one well worth dying for. His parents hailed from County Sligo, but he had never actually drawn a breath in the country, and had no plans to ever do so. Dillon made it clear that he also didn't want to be buried in Ireland lest he "might be compelled to sleep beside some one who had not been true to Erin."[14]

Dillon was born in Leeds, Yorkshire, in 1850, after his parents were driven out of Ireland by evictions. He moved from England to the U.S. when he was six years old, first to Trenton, New Jersey, and then Philadelphia. His father fought for the Union in the Civil War and Dillon became a soldier, too, when he was 17-years-old. He served for three years with the 27th Cavalry in Montana and Wyoming, in wayward outposts like Boconstitutionzeman, Fort Union, and Wind River. He developed affection for Native peoples, and learned some of their phrases. However, he also fought against them in the Indian Wars, including battles against Oglala Sioux chief Red Cloud, who rightly feared that White encroachment meant death for his people's way of life.

At age 20, Dillon left the cavalry, and he eventually found work as a clerk in a bank. More importantly, he joined the Clan na nGael in Philadelphia, in what was known as the Free Soil Club. He was given membership number 448, an indication that the chapter was thriving, although its members also included at least one British spy—Red Jim McDermott. Dillon continued to carry himself with the erect bearing of a military man, and was known in Irish ranks as a "hard man." Soon, he was also nicknamed Dynamite Dillon.[15]

The Clan na nGael met in Faneuil Hall in Boston for its annual convention in mid-August 1884 in what was publicly billed as the Convention of the Irish National League of America. It was a wholly suitable venue as Boston was home of the Ninth Massachusetts, one of the Civil War's first Irish regiments, and Faneuil Hall was the site, a little more than a century earlier, where Samuel Adams and his compatriots planned the American revolution against the British.

Among those in attendance that August were MPs Thomas Sexton and William Redmond of Parnell's Irish Party, and P.J. Tynan, believed to be the guiding hand of the Phoenix Park murders. The convention gave Le Caron a chance to renew relations with the fugitive Patrick Egan, now a prosperous Nebraska miller. Egan treated him to a graphic description of his recent escape from Dublin, boasting he had a source inside British government headquarters at Dublin Castle, who told him that there was a warrant issued for his arrest, just twenty minutes after the order was signed. Egan described how he rushed home to pack his satchel and destroy a number of incriminating Irish Republican Brotherhood documents. Some of these papers, he said cryptically, connected himself to the Invincibles.[16]

At the Boston convention, Alexander Sullivan's men acknowledged that they had received $118,000 for dynamite attacks on Britain since the Chicago Dynamite Convention of 1881. Cronin supporters demanded receipts for their expenditures with the money, and Sullivan's backers dismissed this as ridiculous. They were revolutionaries, not accountants. Wouldn't such records only risk the lives of brave men in their ranks?

Sullivan was nominated for Land League president, but declined the honour, clearing the way for newly arrived Patrick Egan. Egan then declined the presidency, saying his election might hurt Parnell, as the British government likely knew about Egan's connection with the secret terrorist movement. However, the mood toward him was so warm and the pressure so powerful that his resolve appeared to weaken. Le Caron shuddered as Egan was praised as "that clean handed, that patriotic, that heroic exile," although it wasn't explained that his "heroic" action included helping to plot the fatal knifing from behind of two British politicians in Phoenix Park, or to help plan the bombing of innocent strangers on English streets.

Perhaps Le Caron had a flashback to several conversations he had with Egan, including one in which the redhead told some 60 fellow revolutionaries in Philadelphia that they could learn valuable lessons from the Italian underworld. "I have been reading up the records of the Italian banditti," Egan told them, "and from them I have come to believe in this rule: Let us meet our enemies with smiling faces, and with a warm grasp of the hand, having daggers up our sleeves ready to stab them to the heart." Le Caron also couldn't help but think about how Egan had smiled and squeezed his hand the night in Paris when they first met and went to the opera.[17]

Egan left the convention with a smile as the newly elected president. He cheerfully told Le Caron that the stage was set for more violence in England. The next wave of bombers would be men who, unlike Dr. Gallagher, would know how to follow orders.[18]

They landed on England's shores within a few months of the Boston convention, and their ranks included Le Caron's old Detroit neighbour, William Mackey Lomasney. Le Caron saw him in Chicago two days before Lomasney set off to England, and couldn't help but like the man to a point.[19] Lomasney badly wanted to attack English symbols, but not English people, and Le Caron noted that he "devoted much of his time to transporting dynamite and rifles to England and Ireland, yet hoped above all to avoid bloodshed in his efforts to frighten the British Government." Devoy shared the same view of Lomasney, and his relatively gentle approach to terrorism, writing, "He wanted simply to strike terror into the Government and the governing class and 'would not hurt the hair of an Englishman's head' except in fair fight."

Around 5.45am on 13 December 1884 Lomasney and two other men paddled a rented boat through the fog on the Thames River toward London Bridge. Associates onshore held flickering lamps, watching the tiny boat's quiet progress. If others also saw it, they wouldn't have been alarmed as it wasn't unusual for boats to navigate the Thames in the early morning hours. The Little Captain's boat carried dynamite that had been imported from America, hidden under the clothing of an employee of the National Steamship Line, who belonged to the organisation. They stopped paddling when they reached the arch of the bridge. Moments later, the morning calm was broken for an instant with the loud boom of an explosion, a flash of yellow, and a gust of smoke. When the smoke cleared, there was next to no damage to the bridge, nor any traces of the three men and their boat.

Back in America, Lomasney's mourners included his aged father, his widow, Susan, and his four children, who lived at 96 Michigan Avenue in Detroit. Another man involved in the scheme, James Moorehead (a.k.a. Thomas J. Mooney) escaped to New York, where he eventually became a police informer.

Lomasney was a valuable, respected man within the movement, and he would be missed. However, there was still plenty of dynamite and plenty of men willing to use it. Another Clan na nGael member, Jack Daly, sought nothing less than the blowing up of the House of Commons while it was in session by heaving bombs onto the table in front of the Speaker. Twice, Daly gained admission to the strangers' gallery of the House to plan his attack. His actions were noted, he was arrested, and his explosives were taken. One of those bombs was powerful enough, in Le Caron's words, to "send every stick and stone, to say nothing of the members of the House of Commons themselves, heavenwards or thereabouts."[20]

On 24 January 1885 Luke Dillon was back in London on a guided tour of Parliament, more properly known as the New Palace of Westminster, and hailed by the British as the cradle of Western democracy. His tour guide referred to the delaying tactics of Parnell's Irish Party as he remarked, "This is where the Irish members are creating so much trouble." An English member of Dillon's tour group added, "I'd have them all hanging at the end of a rope."[21]

Their observations about Irish revolutionaries were interrupted by the loud boom of an explosion at the far end of the great building, inside the great ornamental gates leading to the abbey's crypt. As members of the tour fled the building, Dillon ran in the opposite direction, toward the strangers' gallery. Once there, he planted another bomb. At least half a dozen men were injured by that blast, which released a force so great that a man standing some three hundred yards away was knocked down. Several chairs inside the House of Commons, including Gladstone's, were toppled. The gates to Westminster were immediately locked shut, and Dillon's confederate, James Cunningham from Philadelphia, was arrested while trying to escape. He would be sentenced to life imprisonment for his role in the attacks.

Dillon was stopped at the Westminster gates. Looking every inch the military man that he was, he put his hand on a guard's chest and admonished him for not being able to stop the bombers. Possibly because of his official bearing, the guard mistook him for a Scotland Yard detective. Whatever the case, Dillon marched outside to freedom, and celebrated that night with a trip to the theatre. During intermissions, he overheard patrons describe the disgust they felt as they walked past the scene of the Westminster explosion, cursing the Fenians for attacking their hallowed building.

Others in Dillon's ranks now set their sights on Westminster Abbey, a short walk from the House of Commons. The Abbey housed the coronation chair upon which Queen Victoria and other English monarchs were officially granted power. The coronation chair held the Stone of Scone, also called the Stone of Destiny and the Coronation Stone. Irish nationalists argued that the stone rightfully belonged in Ireland, since it had been used, for a thousand years before Christ, in coronation ceremonies of Irish kings on the sacred Hill of Tara. It had been hauled to Westminster by the English as spoils of war, and the Irish nationalists desperately wanted the massive chunk of limestone back.

Serious men were dispatched from America to London to deal with the throne and the stone. The plan called for some of them to hide inside the Abbey, and then pass the stone out a window to their confederates, under cover of night. Police caught wind of the plot and stepped up patrols around the Abbey. Conspirators waited for months for an opportunity, but that right moment never arrived. It remained easier to blow up buildings and murder people than to steal a stone.

CHAPTER 18

BLACK BAG IN PARIS

1885-1886

Mr. Pigott was perfectly impartial in his scheming propensities.
—**Irish revolutionary Michael Davitt on journalist Richard Pigott**

I rish nationalist A.M. Sullivan noted that journalists Patrick Ford and O'Donovan Rossa both advocated using dynamite to further the Irish struggle for independence, but added that Rossa had reached this conclusion "without any preliminary spiritual exercise. He declared he was in favour of 'dynamite, Greek fire, or hell-fire if it could be had.'" Rossa enthusiastically encouraged *Irish World* readers to contribute to the dynamite fund, printing their names in his "Roll of Honour," as other newspapers might record contributions to a Christmas Santa Claus fund.

Yseult (Lucille) Dudley, a 24-year-old Englishwoman, announced she wanted to make such a donation when she walked into Rossa's office in February 1885, in Manhattan off Broadway Avenue. She was saying something about dynamite as she approached him, and Rossa loved a lively chat, especially about this, his favourite topic. They took their conversation outside onto Chambers Street and hadn't taken many steps when Dudley pulled out a pistol and shot him point-blank. As Rossa lay bleeding on the pavement, she pumped several more bullets into him. The shots weren't enough to kill him, but they were enough for English newspapers to gleefully write that Rossa's life was almost ended by a madwoman. Meanwhile, Rossa's newspaper reported the story under the screaming headline, "ENGLAND'S BULLET—A HIRED BRITISH ASSASSIN ATTEMPTS TO MURDER O'DONOVAN ROSSA—ENGLAND WILD WITH REJOICING."[1]

Back in Chicago, the worst enemies of Dr. Philip Cronin weren't strangers like Yseult Dudley, but rather fellow members of the Clan na nGael. In 1885, Alexander Sullivan succeeded in putting Cronin on a secret Clan na nGael trial for treason. Le Caron was named to the jury, along with Chicago police detective Daniel ("Big Dan") Coughlin, one of many members of the force who got his job through Sullivan's graces. As usual, Le Caron voted with the majority, who decided to expel Cronin from their ranks. The move backfired, driving Cronin and his associates further from their control, and making tensions among the revolutionaries even more volatile.

In London, by mid-1885, Parnell's Irish Party held the balance of power in the House of Commons. This made him a virtual dictator in Parliament, with the power to grind all legislation to a halt. Richard Pigott, a seedy Dublin newspaper owner, sensed an opportunity, and approached Liberal chief whip, Lord Richard Grosvenor, with a plan. Widely known and poorly regarded, Pigott was a photographer, pornographer, and former proprietor of *The Irishman*, *The Flag of Ireland*, and *The Shamrock* newspapers. He was also an Irish nationalist when the price was right. To his credit, in nationalist eyes, he had served six months in prison for publishing seditious articles, and he also published Rossa's letters from prison about his harsh treatment, and lent money to Rossa's wife so she could move to America. In a less flattering light, there were whispers that he had sold lewd publications to Anglican clergy, and troubling suggestions that he raised money for the wives and children of imprisoned Fenians, only to pocket the donations. He was also known for a curious ability to imitate handwriting.[2]

Irish Party MP T.J. O'Connor certainly found Pigott distasteful, commenting, "A look at the man betrayed his essentially epicurean character; he was rather stout, and had a full, rather bloated face; he looked, as he was, a thorough sensualist."[3] The official history of *The Times* newspaper was less judgmental, describing him as "an elderly man with a large beard, a soft voice, and a hesitating manner."[4] Michael

Davitt, who sometimes abbreviated Pigott's name to "Pig," struggled to find the good in everyone, and concluded, "Mr. Pigott was perfectly impartial in his scheming propensities."[5]

If Pigott had a truly redeeming quality, it was his love for his young family. In the mid-1880s, he dearly wanted to keep his children in a privately funded Jesuit school. To this end, he suggested that Lord Grosvenor commission a pamphlet, entitled "Parnellism Unmasked." It would, he promised, expose the Home Rule movement as nothing more than a front for violent terrorists. Worse yet, Pigott alleged, they weren't even honest terrorists, since the Parnellites couldn't account for £100,000 of Land League finances.[6]

It was a tempting prospect for Lord Grosvenor, who, like others in his party, was frustrated by Parnell's embarrassing stranglehold over the legislative process, with his seemingly endless speeches in Parliament. He put Pigott in touch with Edward Caulfield Houston, a journalist in his early twenties who had worked for the pro-landlord *Daily Express* and served as *The Times* correspondent in Dublin. Now, Houston was private secretary of the Irish Loyal and Patriotic Union, an association of landlords and Ireland's leading Unionist organisation. In Houston's words, the union was "a sort of anti-Land League."[7] Houston had attended all of the Phoenix Park murder trials, and had written a descriptive account of them for *The Times*. Since then, he said he had heard of plots to murder the Prince of Wales and Gladstone while they visited Cannes on the French Mediterranean, which was fast becoming a popular spot for Britons who wanted to flee England's damp winters.[8] Houston, who had far more ambition than experience, listened to Pigott's allegations about Parnell's links to terrorists and was instantly hooked.

Houston agreed to pay Pigott £60 to begin his anti-Parnell pamphlet, and Pigott promptly pocketed the money, and set off for Paris, Lausanne, and America.[9] Houston prepared an anti-Parnell pamphlet based on Pigott's information, and then amended it because it was clearly libellous. He met with Pigott again, this time agreeing to pay him a guinea a day, plus hotel and travelling expenses, for further anti-Parnell research.

The year 1885 ended with Liberal Prime Minister Gladstone's announcement of his conversion to Irish Home Rule. Shortly after those words were spoken, the Clan na nGael, or United Brotherhood, issued a secret circular, calling on members to temporarily shelve their violent plans:

> The operations so far conducted have compelled the enemy to recognise the Constitutional party, and we are now in a fair way to reap the benefits and results of the heroic work of the members of the u.b.[United Brotherhood]. . . We expect to resume active operations after the present exigencies of the Constitutional party are passed. We have purposely and advisedly abstained from doing anything likely to embarrass them during the crisis of the elections. . . The mystery of an unknown power striking in the dark, always able to avoid detection is far more terrible than the damage inflicted. We caution you, therefore, above all things, to be silent; but if compelled to speak, disavow all knowledge, or better still, mislead all inquirers. In the meantime, we wish to impress on you the necessity of mutual forbearance and faith.[10]

Notwithstanding the bold words, the British weren't the only ones who enjoyed the sudden outbreak of peace. For all of its drama, the dynamite attacks of 1885 caused little actual damage to England, while sending at least 25 terrorists to prison, 16 of whom were serving life sentences. The only people who seemed to truly profit from the terror campaign were the informers.

As the hostilities cooled, Parnell secretly moved into Womerish Lodge in Brighton on the English coastline with his lover, Katharine, who remained legally married to Captain Willie O'Shea. Shortly afterwards, Parnell had his horses Dictator, President, and Home Rule shipped down from Ireland, followed by some of his hunting dogs, including his retriever, Grouse.

In April 1886, Gladstone introduced his much-anticipated bill calling for limited Home Rule for Ireland. The Irish would gain their own Parliament based in Dublin, but Britain would still control foreign affairs, as well as customs, currency, trade, and the postal service. The bill was defeated 343 to 313, and in July, Gladstone was ousted from office by a Conservative-Liberal Unionist coalition, effectively killing the initiative. The failure of the Home Rule bill was a cue for the Irish nationalists to end their silence, and to seek change through bombs, not ballot boxes.

Pigott continued to enjoy his newfound income, courtesy of Houston. He went about his research in a leisurely manner, living in comfort on his daily allowance, plus expenses, provided by Houston, while travelling twice to Lausanne, once to America, and several times to Paris. Eventually, in March 1886, Pigott reported to him that illuminating documents were to be found in a black bag in Paris. He told him that his sources included a mysterious expatriate Irish nationalist in Lausanne named Eugene Davis, who sometimes answered to the name Owen Rowe, and who was extremely bitter about Parnell and his efforts for parliamentary reform.

Pigott reported that he had to go to America to get the "open sesame" to have the bag with explosive Parnell papers turned over to him. Aside from the shadowy Davis, Pigott also told of meeting men named Casey and Hayes, who might help him gain access to the black bag. This information was promising, but not cheap, and Houston continued to make his payments to Pigott in cash to avoid any embarrassing paper trail.

Houston told Pigott that he would need originals of any documents before he travelled to Paris yet again in July 1886. Soon Pigott summoned Houston to join him there. Houston was accompanied by a pro-British Irishman, Dr. Thomas Maguire, a professor of Moral Philosophy in Trinity College in Dublin. Maguire had loaned Houston £850 to pay for letters that incriminated Parnell. It was all very cloak-and-dagger, with Houston using the nom de guerre Wilson, and he and Dr. Maguire checked into the Hotel du Monde, near the opera house, to await further instructions from Pigott.

Pigott called them to meet him at the Hotel St. Petersbourg, and said the black satchel was in the building. The men who controlled it, Maurice Murphy and Tom Brown, could be persuaded to part with it—for a price. Nothing but cash would do, and the men would not give up the satchel if Houston or Maguire saw their faces. Pigott stressed that he was duty-bound to protect his sources' identities. Soon, Pigott pocketed 100 guineas from Houston to cover his own services and disappeared downstairs, this time carrying £500 for the letters. Houston agreed not

The Battle of Nashville. Le Caron and some six hundred soldiers refused to risk their lives at the front on 26 December 1862. Instead they stacked their weapons in front of their tents and refused to fight.

Battle of Ridgeway, 2 June 1866. This print shows Fenian Brotherhood (Irish-American) troops under the command of Colonel John O'Neill charging the retreating Queen's Own Rifles of Canada commanded by Colonel A. Booker at Ridgeway, Ontario, during the Fenian invasion of Canada.

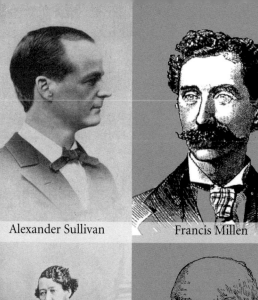

Alexander Sullivan

Francis Millen

Patrick Ford

Thomas D'Arcy McGee

Richard Pigott

British prime minister
William E. Gladstone

Sir Charles Russell

Patrick Egan

Sir Richard Webster

Dublin Castle, the nerve centre for the British government in Ireland for eight centuries. © *Peter Edwards*

The serpents above the door to Kilmainham Gaol. The stone carvings, like a scene from Hell, seemed appropriate.

Kilmainham Gaol cellblock, rebuilt in 1862. Overhead windows were installed to symbolise God's love and hope for sinners.

For Luke Dillon (left), Ireland was an abstraction, but one well worth dying for. His parents hailed from County Sligo, but he had never actually drawn a breath in the country, and had no plans to ever do so. His nickname was "Dynamite Dillon".

The explosion at Clerkenwell prison, 13 December 1867, was an attempt by Fenians to rescue Richard Burke. Police secretly watched the events unfold, resulting in the death of 12 people and injuring an estimated 120.

Charles Stewart Parnell

Katharine O'Shea

Captain William O'Shea

Katharine O'Shea, married to Irish member William O'Shea, had a long-standing affair with Charles Stewart Parnell, which eventually ended in her divorcing O'Shea and marrying Parnell.

The Cuba Five
Left to right: John Devoy, Charles Underwood O'Connell, Harry Mulleda, Jeremiah O'Donovan Rossa and John McClure.
The five Irish Fenian prisoners who, under general amnesty, were released by the British to America on 5 January 1871, and were shipped together aboard the Cuba.

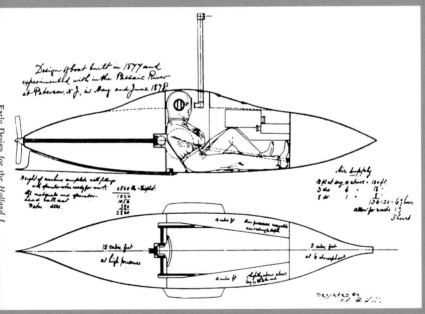

Early Design for the Holland I

Le Caron noted that Rossa was constantly thinking of new ways to attack the English, including launching dynamite from pedal-powered submarines onto British ironclad ships.

The former London townhouse of Robert Anderson (above), Le Caron's British handler. Where the spy often visited.

The London home of Henri Le Caron (above), where he lived with his wife, Nannie, and daughter, May. The house was within walking distance of Anderson's home. Le Caron was confined to his bed and died on 1 April 1984.

An artist's rendition of the Carlson cottage and the crowd gathered around the mutilated body of Dr Patrick Cronin (left). Cronin's body was found in a sewer near Lake Michigan, Chicago, January 1889.

Former Fenian Headquarters, 10 West 4th Street, Greenwich Village, NYC. The brownstone mansion was a far cry from the squalors in nearby Five Points and Hell's Kitchen.
© Peter Edwards

An artist's rendition of Henri Le Caron on the stand at the Parnell inquiry, February 1989, wearing a pin on his collar to denote his Civil War service.

IRA Bond, sold to raise money. Fenians believed once Ireland was a free republic they would be repaid with interest.

An artist's rendition of the Phoenix Park murders. Lord Frederick Cavendish and Thomas Henry Burke were murdered on 6 May 1882. The newly formed Irish terror group, the Invincibles, claimed responsibility for the bloody work.

to try for even a peek at Murphy or Brown. He would have to trust Pigott.

CHAPTER 19

DELUSION

You are cautioned to use every device to mislead those engaged in tracing our operations.

—Irish-American revolutionary circular, summer of 1886

> *IRISH NATIONAL LEAGUE OF AMERICA*
> *Offices of President and Secretary*
> *Lincoln, Neb. November 24, 1885*
>
> *It affords me great pleasure to introduce to all Friends of the Irish National League with whom he may come in contact during his visit in the south my. . . Friend Dr. H. Le Caron. . .*
>
> *Dr. Le Caron although French by name and descent has ever proved himself one of the most devoted Friends of the Irish National Cause and since the formation of the Land and National League has been most indefatigable in promoting the good of the organization.*
>
> *Patrick Egan,*
> *President[1]*

Le Caron was appointed, with much Irish community political influence, to a seat on the Mississippi Valley Sanitary Commission. His letter from Egan, which he called his "Passport for the Faithful," opened doors for him with Irish revolutionaries throughout the Deep South. When Le Caron felt this posting had run its possibilities for letting him gather information, he developed an association with one of the largest pharmaceutical houses in the United States, travelling as its representative.

By the summer of 1886, a revolutionary circular reached Le Caron's hands that must have given him a chill. High hopes over Irish Home Rule had evaporated, and plans were afoot for more bombs and bloodshed in Britain:

> The indications all point to the conclusion that the measure of Home Rule offered will be emasculated and pared down in such a way as to make it unacceptable to those for whom it is intended. We are now preparing for those contingencies, and the estimates for the cost of making a rigorous campaign with "delusion" [dynamite] will absorb more funds than are present available from the prescribed percentage . . . in the next few months, important operations are likely to take place; you are cautioned to use every device to mislead those engaged in tracing our operations.[2]

The Times was advocating for a tougher crime bill regarding Ireland. It planned to back its argument with a handwritten letter dated 15 May 1882 from the black satchel that Pigott had sold to Houston in Paris. It was presumably sent from Parnell to Patrick Egan, and read:

> I am not surprised at your friend's anger but he and you should know that to denounce the murders was the only course open to us. To do that promptly was plainly our best policy.
>
> But you can tell him and all others concerned that though I regret the accident of Lord F. Cavendish's death I cannot refuse to admit that Burke got no more than his deserts.
>
> You are at liberty to show him this, and others whom you can trust also, but let not my address be known. He can write to House of Commons.
>
> Yours very truly,
> Chas. S. Parnell

If true, the letter meant that Parnell was lying when he publicly denounced the Phoenix Park murders of Burke and Cavendish. If true, it was clear, damning proof in Parnell's own hand that he was a violent terrorist, comfortable with orchestrating murder, and even gloating about it. The three paragraphs were easily enough to inflame public opinion to support tough anti-Irish legislation and end Parnell's career in Parliament. If false, *The Times* had been duped by Pigott, and was being set up to commit a libel of monumental proportions.

Before it published the letter, *The Times* needed reassurance that it was genuine. They needed a Parnell signature, which wasn't an easy thing to obtain as the Irish Party leader was famously cautious about writing his name for just anyone. *The Times* ran an advertisement in the 21 December 1886, paper under the heading "autographs wanted." The hope was that some readers would send in Parnell signatures.

Three readers sent in what they claimed were samples of the Irish Party leader's writing. To the untrained eye, they certainly looked like the signature on the 15 May 1882 letter from Pigott's black satchel. If it was a forgery, it was a good one. A copy of Pigott's incriminating letter was prepared for publication in *The Times* for 27 January 1887 the opening day of Parliament. Just before the letter was to be published, editors at the great newspaper thought perhaps their lawyer, Sir Henry James (who later became Lord James of Hereford), should take a look at it. According to *The Times* official history, they were in for a shock.

It then transpired, entirely to the surprise of the newspaper's representatives, that Sir Henry had seen the letters before. They had been brought to him by Houston in the summer or early autumn of 1886, and he had then advised that they were not adequate in law to sustain the case it was proposed to put forward. Further, Sir Henry expressed doubts about the authenticity of the letters, begged the newspaper to be most careful, and discouraged publication.[3]

In short, *The Times*' lawyer thought Houston had been tricked when he bought the black satchel full of documents in Paris. The letters from Pigott would remain out of print, at least for the time being.

An odd era was ending at Scotland Yard in January 1887 when Edward Jenkinson, the man who had fired Robert Anderson three years earlier, was sacked from his post as spymaster general and ejected from his office at Room 56 of the Home Office, Whitehall. Like Anderson, Jenkinson certainly safeguarded secrets, having run the Millen files from 1885 to 1886, and another undisclosed agent from Philadelphia. A source of frustration for Jenkinson as he left office was that he still did not know the identity of Robert Anderson's top agent in America, Henri Le Caron. On his last day at work in his office, Jenkinson stoked his fireplace, gathered up all of his files, and heaved them into the flames. Within a month, his successor, James Monro, hired Anderson back into his old post, with a raise in pay.[4]

Evictions and violence accompanied a downward spiral of agricultural prices in Ireland, while in Westminster the government refused to reassess rents. The ruling Tories planned to meet nationalists with force, not concessions. As was his nature, Parnell appeared aloof, still publicly supporting constitutional means to better the lot of Irish peasants. Such a moderate public stance appealed to many English until they read the 18 April 1887, *Times*. The paper published a reproduction of the 15 May 1882 letter from Pigott's black satchel. Now *The Times'* readers could read, in what was presumably Parnell's own handwriting, of the Irish Party leader's support of the Phoenix Park murders and his satisfaction that "Burke got no more than his deserts." Sir Henry James hadn't changed his legal opinion about the dubious authenticity of the letter. The editors had simply decided to ignore his advice, and published it anyway.

Parnell propped up his copy of *The Times* against a teapot that morning as he began breakfast in Eltham with Katharine O'Shea. "He read it silently over his toast and marmalade," she later recalled, "and only when he had finished and had clipped the end off his cigar did he smile and say: 'Now for that assaying I didn't finish! Wouldn't you hide your head with shame if your King were so stupid as that, my Queen?'" For the next two hours, as she later recalled, Parnell busied himself with his scientific experiments. It was only after much coaching from her that he left the house to "attend to *The Times*." In Katharine's recollection, he returned home that evening, noting briefly that he had consulted with a famous lawyer, Sir Charles Russell, about the matter. Then he went back to trying to extract tiny particles of gold from a stock of minerals from his Irish estate.[5]

The Irish Party saw *The Times* as an unofficial branch of the Conservative English establishment. As Davitt later noted, "The part played by *The Times*' manager in this whole business. . . was that of a whipping-boy for his master."[6] There were those within the Irish Party who wondered if Captain Willie O'Shea didn't have a hand in the publication of the letters. His ambition to curry favour with English politicians, and his resentment that Parnell was still living with his wife, offered more than enough incentive for him to plant a damning letter in the newspaper. Even those who argued that O'Shea wasn't behind the publication weren't particularly flattering, Davitt noted: "Not that they had any great trust in his honor or reputation but because this act was above his capacity to execute, even though the motive might not be far removed from the character of his friendship."[7]

Around this time, a new phrase—"Bob's your uncle"—was becoming popular among Britons, and it had to gall Arthur Balfour every time he heard it. The expression was used to show just how simple it could be to do something if conditions were right. The interjection came into vogue shortly after Balfour was appointed Irish secretary in March 1887, at the almost tender age of 38. He was considered by many to be a dilettante, a pampered product of Eton and Trinity colleges, who only got the Irish posting because of the graces of his uncle Robert "Bob" Cecil, better known as Lord Salisbury, who was then British prime minister. Balfour had attracted some public notice when he entered Parliament in 1874 at age 25, but much of it was sneering, with critics in the press calling him "Prince Charming" and even "Miss Balfour."[8] Now, every time someone quipped, "Bob's your uncle," it was a smiling dig at Balfour and his seamless rise to power on his uncle's coattails.

No one was snickering or questioning his masculinity when Balfour came down hard with a new Crimes Act, which threatened stiffer penalties for anyone involved in boycotting, fighting evictions, and conspiracy. Balfour and his uncle, Lord Salisbury, felt the eyes of the world were upon them. What hope did the British Empire have to dictate affairs in Armenia or Macedonia if they could not control the

Irish in their own backyard? His tough stance was a pleasant surprise to Conservatives, and a shock to Irish nationalists, who soon began calling him Bloody Balfour.

The Irish Party looked for leadership, and Parnell was nowhere to be found. He had literally vanished from the public stage, and only the few political insiders who knew of his relationship with Mrs. O'Shea had an inkling of his whereabouts. As Irish Party MP T.P. O'Connor noted, "As far as his colleagues were concerned, with the possible exception of his secretary, Mr. Henry Campbell, he might as well have lived in the moon."[9]

Luke Dillon was hearing strange, wild things in early 1887. Fellow Clan na nGael members were planning to leave America en masse for London, and their goal was nothing less than to blow up Queen Victoria on 24 May as the tiny monarch celebrated her 68th birthday. Somewhere in the background, pushing the plot, was General Francis Millen. Dillon wrote on 7 February to John Devoy, describing his confusion:

> They claim that they intend celebrating the Queen's birthday, and that one hundred and fifty men are prepared to work with Greek fire with which they are at present supplying them. I would not mention this, even to you, if I felt there was a possibility of these men accomplishing anything. I know, however, it is impossible for men who are forced to proclaim their intentions in order to raise money to do anything more than get men into prison. . . I may possibly be able to get at the bottom of Millen's overtures.[10]

Henri Le Caron also heard that a horrific explosion was planned for London that spring, but his information was that the planned attack on Queen Victoria was set for June. That was when celebrations were planned across the British Empire to mark the 50th anniversary of her ascension to the throne. Le Caron left for Europe in April 1887. To explain his absence, he first claimed that he was helping to set up an English headquarters for the wholesaling of American patent medicines. Then he amended his story and said he was travelling for a syndicate that was attempting to buy up breweries in Chicago and other key American cities.

Le Caron sought answers from Dr. James G. Fox, a former Troy, New York, resident who was now an Irish Party member of Parliament. His search for Fox brought him to Gatti's Restaurant in Adelaide Gallery off the Strand, near Westminster. The Gallery was a showcase of sorts for inventors, and diners marvelled at dazzling, cutting-edge technology, like steam engines powering model boats, daguerreotype photographs, diving suits, and electrical lighting devices. Le Caron had heard that Fox liked to dine there, amid this explosion of ideas, and before long, they were seated at the same table. If Fox recognised him from Clan na nGael meetings in North America, he hid it well.

Le Caron noted that Fox was reading Patrick Ford's *Irish World*, and asked where he might buy a copy in London. Fox's tone was cordial as he replied that his copies were mailed to him from America.[11] He then offered Le Caron the newspaper he was reading, and asked if he was American. Le Caron replied in the affirmative, pulling out his business card.

"Why, I ought to know you," Fox said, looking directly at Le Caron now. "I have met you in conventions. My name is Fox."

Le Caron flashed him the secret Clan na nGael hailing sign, but Fox didn't respond with a secret hand gesture of his own. Instead, he curiously told Le Caron that he wasn't a member of any secret society.

Perhaps Le Caron would have more luck with the shadowy General Millen, who was now in Paris. He was still unaware that Millen was a fellow agent, also reporting to Robert Anderson, when he visited the general, who was comfortably ensconced in the Hotel des Anglais on Cour de la Reine by the River Seine, near the Place de la Concorde, with his wife and two daughters.[12]

Millen now had the uneasy expression of a heavy drinker, with a reddish, pronounced nose, and his former good looks were many years and bottles of alcohol in his past. He still played the role of an Irish patriot, with an Irish harp and shamrock on a locket on his jacket, more than two decades after he began to sell nationalist secrets to their British enemies.

He told Le Caron that he was in Europe to mend relations between different revolutionary groups. At the core of the current tensions was Alexander Sullivan's assertion that the Irish branch shouldn't have any more money as weapons already lay hidden and unused in Ireland. He volunteered nothing about the rumours of a Jubilee dynamite plot against the Queen, but Le Caron remained convinced that something major was happening. Most likely it was some sort of joint operation, fusing the resources of more than one group, Le Caron concluded. "The whole undertaking was shrouded in mystery, but it is pretty certain that it was not a Clan na nGael affair alone."

It's understandable that Le Caron was befuddled by the Jubilee affair. Millen wasn't about to tell him that he worked with the British Home Office to encourage the plot. Like Alexander Sullivan, the Home Office wanted to humiliate Parnell and destroy his effectiveness. Unlike Sullivan, they also wanted to nip the plot in the bud at the last moment, make a series of spectacular arrests, and heroically save the Queen's life.

Spontaneity wasn't on the itinerary for Queen Victoria's Golden Jubilee celebrations of 20 and 21 June 1887. Her Highness intended to ride between ten miles of scaffolding and terraced benches holding throngs of her faithful, along a parade route in an open, gilded landau, behind six cream-coloured horses, escorted by the Indian cavalry, to Westminster Abbey. The tiny monarch did not want to wear a crown as they were heavy and uncomfortable, so hatmakers strove to create for her the perfect bonnet. Jewellers crafted special broaches so that the Queen could give them to her family in the palace ballroom, and tailors embroidered a special gown with silver roses, thistles, and shamrocks for the evening gala. The plans called for a palace reception with diplomats and princes, and then she was to be wheeled in her chair to watch fireworks in the royal garden. At the same time, all across her empire, from the Arctic Circle to Antarctica, beacons and bonfires would be lit in her honour.

In the months leading up to the Jubilee celebration, undercover Scotland Yard officers working for James Monro shadowed Millen, apparently clueless that he was a British government spy working for the Home Office. Spies tailed spies who pretended to be revolutionaries, oblivious that they were all on the same side. While Le Caron had burrowed deep into the Irish independence movement, he operated in a virtual vacuum, unaware of the identities of his fellow spies, who also didn't know his true identity. The man with the fullest picture of the multilayered intrigues was Anderson, who had served in the espionage branches of both Scotland Yard and the Home Office. However, Anderson was not about to simplify things for anyone as he regarded secrecy as a sacred trust.

Monro's agents watched from a discreet distance in mid-April 1887 as Millen left Amsterdam for New York, and were particularly interested in his agent, Joseph Melville, whom they considered the smartest of the gang.

Monro knew that Melville's real name was Moroney, and Monro also likely knew that Melville/Moroney sometimes used the name James Moorhead, and that he ran a Philadelphia bomb school for the Clan na nGael. Police watched from a discreet distance as Melville and his associates, Thomas Callan and Michael Harkins, arrived at New York harbour with their clothes lined with 100 lbs of dynamite, ready to put their months of planning into bloody action. Their agents had scouted Windsor Castle and the procession route, and used a watch to determine how long it would take them to escape once the dynamite was ignited. They did not, however, put as much effort into their travel plans. The ship they had planned to board in New York was full. They caught the next ship out of New York, the steamer City of Chester, but did not arrive in England until 21 June the second day of the two-day Jubilee. There wasn't time to celebrate with "Greek fire." The would-be assassins had literally missed the boat.

Police trailed Melville through London, noting that he stayed in modest quarters on Gladstone Street, apparently having little money. They watched from a distance as he called twice upon Joseph Nolan, MP, at the House of Commons, but had no clues about the content of the meetings. When the matter finally came to court, Melville, Callan, Harkins, and an associate named Joseph Cohen were all convicted of conspiring to endanger lives and property with explosives and each was sentenced to 15 years' penal servitude.

For Queen Victoria, it was as if all of the plotting and spying never happened. Her Jubilee celebrations went off without a hitch, and she wrote in her diary of the 20 June event: "All the Royalties assembled in the Bow Room, and we dined in the Supper-room, which looked splendid with the buffet covered with the gold plate. The table was a large horseshoe one, with many lights on it. The King of Denmark took me in, and Willy of Greece sat on my other side. The Princes were all in uniform, and the Princesses were all beautifully dressed. Afterwards we went into the Ballroom, where my band played."[13]

CHAPTER 20

STRESS LEAVE

1888

The American people now have more respect for Irish Nationalists and less condemnation for the use of dynamite.

—**Henri Le Caron describes change in US public opinion**

As police rounded up suspects in the Jubilee dynamite plot in July 1887, Henri Le Caron was in London, quietly meeting with Robert Anderson. The spymaster dispatched him to Paris to meet again with General Millen, who was now at the Hotel du Palais, 28 Avenue Cours de la Reine, a short walk from the Champs Élysées. Anderson's reason for arranging the meeting remains mysterious. Perhaps Le Caron finally had somehow divined that Millen was a fellow spy. More likely, Anderson was using Le Caron to keep tabs on Scotland Yard's Agent X. Whatever the case, according to Le Caron, Millen professed to know nothing of the assassination plot. Le Caron might have been guarding a secret for Scotland Yard to protect his friend Anderson when he later wrote: "I did not, however, gain very much by my visit, for the simple reason that at this time Millen had not, as far as I believe, any close connection with the dynamite business known as the Jubilee Plot, with which his name was subsequently associated."[1]

For his part, Le Caron was understandably nervous when he heard that many of Anderson's colleagues were now asking questions about him and his whereabouts. At least one British government official was bent on learning the identity of Anderson's top American spy. Perhaps it was just raw curiosity, or perhaps the government official felt this information would give him professional advantage. Perhaps it was something more sinister. Whatever the case, the Briton was determined to learn the identity of the mole, even if this might jeopardise Le Caron's work and his life. The curious man somehow managed to learn that the spy's first name was Thomas. He also suspected that Thomas lived in Chicago, and sent a detective there to find him. The attempt failed, but Le Caron was left to wonder how his survival and the safety of his family could all have been easily and irrevocably compromised. A few careless words and Le Caron would be a dead man.[2] Perhaps he thought of how he had agreed that death was a fitting punishment for betrayal when he swore his allegiance to the Clan na nGael.

After his failure in Chicago, the curious British government official began asking questions of Le Caron's Canadian contacts, John Rose and Gilbert McMicken. The official must have been powerful, since he was able to put so much pressure on McMicken that the spymaster went to Chicago to see Le Caron about it. Le Caron stressed that he wanted to keep his distance, and McMicken respected his wishes. The curious man would have to stay curious.

The Clan na nGael's plans for a massive Jubilee explosion had blown up in their faces, and now its members were impatient for action. Le Caron wrote Anderson on 20 February 1888 noting that American general Philip Henry Sheridan had boasted that he could free Ireland from England if given an army of just five thousand men. Sheridan wasn't the only one who was sick of debate and eager, in Le Caron's words, to "get down to something more practical." Le Caron continued in the letter that he remained close with Chicago lawyer Alexander Sullivan, who escaped prosecution in the Jubilee dynamite plot. Le Caron noted that he had attended the wake for Sullivan's brother Florence. The cause of Florence Sullivan's death wasn't explained, but Le Caron did note that the Sullivan brothers drank a lot.[3]

On 27 March Le Caron wrote to Anderson informing him that negotiations were underway to unite the Vera Cruz wing of the Clan na nGael, which was under John Devoy and Dr. Philip Cronin, with

Alexander Sullivan's Unlimited Security wing. He also noted that an Irish agent named W.L. Wilkinson had gone missing since travelling to Dublin on Patrick Egan's orders. The Clan na nGael man had run into British detectives in Dublin and before he was taken away he apparently managed to destroy all the secret documents in his possession. No one seemed to know where Wilkinson was except that he was gone, and no one seemed to expect him to return.[4]

That spring, Le Caron's son William contracted spinal meningitis, an inflammation of the membranes covering the spinal cord and brain. As a doctor, Le Caron knew about the sad effects of the disease, which were often brain damage, followed by death. While he could describe the condition that afflicted his son, he was helpless to do anything to save him. Le Caron was in England again when, at 10.15am on 3 April his son was pronounced dead in Chicago. He had been sick for 22 days, and death came just five days after his 15th birthday.[5]

Le Caron would seldom talk of William's death, or express guilt that he was on the other side of the ocean as his son lay dying. It's highly unlikely that he knew about William's death when he wrote a report that day for Anderson. In that letter, Le Caron discussed the possible consequences if the Devoy and Sullivan factions of the Clan na nGael were united. Clan na nGael members wanted an end to infighting and bickering, but faction leaders wanted to protect their fiefdoms and settle scores. Le Caron speculated that if the two sides came together, an explosion of violence in England would quickly follow. Le Caron predicted that a revitalised Clan na nGael would likely break with Parnell and parliamentary reform, and focus instead on dynamite attacks in Britain. However, Le Caron was suspicious that neither side genuinely wanted unity, writing, "It now looks as if a very sharp game was being played by both sides."

Le Caron was writing Anderson about every ten days now. He called attention to a man named McKenna, whom he described as an "inside sentinel," or Clan na nGael internal security detective, working for Patrick Egan. For some reason, Le Caron said, McKenna had been dispatched to Mexico. As talk of a Clan na nGael unity convention continued, there was also considerable interest in the upcoming American presidential election in November. By mid-June 1888, Patrick Egan had put his support behind Republican James G. Blaine, a Protestant congressman with an Irish Catholic mother.[6] Soon afterwards, John Devoy and Patrick Ford also pledged their support to Blaine.

Alexander Sullivan publicly withheld any announcement about his preferred presidential candidate. One reason appeared altruistic to those who didn't know Sullivan better. It would be improper, while Sullivan held the title of president of the Irish National League of America, for him to back a partisan candidate in American politics. However, Sullivan schemed as naturally as he breathed, and generally confined his morality to pious speeches that aided his career and created a smokescreen for his actions. It's more likely that Sullivan realised that the longer he waited with his announcement of support, the more leverage he gained. Certainly, Le Caron looked for hidden motives in almost everything Sullivan said or did. He even wrote to Anderson that he suspected Sullivan of feigning grief about his brother's recent death to dodge debate about public statements by the Pope against secret societies.[7]

Suspicions lingered that Sullivan, who was at this stage a Democrat, had nursed grand ambitions of winning the Democratic vice-presidential nomination. A lack of support from many Irish-American Democrats for the candidacy effectively killed that dream. Now, Devoy reasoned, Sullivan declared his support for Blaine and the Republicans only after winning a secret agreement that he would be appointed secretary of the interior should Blaine win the presidency. Le Caron also suspected that Sullivan was drawn to Blaine because Blaine was a fellow revolutionary, capable of extreme violence. The more Sullivan talked of peace, the more Le Caron feared bloodshed. Anyone connected to Sullivan also fell under suspicion in Le Caron's mind. In the end, it was moot as Blaine's bid for the presidency fizzled.

A 23 June letter from Le Caron to Anderson warned again that Clan na nGael members were exhausted with parliamentary agitation and wanted "dynamite or any other mite."[8] A Clan na nGael unity convention had been scheduled that month for the Madison Street Theatre in Chicago, but was moved to the Westminster Hotel in Buffalo at the last minute, amid fears that British detectives had infiltrated the first venue.

Despite the convention's goal of reconciliation, Le Caron noted, "I never heard such a row in my life."[9] At first, it appeared that Sullivan's Ultimate Security faction, with 9,000 members, clung to control, but the Vera Cruz group, with 5,000 members and led by Cronin and Devoy, kept threatening to quit if they didn't get a thorough hearing. They dug in their heels, accusing Sullivan of misspending and of tarnishing noble ideals with base, machine politics.

As Le Caron surveyed the tensions from his seat, a husky delegate from Troy near him climbed onto a chair and demanded to be heard. He held up a *Times* pamphlet, entitled, "Behind the Scenes in America." Thousands of copies were being sold for a penny each in London, and the information they contained obviously originated with a highly placed traitor to the Clan na nGael cause. The husky man on the chair demanded an investigation into the source of the pamphlet's information. He had no clue that its source was Henri Le Caron, the wiry little man with the ferret-like eyes, sitting next to him, or that the pamphlet's anonymous author was Le Caron's British spymaster, Anderson, who moonlighted as a writer.[10]

On 1 July Le Caron reported back to Anderson that the Vera Cruz and Unlimited Security factions had reached a peace of sorts at 3am after an eloquent speech by *Chicago Citizen* editor John J. Finerty, who declared, "This organization is greater than any man."[11] These grand early-morning words moved the audience to stamp their feet and raise their hats in approval, Le Caron later recalled, adding the agreement was finalised after "liquids and cigars [were] served."[12]

Le Caron noted to Anderson that a delegate named Scanlan declared that informers deserved sharp, fast treatment or, in his words, "Such men should have their ears nailed to the pump. . ."[13] No one seemed to oppose the idea. There was also no visible opposition to spilling blood for Irish independence, and the nationalists felt buoyed by what they considered growing support from the American public, and high-placed political friends. "The American people now have more respect for Irish

Nationalists and less condemnation for the use of dynamite," Le Caron noted.[14]

Devoy wasn't in Buffalo for the excitement. Instead, he was at the Republican Convention in Chicago, pressing for wealthy Philadelphia merchant Hugh McCaffrey to be made secretary of the treasury should Benjamin Harrison win the presidency. Harrison's name was of more than passing interest to Le Caron as he was the son of Congressman John Scott Harrison, whose corpse he had stolen a decade earlier in Ohio when he was known as Dr. Morton.

On 3 July Le Caron wrote Anderson that the newly forged union of the Clan na nGael was called the United Brotherhood, a name that had sometimes been used by Clan members for their movement. This new organisation promised an exciting future both for Irish-American nationalists and Le Caron. "I worked as industriously [and] as descreetly [sic] as humanly possible," Le Caron wrote, estimating he logged twenty-hour workdays at the convention. "The prospect for [my] advancement under the new regime will also be better than under the old."

A trial committee was struck to examine embezzlement charges that Cronin had raised against Alexander Sullivan and his associates, Colonel Michael Boland of Kansas City and Timothy Maroney of New Orleans. Sullivan also stood accused of betraying a bomb plot against the Tower of London, attempting to bribe Luke Dillon, and refusing to aid William Mackey (Michael) Lomasney's widow after he was killed in the London Bridge attack.

Key evidence was missing when Sullivan's embezzlement hearing began in August at the Westminster Hotel in New York. The hearings shifted upstate to Buffalo in what was likely another attempt to shake off British spies. Le Caron provided affidavits for Sullivan, and Cronin struck back, suggesting that any statement by Le Caron was tainted. Cronin noted that Sullivan had sponsored Le Caron into the organisation, and put him into a position of trust. Le Caron wrote Anderson that the infighting promised a gold mine of intelligence: "This trial is bound to develop some rich information for our use."[15]

Perhaps the strongest witness against Sullivan was Lomasney's widow, who accused Sullivan of financially abandoning her after her husband's death under London Bridge. Now, she could not afford to pay the $30 monthly rent for her family's apartment.[16] Were it not for the $1,000 that Dillon raised for her, her family might have gone hungry.

Notes that have survived from the secret trial also describe what seems to be the shabby treatment of another member of Lomasney's group. The man, identified only as O'Neill (not the Civil War general John O'Neill, who had died in 1878), testified that he had to sell much of his clothing to be able to escape from England. Referring to O'Neill, the meeting notes state: "Received £20 and one steerage passage. . . No shoes. Sold clothes and trunk to get home. No bed."

With that, the secret trial was over. The verdict would be announced at an undisclosed date.

On 31 August 1888 Robert Anderson was appointed assistant district commissioner for crime for Scotland Yard, replacing James Monro, who stayed on as head of the Scotland Yard Secret Bureau. Anderson must have felt some sense of vindication from the appointment. It was just four years after he had been sacked by Wilkinson, and relegated to work as secretary to the prison commissioners.

The promotion came just as Anderson's doctor ordered him to take two months off work to rest and recuperate from stress.[17] Anderson was making vacation plans for a trip to the continent when, hours after he received his promotion, a prostitute named Mary Ann (Polly) Nichols was carved to death in London's East End Whitechapel district. At first, the slaying was dismissed as a horrifying, but isolated, incident. Life was pitifully cheap in the East End, especially for its prostitutes.

Anderson decided to follow his doctor's orders and take the stress leave in Switzerland, leaving for the continent on 8 September. Hours after Anderson boarded his train, the body of prostitute Annie Chapman was discovered in a Whitechapel backyard. Her throat and torso were sliced open, as a butcher might gut a pig.

Anderson didn't mention later in his memoirs, which were published in 1910, that he met, during a stopover in Paris, with his agent, General Millen. The two men clearly had plenty to discuss. A commission of inquiry had been called to investigate *The Times*' publication of letters from Pigott's black satchel, which supposedly linked Parnell to terrorism and murder. It's possible that Anderson considered trying to convince Millen to step forward as a witness to help out *The Times*, which had faithfully supported the Conservative government. There were obvious negatives to that course, however. Testifying would abruptly end Millen's work as a double agent. Also, Millen's name had surfaced in connection to the Jubilee dynamite plot, and it was doubtful that a man linked with an attempt to blow up the Royal family would be viewed too favourably by the British public or Her Majesty.[18]

Back in London, Scotland Yard detectives studied a letter that was dated 25 September 1888, and was written in red ink. The writer claimed to be the Whitechapel killer, and threatened to strike again. He signed his name, Jack the Ripper.[19]

Anderson was still in Paris when the mutilated bodies of two prostitutes were found in London's East End on 30 September. Even Queen Victoria demanded action and Anderson later wrote that the "next day's post brought me an urgent appeal. . . to return to London; and of course I complied."[20] His stress leave would have to wait.

Patrick Egan had settled in Lincoln, Nebraska, when *The Times* had published its letters from Pigott, all suggesting that Parnell was in league with violent terrorists. When Egan saw the handwritten facsimiles in *The Times*, he found something just a little off about the letter r. He also noted that "hesitancy" was misspelled "hesitency." Such sloppiness was very un-Parnell-like. The Irish Party leader had a compulsion for proper spelling, and once refused to finish reading a letter because the word "agriculture" was spelled incorrectly. Egan, who was now a prosperous grain merchant, dismissed the published letters as "villainous concoctions." Then he and Sullivan contacted Parnell to relay Egan's handwriting analysis.[21]

On the home front, Le Caron had fallen once again onto hard financial times. As a doctor and pharmacist, he would have made more money than the average worker; however, his passion for gathering information didn't extend to money management until things reached a crisis point. He told Anderson in a 26 September letter that it had taken him six months to afford a headstone for his teenaged son William's grave. The money Le Caron received from Anderson on that day—coincidentally Le Caron's 48th birthday—was a godsend, he wrote:

> My dear Sir,
>
> Your kind favor of Sept. 8th containing five hundred dollars came duly by hand yesterday. . . it has enabled me to do today what I have been heartily wishing for. . . buying a headstone to mark my dear boys grave, besides forty other essentials. . . I am relieved from immediate need and feel more like facing the world. . . I have no desire to lay down—though personally I would like to settle down quietly for the balance of my days, and others near and dear to me would like to too. And that would not be in this locality. The stigma of Irish Dynamiter sticks to me and kills me in the estimation of many.[22]

On 12 October Le Caron wrote Anderson to relay the news that Luke Dillon had said that Land League funds were diverted to pay for the Phoenix Park murders, apparently to pay for the escape of the fugitives and the legal defence of members who were put on trial. Le Caron added that Parnell knew about the Phoenix Park murder plot. Le Caron further noted that "Luke Dillon described in the writer's presence a bomb device on the scale of a baseball and the tactics for using it." Le Caron wrote that the upcoming commission of public inquiry sparked by The Times letters made Dillon fear that Parnell would be exposed as an advocate of violence.

The inquiry was to take a broad look into violence associated with the Irish independence movement. Its mandate was for fact-finding, public education, and the shaping of public policy. However, it was obvious that it would never have been called if not for the controversy over the correspondence attributed to Parnell published in The Times, suggesting that he supported murder to further his political ends. The inquiry didn't have the power to try and sentence suspects, but it could subpoena witnesses. It could also kill reputations.

After relaying Dillon's fears about the inquiry, Le Caron added that Dillon's hometown of Philadelphia now seemed to be at the centre of Clan na nGael activity for America. He sent Anderson a picture of Dillon, and also relayed a new phrase for killing—"giving a quietus."[23]

CHAPTER 21

SURFACING

No. 3 Cork Square, London, 1888

I gazed suspiciously at the tall youthful figure which met my view.
  —**Henri Le Caron prepares to tell a stranger about his double life**

The commission of inquiry called after the publication of *The Times'* letters was to be held in London's massive Royal Courts of Justice on the Strand. It was located close to Fleet Street, home to the newsrooms of the world's most widely read English-language newspapers.[1]

Opened less than six years before by Queen Victoria, the courts were built on eight acres of land where some 450 houses had stood. The massive new legal complex that replaced them fused Edwardian style with modern efficiency, housing 19 courts and 700 rooms and offices, and heated by about eleven miles of pipes. It was ambitious in its detail as well as its scope, with oak and multicoloured carved granite pinnacles and soaring ceilings.[2]

Parnell wasn't impressed that the inquiry had been called. He didn't sue *The Times* for libel since he didn't trust English courts to hear a case against the mighty, pro-Conservative Party newspaper. Instead, Parnell wanted the House of Commons to set up a select committee to determine if the letters that were published in *The Times* and attributed to him were indeed authentic. He was denied this wish. Instead, the government ordered a wide-ranging inquiry into Irish political violence, headed by a trio of Unionist judges: Sir James Hannen, who was named president of the commission, from the Prolate and Divorce Division; Sir John Charles Day; and Sir Archibald Levin Smith, all of whom were political opponents both of Parnell and Gladstone's Liberals. The inquiry's mandate might be on Irish violence, but there was no question whose reputation was really at stake. The Special Commission of Inquiry on Irish violence quickly became referred to publicly as the Parnell Inquiry.

Representing *The Times* was Sir Richard Webster, the attorney-general of England. Aside from his title, Webster was also notable for what Davitt called his "bulldog tenacity," enormous work ethic, and fine singing voice in his church choir. Representing Parnell was Sir Charles Russell, an Ulster Catholic, and his bright junior counsel, Herbert Henry Asquith, who would one day be prime minister. Asquith brought a towering intellect, as well as a massive distrust of zeal, to the Parnell team. "He understood everything and originated nothing," scoffed *Daily News* editor A.G. Gardiner.[3]

Even in this who's who of legal talent, Sir Charles Russell clearly stood out above the rest, Davitt thought: "Sir Charles Russell towered in personality and in voice above all the able men engaged in the case. He was a combination of the Celt and the Saxon in some features of his individuality. His sympathies towards Ireland, his ambition towards England. He was in no sense an Irish nationalist, but held a warm feeling and an attachment for the land of his birth."[4]

Sir Charles liked to control his clients, a trait that made Parnell bristle. As Davitt observed, "They seem never to have taken to each other and although on one occasion during Russell's opening speech Davitt was startled to observe Parnell actually in tears (for the first time in his life, he told Davitt) when the great advocate was describing the poverty of the west of Ireland." Russell wasn't placated, grumbling, "I'm glad something can move him."[5]

22 OCTOBER 1888

There were three rows of lawyers in black silky gowns seated in Probate Court No. 1 of the Royal Courts of Justice as the inquiry began. They looked impressive in their powdered white wigs, fashioned from horsetails, if one did not think too long about the horsehair's former function. Behind them, journalist John Macdonald observed, there were:

> Witnesses from every level of Irish society, the Paddy of Punch's shop-windows, in the flesh, in his traditional costume. He wears knee-breeches and woollen stockings. The style of his tall hat is unknown in Piccadilly. His starchless collar of blue-striped cotton falls round his lean, weather-beaten neck loosely as an aesthete's; and the swallow-tails of his baggy dress-coat of grayish brown shaggy frieze impinge upon his calves. Just as he appears at mass, or on market-days—say at Galway or archiescopal Tuam—while he waits, mutely, through the irresponsive hours, straw rope in hand, beside his pig.[6]

1 NOVEMBER 1888

An ugly tone to the inquiry was quickly set when a man identified as J. Cavanaugh pulled out his revolver inside a tavern opposite the law courts and opened fire on another Irishman, Phlanche Cox. Both men were slated as inquiry witnesses, and Cox survived the shooting to testify. Cavanaugh said he fired the shot because he had been "threatened with death for making certain disclosures."[7]

7 NOVEMBER 1888

Le Caron wrote to Anderson from his home at 177 La Salle Avenue in Chicago, with money and politics on his mind. "My dear Sir," he wrote. "Your kind favor of Oct 27th containing three hundred dollars was duly received this day. Accept my heartful thanks..." Then Le Caron again said he had no future in mainstream politics because he had been tainted by the Irish cause. "Political preferment is now out of the question for me." He sniped at Republican presidential candidate Benjamin Harrison, adding, "The Irish vote has been a potent factor and will demand and obtain favors from Harrison. As soon as excitement is over I look for something in National affairs, always faithfully yours, TB"[8]

It's not surprising that Le Caron omitted to note his connection with Harrison from a decade earlier when he fled prosecution for robbing the grave of the president's father and selling the corpse to a medical school.

9 NOVEMBER 1888

Early that morning, the landlord's assistant in a sad building at Miller's Court, Whitechapel, London, heard no answer when he knocked on the door of Mary Jane Kelly. He stepped inside into a crime scene that was even more horrific than the previous bloody work of Jack the Ripper. The stress on Anderson to solve the case was only getting more intense.

17 NOVEMBER 1888

Parnell's lawyer, Sir Charles Russell, bristled about what he called flimsy, hearsay evidence at the Parnell Inquiry and snapped, "This ceases to be a judical investigation." The *Chicago Citizen*, an organ for the Irish nationalist movement, wrote that "At these words (Justice) Hannen, whose bad temper is aggravated by illness, grew ghastly pale and lost all self control. The admission of the evidence amazed every lawyer in court."

In America, Clan na nGael leaders feared that a report of their investigation into charges that Alexander Sullivan and his associates mishandled funds would fall into hands of officials with the Parnell Inquiry. The verdict on Sullivan et al. wasn't yet released, but Le Caron took it as a given that Cronin would not be recommending mercy.[9]

In early December 1888, Le Caron received news that his father was dying, and he rushed to be with him, thinking he would return home within a month. By the time Le Caron's ship docked in England, his father had lost consciousness, and when he reached the family home on Mersea Road by Colchester's old fortified wall, John Joseph Billis Beach had died. True to his modest nature, his notice in the *Essex Standard* newspaper simply read, "BEACH—December 15, at his residence, 10 Mersea Road, Colchester in his 73rd year, John Joseph B. Beach. Much respected."

Le Caron was ready to sail back to America after the funeral when he was summoned to meet with Anderson. The spymaster told Le Caron that *The Times* sought a witness regarding the American side of the Irish conspiracy. Le Caron would later say that Anderson also told him that he didn't want him filling that role. If Le Caron took the witness box, Anderson knew this would forever dry up a valuable stream of information. Le Caron sorely felt the need for a change in his life.

Gone forever were the letters and nods of approval from the man whose good graces mattered most to Le Caron, who had struggled hard to win fatherly favour in his large family. The death sapped Le Caron's zeal for espionage. Le Caron had never been particularly sophisticated politically, and the politics he did hold didn't reach much beyond seeing his family home on Magdelan Street in Colchester as a metaphor for his English homeland.

There's no record that Le Caron shared his many aliases with his father, but there's also no doubt the senior Beach understood the risks of his son's life as a spy, just as he had appreciated the dangers of his other sons who had died serving the British Empire in South Africa and Egypt. Le Caron had done his father proud with his intelligence work, but he had grown weary. It was time to move on with his life.

The Times badly needed him, and Le Caron was low on money as usual. Soon, he was negotiating for either a one-time fee of £10,000 or a pension of £400 annually for life in return for his testimony.[10] Whatever sum was reached isn't clear. It didn't make Le Caron rich, but it was enough to make him a witness.

Representatives of *The Times* told Le Caron that he should deal with a man identified only as Mr. Houston in his preparations before taking the witness box. Their meetings would take place privately, in Houston's home, east of the Tower Bridge, a few minutes' walk from the River Thames, at No. 3 Cork Square. Le Caron was greeted there by a manservant, identified only as Rogers, who ushered him inside to meet Houston.

"I gazed suspiciously at the tall youthful figure which met my view," Le Caron later recalled. "As Mr. Houston took my letter of introduction from me and carelessly opened it, answering my suspicious glance with a slight smile hovering about his face, I could not help the remark, 'Sir, you are a much younger man than I was led to believe I would meet.'"

The man smiled back at him and said, "I am sorry, but I cannot help being young, you know. However, I am Mr. Houston."[11]

Le Caron later said that he felt that the public needed to know the true face of Irish revolution as he felt they were being deceived by Parnell and his talk of parliamentary reform. Before he would take the stand, Le Caron demanded that his family be safely moved from Chicago to England. Without a word to her friends or landlord, Nannie Le Caron called a furniture dealer, and sold everything in their home at 177 La Salle Avenue. Asked by neighbours where she was going so quickly, Nannie first explained she had found a new flat, and then modified her story to say that she was moving to New York. Their 22-year-old son Henry and daughter Ida, who was in her late teens and married, stayed behind in America, while Nannie took Gertrude, May, Arthur, and Charles with her. When the furniture man arrived to clean out the flat, he noted that the beds were unmade, as if the family didn't want to waste a second in getting out the door.

In her haste, as she fled Chicago with the children, Nannie left behind incriminating copies of letters her husband had written that year to Anderson. Soon they would be in the hands of the Clan na nGael, humiliating reminders of the depth of Le Caron's betrayal.

In mid-December 1888, the verdict was finally delivered in the United Brotherhood's secret American embezzlement trial for Sullivan et al. Only Michael Boland of Kansas City was convicted of misappropriation, even though the expenditure of some eighty-five thousand dollars could not be explained in any way.[12] While Sullivan was acquitted of embezzlement, he and D.C. Feeley were censured for loose business practices. Cronin and Dr. Peter McCathey refused to endorse the report, and Cronin wasn't about to let the matter rest. Soon there were rumblings that Cronin possessed a good deal of information that didn't come out at the trial, and which Cronin planned to publish in Irish newspapers. The heat against Alexander Sullivan would continue as long as Cronin was alive.

In London, Anderson gave Le Caron records of his decades of correspondence, which had been stored in Anderson's townhouse near Notting Hill Gate. Now, in Houston's home, Le Caron and Houston read through hundreds of letters and Clan na nGael documents for ten days, from 10am until 6pm, with Houston taking notes.

After Le Caron left for the day, Houston worked on, assisted by clerks, long into the night.

CHAPTER 22

True Colours

London, 1889

I never forgot yet that I was an English subject and English-born.

—**Henri Le Caron**

I rish nationalists had been eagerly anticipating the testimony of Colonel Charles Boycott at the Parnell Inquiry, even though authorities tried to keep identities of upcoming witnesses secret for security reasons. It was a source of pride for the nationalists that they could divine who would be testifying next and Boycott's testimony promised comic relief for them. In one case, they gathered intelligence by intercepting a Canadian witness and plying him with liquor. Another time, they were able to intercept a mail bag belonging to the British Ministry at Washington. So when Boycott took the stand as expected, they laughed as the colonel told of having to rise at 4am to feed cattle and pick turnips after he was shunned by local workers. However, Parnell's supporters were stunned on the morning of 5 February 1889, when a short, wiry man stepped into the witness box.[1]

Henri Le Caron was 48 years old when, on the 44th day on which the inquiry sat, he strode into Probate Court 1 and out of his double life. He had been a spy for half of his life when Attorney-General Webster asked him, "What is your name?"

"My baptismal name is Thomas Billis Beach. . . I have been known . . . as Henri Le Caron."[2]

With those words, the American phase of the inquiry began. The mood in the inquiry shifted from boredom to shock. Le Caron, who wore a pin on his collar showing his Civil War service, was charged with the drama of the occasion. He later described his emotions as he finally went public after almost a quarter of a century as a spy: "On Tuesday morning, the 5th of February 1889, the curtain was rung up, and throwing aside the mask for ever, I stepped into the witness-box and came out in my true colours, as an Englishman, proud of his country, and in no sense ashamed of his record in her service."[3]

A reporter who was keeping a diary of the commission noted that "He paused at each of his three names, pronouncing them with slow, distinct emphasis. . . Major Le Caron is short and slightish in build; erect—like a soldier—and imperturbably cool; he has a lofty forehead, and smallish, alert eyes, which look straight. The major's is one of the boniest faces in or out of the New World,—a death's-head with a tight skin of yellow parchment. With his arms folded over his chest—like another short man, the great Napoleon—he raps out his answers, short, sharp. 'Yes, yes,' he says, snappishly sometimes, pronouncing it 'yus.'"

Irish Party MP T.P. O'Connor struggled to take the measure of the wiry, intense man who appeared unexpectedly before them. "He was a very thin man, with black hair, piercing black eyes, small, pallid face, with regular features and a waxed moustache," O'Connor noted. "It was curious that a man with such a face—which, to say the least, was a little sinister—should have been able to deceive for two generations the suspicious and ferocious men among whom he passed his life." O'Connor studied the witness further and found a sense of drama about him. "There was something also in the pallid and cadaverous cheeks that suggested the long years of peril through which he had passed."[4]

Clan na nGael members who had known and trusted Le Caron for a quarter century weren't the only ones shocked to see him on the witness stand. So were long-serving Scotland Yard officials, as Anderson's son, Arthur Ponsonby Moore-Anderson, later wrote: "[Liberal statesman and author John] Morley's Life of Gladstone states that for more than twenty years le Caron [sic] was in the pay of Scotland Yard. 'Scotland Yard,' replied my father, 'was not aware of the man's existence until he appeared as a witness at the Parnell Commission.' As a matter of fact the correspondence was carried on through his wife in America and a relative of my father's in England, and was always treated as private. On his visits to London, Le Caron used to see my father at our own house; I have a clear recollection of seeing him there and wondering who he was."[5]

6 FEBRUARY 1889

Visitors rushed in for seating when the courtroom doors opened for the second day in which Le Caron would recount what he later called "my strange and weird but true story." The buzz of excitement was particularly strong when, shortly after noon, Charles Stewart Parnell appeared in the spectators' gallery. Parnell was an infrequent visitor at the inquiry, and appeared this day with the collar of his brown overcoat pulled up to his ears, as if to shield him from a chill. His gaunt face looked particularly thin and sickly, but his eyes remained sharp and bright, and Le Caron couldn't help but follow him with his gaze as he moved to his seat. Parnell carried a handful of papers and a black handbag. An animated group of supporters settled around Parnell, including Davitt, O'Connor, and Sir Charles Russell. A reporter noted that, "For the first time perhaps since the Commission began its very intricate labours, the Parnellites showed a real interest in the proceedings. They looked as if at last they felt the delight of battle—felt that they were coming to close quarters. The expression of boredom vanished from their faces; and at various stages in the proceedings they even became merry."[6]

7 FEBRUARY 1889

In Le Caron's curious accent, which some thought was American and others considered to be faintly English, he laid bare the carefully guarded inner secrets of the Clan na nGael. He explained that the VC or United Brotherhood and the Clan na nGael are the same entity, and that its governing body was called the "FC," using the letter that followed the first letters of "Executive" and "Body"; its secretary "Y," treasurer "Z," and chairman "X." America was divided into districts, known by letters from A to N. The Clan's codes seemed a little foolish, like something concocted in a boys' treehouse, as Le Caron described almost twenty secret signs, including a cross for the treasurer and a triangle for the three-man executive body.

He then supplied a copy of the constitution of the United Brotherhood.

"And what was the object of this UB?" he was asked.

"It was to bring about the establishment of an Irish Republic, of an independent Irish Republic in Ireland, and the independence of that nation, and it was believed that the only method whereby that could be accomplished was by the force of arms."

"Were you appointed to any office in that organization?"

"Yes, sir."

"What?"

"That of senior guardian."

"Of what?"

"Camp 463."

"Where was that?"

"Illinois."

Soon, Le Caron was describing how "skirmishing" meant striking at the heart of the enemy with violence, which generally meant using dynamite. He noted how Devoy and Millen were dispatched to Europe in 1879 with some ten thousand dollars for this purpose.[7] It's likely that Le Caron still didn't know another of Anderson's tightly guarded secrets—that Millen was another British spy.

Le Caron produced a copy of a document from the Clan na nGael headquarters. Dated 19 April 1880 it sounded much like the American Declaration of Independence, with its assertion that just power must flow from popular consent:

> The world beholds the spectacle of a nation of enforced paupers and beggars who suffer the pangs of hunger and the humiliation of beggary and although their land produces and exports twofold more than sufficient to sustain them in comfort. This condition is the result of the infamous alien misrule which it is our purpose and duty to overthrow . . . a great revolution is being wrought, and that aristocracy and feudalism must give way to democracy, and the distribution of the soil among the people.

Next, the attorney-general read the letter of introduction written for Le Caron by Patrick Egan, which described him as "one of the most devoted Friends of the Irish National Cause." Journalist John Macdonald wrote, "The major smiled. His thin, yellow face rippled, so to speak, into wrinkles. Then he blushed. He appeared to appreciate the fun of the situation."

Le Caron told the commission of his meeting in Paris with O'Leary, the grand old man of the Irish independence movement. "He mentioned the name of Mr. Parnell as being a thorough Nationalist in sentiment, as he had always been, but a revolutionist to the backbone."

"Did he say anything further about him?"

"Yus. He cited to me, as proof of his statement in reference to Mr. Parnell, that about a year previous to this conversation, Mr. Parnell had made application and had endeavoured to join the Irish Republican Brotherhood, the organisation upon this side of the water."

Le Caron testified that Parnell never did join as members thought it was better for him if he remained on the outside of the revolutionary group. Le Caron stated that Parnell left no doubt about his meaning when he told him in the corridor of the House of Commons: "I have long since ceased to believe that anything but force of arms will ever bring about the redemption of Ireland." In another description of his talks with Parnell, Le Caron said, "He told me that he did not see any reason why an insurrectionary movement, when we were prepared to send money and men who were armed and organised—why a successful insurrectionary movement should not be inaugurated in Ireland."

Le Caron didn't falter as the questioning pressed on, and he explained how "the Castle" was slang for the British government in Dublin and dynamite attacks were referred to as "the delusions." Revolutionaries must have cringed when he noted the submarine torpedo boat, which, "after being partly completed, was discovered to be a failure. . . It is still possessed by the organisation, and has never been used to attack British vessels under water."

He noted how Clan na nGael fund-raisers like picnics and excursions were often held on 4 July so that they could serve the double purpose of aiding the organization and celebrating American independence from Britain. Then he read from a Clan na nGael circular about how its fighters were trained in America:

> It is much better for our men to join the State Militia, when they receive the best instruction, uniforms, and arms without cost, and where they are compelled to obey orders and become disciplined. In places where it is impossible to join the State Militia, the men without going to the expense of supporting companies, can practice target shooting and in other respects make themselves useful. In many of the mining and other regions they can acquire knowledge of the use and preparation of certain articles of modern warfare.

Sir Charles Russell stepped away from his client, Parnell, to begin his cross-examination. There was plenty to challenge if his client's reputation was to be salvaged. Standing straight and powerful, his arms crossed, Russell asked *The Times*' star witness how he came to join the Fenians in America.

"Did you take any oath?"

"I did."

"What was that oath?"

"That I would fight for the cause of Irish independence and the establishment of a republic of Ireland. I took a military form of oath as a military officer."

"Of obedience?"

"Yus, Sir."

"And you say, although you took the oath, it was not at that time a secret organisation?"

"It was not at that time."

"Were there any signs or passwords?"

"None, whatever, at that time."

"When did it become a secret organisation?"

"It first became a secret organisation, to my knowledge, in 1869."

"Up to that time, there had been no oath or secrecy?"

"Yus. Periodically, I took an oath that I would keep inviolate all secrets on military matters that were disclosed to me."

"Was that oath periodical?"

"It was an oath that was given at councils of war, and also, when important business was transacted, all that were present were sworn to keep it secret."

"Of course, you took this oath intending not to observe it?"

Le Caron didn't flinch, replying, "Decidedly yus, sir."

"And your purpose in joining was to learn all that you could about the organization?"

"Yus, sir."

"With the view of disclosing it?"

"Yus, I might be allowed to state, my Lords, I have thought of the oath many times. . ."

"Never mind," Russell said.

"The witness is entitled to explain," Attorney-General Webster protested.

"My Lords, I claim indulgence," Le Caron said.

"I will give you every opportunity of explaining, but I do not think it necessary for you to interpose now," the commission president, Sir James Hannen, said.

Le Caron wasn't fazed, continuing, "I never forgot yet that I was an English subject and English-born."

It was clear that Le Caron understood the difference between a traitor and a spy, and he wanted to impress this upon everyone who was now judging him. A traitor was the lowest of the low, someone who turned on his own people for a price. A spy was a military man on a lonely, dangerous, seemingly never-ending secret assignment. In case the point hadn't been made, Le Caron restated his mission moments later, saying, "I looked upon myself as a military spy in the service of my country."

The innermost secrets of the Clan na nGael were now available to anyone for the price of a newspaper. Dr. William Carroll of Philadelphia was stunned that things could go so wrong so quickly. He wrote to John Devoy on 6 February asking, "Who is this latest ruffian, 'Major Le Carron' [sic] or 'Dr. Beach,' who has turned up in the Parnell trial? Some scoundrel, I suppose, who has got into camps here, picked up the names he supposed were on the Directory, and got possession of some papers and reports and is earning his money by making up a 'cock and bull' story for *The Times*."[8]

8 FEBRUARY 1889

Sir Charles Russell pressed Le Caron on why he felt the need to testify.

"I saw what I considered a lame presentation of the prosecution," Le Caron replied, his face deadpan, to a ripple of laughter.

"That is rather hard on the attorney-general," said Russell, as Attorney-General Webster joined in the laughter.

"I saw the moral effect it was having among my then confreres," Le Caron continued. "I saw that erroneous information was being published. In the public press and claims being made by the *Irish Press*. . . I felt it my duty to write, and I did write, and offer to take all risks and testify to that to which I could testify."

"Then for twenty years you have been following the patriotic role of military spy?" Russell asked.

"I consider that my duties as military spy."

"I mean for pay as well as patriotism?"

"I have received since that date. . ."

"Will you kindly answer me, yes or no?"

"No sir. I have only received in part remuneration for my services."

"From the Government?"

"Yus, undoubtedly."

"You have not, then, received as much as you think you ought to receive?"

"Not as much as I have expended at times."

Sitting in the gallery, soaking in the drama, were Irish playwright Oscar Wilde; Mrs. Helen Asquith; Mrs. Catherine Gladstone; numerous fashionable women of society; Alexander Sullivan's wife, Margaret, and 15-year-old Winston Churchill. Wilde later quipped, "He [Le Caron] says he is out of pocket by his patriotism."

Sir Charles switched his interrogation from money to dynamite.

"You have suggested rather than stated in your evidence that you had to do with Gallagher and Lomasney," he asked. "Did you take part in any deliberation at which either of these wicked plots was devised?"

"Yus sir."

"You yourself took part?"

"Yus sir."

"And advised them?"

"I did not deem myself of sufficient importance to make suggestions and put myself too forward in these matters."

"You appeared to advise?"

"I offered no objection."

"And gave information at once?"

"Immediately. On the first opportunity that presented itself."

Soon, Le Caron was fielding questions about his Chicago neighbour, Alexander Sullivan. The interrogation was withering, but Sir Charles still hadn't broken, or even noticeably bent, the surprise witness.

"What is his position?"

"As a lawyer or in society?"

"As a lawyer?"

"Very good, as a lawyer."

"He does not move among the aristocracy of Chicago?"

"By no means."

"Have you partaken of his hospitality? Were you intimate with him socially?"

"Yus."

"Then he was not unworthy of your society?"

"No. He was very useful."

Laughter again rippled through the courtroom with the nimble response.

Under pressure from Sir Charles, Le Caron modified a statement in which he stated that Parnell's 1880 American tour was organised by violent revolutionaries. Pressed further, Le Caron said this only applied to Chicago, Cincinnati, and St. Louis.

Then Sir Charles zeroed in on terrorism.

"Did you vote for dynamite?"

"I always voted on the side of the majority," he replied, again to laughter.

"Were the majority in favour of dynamite?"

"Yus, they were unanimous."

Outside the courtroom, Secret Service agents quietly moved Le Caron's family into new quarters in the south London district of Brixton. Nannie and the children would continue to live apart from him as long as the danger against Le Caron remained intense.

9 FEBRUARY 1889

The *Chicago Tribune's* correspondent was impressed that Le Caron seemed a match for Sir Charles, who was widely considered without peer as a courtroom interrogator. The newspaper quoted someone identified as an "eminent counsel" as remarking, "No better witness ever has been in a witness box."

Le Caron was protected by five detectives, and a courtroom bystander commented to him, "You will take a good deal of guarding."

Le Caron didn't flinch at the lightly veiled threat, replying, "I have carried my life in my hands for twenty-five years. Do you suppose I am afraid of these fellows now?"

The Tribune reporter, impressed with the exchange, wrote, "He looks like a man who would shoot quick."

12 FEBRUARY 1889

Le Caron told the inquiry that he estimated there were between 250 and 275 revolutionary Clan na nGael camps in America, with a total membership of 23,000 men.

"Now, were all these 23,000 men in favour of the use of dynamite?" he was asked.

"Yus," replied Le Caron, not requiring time to think.

"Deliberately and knowingly?"

"Yus," he replied again.

Not long afterwards, the questions finally ceased. Le Caron looked up at the judges and asked, "Is that all?"

There was no answer, except a tap on the shoulder from an usher.

"I have to thank you all for the courtesy and forbearance you have shown in hearing me," Le Caron said. "I know I have been impertinent, but I did not know the rules, and I thank you exceedingly for the courtesy you have shown me."

As Le Caron went public on the witness stand, Benjamin Harrison was sworn in as the 23rd president of the United States. There's no record if he saw Le Caron's picture in a newspaper, or if he recognised him as Dr. Charles O. Morton, the fugitive grave-robber who had stolen his father's body a decade before.

14 FEBRUARY 1889

On Valentine's Day, two days after he left the witness stand, Henri Le Caron met with Colchester lawyer Asher Prior to draw up his last will and testament. He appointed "my dear wife Nannie" as the sole executrix and trustee of the will, and guardian of his underaged children. "I give all my plate linen china glass books pictures prints wines liquors furniture and other household effects to my said dear wife absolutely and I also give to her the sum of five thousand pounds."

CHAPTER 23

SPELLING BEE

London, 1889

... not a subject fit for laughter.

—Judge's comments on evidence of Richard Pigott

20 FEBRUARY 1889

The Special Commission was into its 53rd day of hearings when, shortly before 3pm on 20 February 1889, Richard Pigott was called to the witness stand. In happier times, the portly man with the monocle was known for his amateur photography, champagne parties, and grand, military-style moustache, which earned him the nickname The Major. As he stepped forward at the inquiry, Pigott seemed much older than his 54 years. He also looked very much alone. "The rat is caught in the trap at last," Davitt thought.[1]

Irish Party MP T.P. O'Connor considered Pigott a "cowering, miserable, despairing figure," while a reporter wrote that his appearance suggested he "might be a church deacon." A writer for the *Birmingham Daily Post* was less sympathetic, writing of Pigott as "having the general appearance of a coarsely composed and rather cheapened Father Christmas."

21 FEBRUARY 1889

For his part, Pigott seemed to enjoy the attention, at least at first. He told of how Edward Caulfield Houston originally approached him in December 1885 and asked if he knew anybody who might compromise

Charles Stewart Parnell. Pigott described furtive meetings in Lausanne, Switzerland, London, Dublin, and Paris, in which he said he tried to gather letters from Irish-American revolutionaries, who were unhappy with Parnell. There was a general feeling of mistrust from the Irish-Americans towards him, he told the inquiry. "I was charged with being in the employment of the Government, hunting up evidence for a prosecution against Mr. Parnell, and therefore I was regarded with suspicion, and I have reason to believe they all gave me assumed names."

Pigott seemed to be entertained by the questioning, as he testified that Henry Labouchere, the radical member of Parliament for Northhampton and publisher of a journal with the grand name of truth, had tried to get him to lie and testify that he had forged the letters that appeared in *The Times*.

"He urged as a further inducement to me to do this that I would become immensely popular in Ireland," Pigott testified, to a ripple of laughter. "The fact that I had swindled *The Times* would be sufficient in itself to secure me a seat in Parliament." There was more laughter from the gallery, as Pigott continued, "And he added that, if at any future time I should decide to go to the United States, he would undertake that I should be received by a torchlight procession."

Pigott paused to let the laughter subside a little, as a dancehall comedian might, and then continued, "Of course, I could scarcely believe he was serious."

At this point, the president of the commission interjected, saying, "I must say, whether this is true or not, it is not a subject fit for laughter."

Sir Charles Russell began his cross-examination of Pigott with a great show of politeness, as an executioner might show a condemned man by offering him a final cigarette and the opportunity to say a few words. Russell hadn't done so well in his cross-examination of Le Caron, and Pigott offered a far less agile target. Sir Charles was a man who seldom missed once, and never twice.

Sir Charles remained the personification of good manners as he asked Pigott for a demonstration of his handwriting.

"Mr. Pigott, will you be good enough to write some words on that sheet of paper for me?"

Pigott dipped the tip of a quill pen in ink and wrote, upon Russell's request, "livelihood," "likelihood," his own name, then "Proselytism," "Patrick Egan," "P. Egan," and, in what seemed almost an afterthought, "hesitancy," with a small "h." Pigott misspelled the word as "hesitency." He wasn't grinning any longer. Were his hands trembling now? Was his fleshy face getting redder? Did the rat smell a trap?

Russell handed the paper to the attorney-general, who suggested it be photographed as evidence.

22 FEBRUARY 1889

Probate Court No. 1 was packed to capacity as Sir Charles Russell opened his third day of questioning Pigott with a spelling bee. He noted that Pigott had written the word "hesitancy" for him.

"Is that a word you are accustomed to use?" Russell asked Pigott.

"I have used it."

"Did you notice that you spelt it as it is not ordinarily spelt?"

"Yes, I fancy I made a mistake in the spelling."

"What was it?"

"I think it was an 'a' instead of an 'e' or vice versa. I am not sure which."

"You cannot say what was the mistake, but you have a general consciousness that there was something wrong?"

"Yes."

Sir Charles referred Pigott to a letter from the black satchel of correspondence he had sold to Houston. It was allegedly sent from Parnell to Egan on 9 January 1882, pressing him to take violent action. The letter refers to William Edward Forster, former chief secretary for Ireland, and reads:

> Dear E
> What are these people waiting for? This inaction is inexcusable. Our best men are in prison and nothing is being done. Let there be an end to this hesitency. You undertook to make it hot for old Forster and Co. Let us have some evidence of your power to do so. My health is good, thanks.

Yours very truly
Chas. S. Parnell

Was Pigott squirming now as Sir Charles asked, "Supposing you wanted to forge a document, would it be any help to you to have before you a genuine letter written by the man whose writing you wished to forge?"

"Yes."

"How would you use it?"

"Copy it, of course."

"How would you proceed to use it?"

"I cannot say."

"Just give us your best idea."

"I do not pretend to have any experience in that line, so I cannot say."

There was more laughter in the gallery, but now Pigott wasn't controlling or enjoying it. The questioning had the tone of an encounter between a cat and its cornered prey as Sir Charles pressed on.

"Is Mr. Parnell's a difficult signature to copy?"

"I cannot tell."

"What do you think?"

"It is a peculiar signature."

"A strongly marked signature?"

"Yes."

"Do you think that it is a kind of signature more easily or less easily copied?"

"Really, I am not competent to give an opinion."

"But I am anxious to have your opinion. Speaking offhand, should you say that it is a signature easy or difficult to copy?"

"I should say difficult, considering the peculiarities of the handwriting."

"More difficult than a free, flowing signature?"

"I think so."

Russell noted that whoever wrote that letter misspelled "hesitancy" as "hesitency," just like Pigott.

"Have you noticed the fact that the writer of the body of the letter of the 9 of January 1882—the alleged forged letter—spells it in the same way?"

Pigott could only fumble for a reply. "I heard that remark made long since, and my explanation of my misspelling is that having that in my mind I got into the habit of spelling it wrong."

Russell turned to Hannen, high up on the judge's bench, to make sure this critical point was not missed, asking, "Did you Lordship catch that last answer?"

"Oh yes," Hannen replied.

The pitiful display continued as Sir Charles pressed Pigott on how he might explain his misspelling of "hesitancy" on the witness stand, and the similar mistake in the letter attributed to Parnell.

Pigott, drained of jokes and clever answers, replied flatly, "I cannot account for it."

Russell was not about to let the matter die easily or quickly or painlessly.

"Does that strike you as an extraordinary coincidence or not?"

"It appears to be horribly stupid. If I were to commit forgery I would not make such a mistake as that. I do not think I would repeat as many words. I am sure of that."

"Not intentionally, with your eyes open?"

"I would consider myself very stupid if I did so."

"You would be rather ashamed of yourself."

"No."

"You do not feel ashamed of yourself?"

"No, and I must object. . ."

"You do not?"

"No, and I think it is scandalous to be so questioned. I affirm distinctly. . ." Hannen didn't halt things, or surrender control to Pigott. Instead, the judge said, "But, witness, we are the judges of how counsel should proceed."

"I beg pardon, my Lord," Pigott replied lamely. "I think I ought to be allowed to say that I positively deny that I forged the letters. If I did I would not be here."

"Not if you could help it," Russell said.

"Why could I not help it?" Pigott asked.

It was a pitiful display, and Pigott left the stand appearing utterly broken, smiling the empty smile of an idiot. "Poor Pigott looked as if he would prefer even the grave to the witness-box," journalist John Macdonald of the *Daily News* wrote.[2]

26 FEBRUARY 1889

There was no answer when Richard Pigott was called in Probate Court No. 1 to return to the witness stand for his fourth day of grilling by Russell. Around the time his name was called out, Pigott was checking into the Hotel des Deux Mondes in Paris. He left Paris within a couple of hours, and headed toward Madrid. It was an odd move since Pigott knew Paris well and apparently had never visited Madrid before. The only person he likely knew who had any strong connection to the Spanish city was Captain Willie O'Shea.

Pigott registered at the Hotel Embajodores under the name Roland Ponsonby. Perhaps he was regaining his sense of humour and this was a joke to himself as the Queen's private secretary was Sir Henry Ponsonby. Whatever the case, Pigott was travelling fast and light now, carrying just a small valise, with a couple pairs of socks, three shirts, and plenty of paperwork. Those papers included two notebooks with memos and addresses of prominent Irish nationalists, old hotel bills, and catalogues of Sotheby's auctions with margin notes and prices, and a licence to carry a revolver. Aside from the odd collection of paperwork and the clothing, there were several religious medals and a pistol.[3]

Hotel Embajodores's staff considered Pigott a well-to-do British tourist and assigned him to one of their best rooms. Pigott made arrangements to hire an interpreter and ate a snack. Then he was given directions to a telegraph office, where he sent a message to London. This done, Pigott's mood lightened, and the interpreter guided him on a tour of Madrid's sights, including a museum and a cathedral. Pigott dined well that night, and went to bed early, after asking whether a telegram had arrived for him. He was told it hadn't.

Back in London, Professor Thomas Maguire of Trinity College, Dublin, lay alone in a hotel bed, depressed and weak. He was due to be called to testify at the Parnell Inquiry, and knew that Pigott's flight meant that his questioning would come sooner than expected and would be particularly intense and humiliating. He would be asked how a man of letters like himself could be duped into buying forgeries from a pathetic figure like Pigott. The professor never made it to the witness box, dying that day in the hotel bed of natural causes, no doubt aggravated by stress.[4]

26 FEBRUARY 1889

It seemed that everyone at the Royal Courts of Justice on the Strand was asking about the whereabouts of Richard Pigott. Court officials checked Anderton's Hotel on Fleet Street, and found nothing but a packet of letters in his room. Perhaps Pigott had killed himself, a spectator volunteered. "He is too stupid," another spectator replied. "He is too thick skinned," someone else offered. "Hasn't shame enough."[5]

It was around 6.30pm when Pigott heard a knock on his hotel room door. He opened it to see Spanish authorities, acting upon the request of the British government. "Very well," Pigott said through his interpreter. "Allow me to get my hat, and I will go with you."

The police waited by the door as Pigott disappeared into an alcove. About thirty seconds later, there was the crack of a single gunshot as Pigott permanently calmed his troubled brain.

When investigators opened Pigott's valise, they found a message to Henry Labouchere, the MP and publisher of the journal *Truth*, ready to be posted. It offered an explanation and an apology for the dead man's actions. It read:

> *I say that the first batch of letters which I sold to The Times were genuine. The second lot, however, contained several forged letters. Among the letters in this batch which I forged were two attributed to Mr. Parnell, one purporting to be written by Michael Davitt, one by Mr. James F. O'Kelly, MP, and one by Mr. Patrick Egan. . . I do assure you that I am deeply sorry for all the wrong that I have caused Mr. Parnell and others, and I am ready to place in your hands the*

means of repairing that wrong and I do all in my power to mend matters. All
that I have hitherto said is false, but what I have written under oath is true.

Pigott's confession was entered into the inquiry's record to outbursts
of nervous laughter. "No one save myself was engaged in the work. I
grieve I have to confess that I myself forged them," the dead man
confessed through his writings.

It was all a fraud. The papers in the mysterious black satchel in
Paris were all forgeries. *The Times* now conceded that the letters that
it had published were false, but pressed on at the inquiry nonetheless.
The inquiry had become, in the words of journalist John Macdonald, a
"funeral of dead reputations."[6]

Richard Pigott was buried far from home in Spain, where he knew
no one, and where no one considered him a traitor. He did, however,
achieve his hope of providing for his children. The shame of bearing
his name was considered too much for them to remain in England, and
they were sent abroad, at government expense, under new and secret
identities to continue their educations.

Also that spring, Francis Millen was found slumped in a comfortable
chair in his study in his brownstone at 487 West 57th Street in Manhattan,
dead of supposed natural causes. There were rumours that he had been
killed by British agents, who didn't want him talking at the Parnell
inquiry. If so, it would have been a strange end to an even stranger life.
A later story circulated that his death was anything but natural. In that
account, it was said that when police moved to arrest Millen, he pulled
out a pistol and blew his brains out, just like Pigott.

Whatever the case, Millen wouldn't be going public with his secrets
like Le Caron. He was given a grand patriot's send-off at Woodlawn
Cemetery, an oasis of calm just 30 minutes from the bustle of Manhattan.
The *New York Herald* reported that revolutionaries and diplomats alike
paid their respect at his casket, where a sprig of shamrock was placed
over his heart.

CHAPTER 24

LIVING LIE

He never could have had one moment's security, one moment of certain repose.

— **A sympathetic lawyer describes Henri Le Caron's life as a spy**

12 APRIL 1889

Sir Charles Russell sounded cocky now as he publicly reviewed the inquiry's evidence regarding his client, Charles Stewart Parnell. He sneered as he came to the surprise appearance of Henri Le Caron, saying he made his way through life betraying friends. "Le Caron! He is a living lie!"

30 APRIL 1889

Parnell was thin and sickly, but his eyes were strangely aglow as he stepped up to the witness stand and, despite his frail appearance, he chose to give his testimony standing. His examination-in-chief was handled by Herbert Henry Asquith rather than by senior counsel, Sir Charles Russell, whose mania for control equalled that of Parnell.[1]

"I may ask you here, Mr. Parnell, were you ever a member yourself of any secret society?"

"No, the only secret society that I was a member of was a body called the Foresters," Parnell dead-panned, referring to the fraternal organisation known for selling insurance and financial services to its members.

When the laughter died down, Parnell continued, with a rare comic flourish, "May I add I never wanted to be."

Asquith reminded Parnell that Le Caron had testified that Parnell had wanted to join the Irish Republican Brotherhood. According to Le Caron's testimony, Parnell changed his mind because Patrick Egan said he thought Parnell could do more good fighting for Irish independence as a member of Parliament.

"Is there a syllable of truth in that?" Asquith asked.

"There is not the slightest truth in that."

Next were questions about his speaking tour of America in 1880: "I want to call your attention to a statement by the witness Le Caron with reference to your tour in America, that without any exception the arrangements for both your eastern and western tours were exclusively in the hands of the leaders of the revolutionary organization. Is that true?"

"I believe it to be absolutely false," Parnell replied. Then he complained that, "from what I have heard since and from what I saw then I am absolutely convinced that the arrangements for my tours were in nobody's hands. We had to complain most strongly of the want of any organisation to receive us or to arrange for our tours. . . We went here, there, and everywhere, passing many important cities we had to return to, travelling long distances of country. In one case we went from the eastern seaboard to Indianapolis down in the central west of America, a journey considerably over 1,000 miles, and returned the next day. We travelled thousands of miles needlessly which we should have avoided had there been the slightest organization."

Parnell told Asquith that he recalled a meeting with Le Caron, but it made so scant an impression upon him that he couldn't remember the agent's appearance. He certainly couldn't recall using Le Caron as an envoy. "I have no recollection of him until I saw him in the witness-box."

"Were you in the habit of seeing at the House of Commons from time to time visitors to the House of Commons?" Asquith asked.

"Frequently, I have seen American gentlemen passing through. Beach or Le Caron might have been among the number. He would have had no difficulty in obtaining an interview with me if he had wished to do so."

"Did you ever say to Le Caron or any one else that 'I have long since ceased to believe that anything but force of arms will ever bring about the redemption of Ireland?'"

"I never said that, and I never even thought it. In the worst period of coercion I never for one single moment doubted the constitutional movement of our Parliamentary action would succeed in the end."

Asquith asked Parnell if he ever instructed Le Caron, or any other man, to enter into negotiations with the leaders of the Clan na nGael in America in order to unite them with Irish revolutionaries.

"No, I never sent any message over to the Clan na nGael, or to any of the persons mentioned by Beach."

In fact, Parnell continued, he didn't even know of the Clan na nGael's existence until after he began his 1880 tour.

"You have told us that you had heard when in America of the existence of the body called the Clan na nGael," Asquith said. "Were you aware at this time or at any time until the publication of these libels that the Clan na nGael organization was what has been called a murder club?"

"No, I never supposed such a thing for a moment."

"Were you aware that its policy was a policy of assassination and dynamite?"

"No, I never heard of it."

"Are you aware of it now?"

"No, except in so far as the witness Beach's evidence goes to prove it, and I do not think that carries very much weight."

In his cross-examination for *The Times*, Attorney-General Sir Richard Webster was particularly interested in Parnell's relationship with Le Caron's former Chicago neighbour, Alexander Sullivan.

"Did you see Alexander Sullivan?"

"Yes, I saw him and formed a high opinion of his abilities."

"Was he a Fenian?"

"Not so far as I know."

"Do you really represent that?"

"With regard to Sullivan I wish to answer your question fairly. I had no idea he was a member of the Clan na nGael or the Fenian body until I heard Mr. Beach's evidence. If I had known that Mr. Sullivan was connected, as it is alleged he was connected with it, I should not have agreed to his being president of the National League in America."

He also strongly denied giving Le Caron a signed photograph of himself, saying, "It was not my habit to give my photograph away." Shown the signed photo to refresh his memory, Parnell relented just a little, saying, "I am nearly certain I did not give it to him."

He retreated again only slightly, saying, "I think this is my genuine signature." However, he continued that people often sent him his photograph, asking him to sign and return it.

Parnell still sounded confident and strong as he worked to create as much distance as possible between himself and the Phoenix Park murders. "I regarded the Phoenix Park murder as the greatest possible calamity which could befall our movement." Then he added that the killers might be Americans.

He also curtly dismissed the testimony of Captain Willie O'Shea that he sought police protection. "I never had police protection."

As Parnell testified, Le Caron sat quietly in court, flanked by his bodyguards, and showed almost no emotion.

3 MAY 1889

To someone who didn't know him, Parnell appeared calm on the witness stand. However, if a spectator had the right angle of vision and watched very closely, his hands could be seen to twitch.[2]

"I have always thought that physical force was useless and criminal," he said under cross-examination by Webster. "If the constitutional movement fails—of which there is no present prospect—I should have to consider whether I should not quit public life."

At the end of the long, particularly grinding day of questioning, Parnell was pressed on why he had told the House of Commons on 7 January 1881, that secret societies no longer existed in Ireland.

"I cannot say, without reading the context of my speech, what my view was in urging that argument, but it is possible that I was endeavouring to mislead the House on the occasion."

It was a staggering admission, and the attorney-general bore in on the tired witness. "Did you or did you not intend to mis-state the fact when you made that statement to the House?"

"It is very possible that I did."

"Deliberately?"

"Deliberately, quite possible."

Webster drove home Parnell's startling admission.

"Do you know if that statement did mislead the House?"

"I am afraid it did not, for they passed the Act."

"You wished to mislead the House?"

"Undoubtedly."

4 MAY 1889

Parnell moved quickly to repair the damage of the previous afternoon. Naturally, he wasn't referring to Fenians when he was asked about secret societies in Ireland. What he meant was the older-style, agrarian ribbon societies, who took their name from the green ribbons worn by members, who burned the haystacks and butchered their enemies' animals.

The attorney-general pressed him about quotes from Patrick Ford's *Irish World* newspaper, which suggested that extremists in the Clan na nGael arranged his 1880 North American tour. Parnell replied that he also had a number of press clippings about the tour, "but the mice got into my bureau and devoured many of them." From someone else, it might have been taken as a joke or sarcasm, but those who knew Parnell realised this had a bizarre ring of truth.

25 JUNE 1889

Member of Parliament Dr. Joseph Kenny apparently had no pleasant memories—or recollections of any kind—of entertaining Le Caron in Dublin, as the spy had testified. Le Caron had described riding about with Kenny and his wife in a "jaunting car," and being shown the city's lions in the zoo. Now, testifying as a witness at the inquiry, Kenny said he recalled nothing of this. "I don't believe I showed him the sights of Dublin."

Certainly, Kenny didn't recall taking a message from Kilmainham prisoner Michael J. Boyton to Le Caron, so that Le Caron could deliver it to Boyton's contacts in America.

"Is Le Caron here?" Sir Richard Webster asked.

There was a rustle of movement in the courthouse crowd as Le Caron walked from the doorway to a spot on the floor directly in front of the witness. Le Caron looked at the witness with what appeared to be condescension. The doctor studied the short, alert, rigid man, then paused and put his hands in his pockets. Finally, he replied, "I would never let a man with a face like that enter my house."

Le Caron seemed to redden, and then he returned to the doorway, out of sight.

"What's wrong with the face?" Webster asked, his voice gruffer than usual.

"It speaks for itself," Kenny replied.

"As what?"

The doctor's voice was louder now. "The face is as false as a man ever wore."

26 JUNE 1889

Sir Richard Webster pressed MP Sexton, Lord Mayor of Dublin, about a tour Sexton had made of the United States. Sexton testified that he might have met Le Caron, but he couldn't remember for sure.

"But, in one of your American speeches, did you not say that you met in Boston a Frenchman who was following in the track of liberty and working for Ireland's freedom?" Webster asked.

Sexton said the Frenchman might have been a French-Canadian. Or perhaps it was Le Caron. Whatever the case, he had no memory of any such meeting. Webster asked if Sexton might like to look at Le Caron, who was again in the courtroom. Sexton said that he had seen Le Caron's face the previous day, and that was enough.

10 JULY 1889

Michael Davitt called the inquiry's attention to a note in a London newspaper, which warned there might be a dynamite attack on the commission. Hannen dismissed this as a "silly hoax," but Davitt told the courtroom that he thought it was a ploy by Le Caron to alarm the inquiry, with the sanction of Houston.

"You have no right to say that, Mr. Davitt," Hannen chided.

Testimony continued, uninterrupted by dynamite.

17 JULY 1889

On the other side of London, in the impoverished Whitechapel district, the body of a woman named Alice McKenzie was discovered, her throat cut and her abdomen gutted. For Le Caron's friend and protector, Robert Anderson, it was just another distracting stress from the killer referred to in the press as Jack the Ripper.

25 OCTOBER 1889

When called to the witness stand, one-armed Michael Davitt said there was no proof to support Le Caron's allegations that Land League Conventions were steered by secret clusters of assassins other than Le Caron's "bundles" of documents. He noted that Le Caron's oath was that of a spy, who acknowledged in the witness box that he had lied repeatedly.

Instead of calling him Le Caron, Davitt referred to the spy by his English name of Beach. As he said the name, it was as if all eyes in the courtroom shifted to Le Caron, who sat with his bodyguards in a corner of the gallery, scowling.

Davitt dismissed the secret codes described by Le Caron as "ridiculous ciphers," but did acknowledge that he knew Le Caron. "I was a guest in Beach's house; I had a cold; he gave me some medicine; and I believe the medicine did me some good."

5 NOVEMBER 1889

Le Caron must have felt some measure of vindication when *Times* lawyer Sir Henry James rose to his defence, nine months after the spy had shocked the inquiry with his appearance on the witness stand. If more heed had been paid to him when he gave his cautions about the Pigott letters, there would have been no call for a commission of inquiry. Sir Henry commanded the attention of those in the courtroom as he gave an unapologetic, extended defence of Le Caron, which included these words:

> My lords, who is this man, on whose evidence much depends in this case, on whom I have to ask you to rely, whose word I ask you to accept? As far as I know, that man's character, apart from anything that took place in America in connection with his conduct towards the Clan na nGael, is unimpeached. . .
>
> Shortly after the [American Civil] war came to an end he learnt, by communication with a Fenian, of the intended attack upon Canada. It was a treasonable attack upon an outlying portion of the Queen's dominions, and against men who had taken no part in the misrule, if there had been misrule according to the view of any man, in Ireland. And Le Caron, who was true to his allegiance to his country, naturally communicated what he learnt. . .
>
> And for twenty years that man has held his life in his own hand. He never could have had one moment's security, one moment of certain repose. One letter miscarried, one person unfaithful to his trust in the post office, one accident any hour occurring, and that man's death in a moment was as certain as any person's death must be as the ultimate result of life. An attack has been made upon him by those who personally have appeared in this case, and I suppose that the attack must be concentrated upon this, that he took a promissory oath of secrecy. I ask, "On whose beliefs is it that that complaint is made?" Is it made on behalf of the men who were thus plotting, those assassins who had not the courage to disclose themselves and who required the secrecy only for the purpose of avoiding the punishment which they knew would follow detection, those men who, as enemies of the human race, as the lowest and most degraded beings that could exist, were plotting destruction of human life by dynamite—are these the men on whose behalf is to be made that honour has not been maintained between them and the man who was pledged to secrecy? . . .
>
> If a detective brings a criminal to justice, the community applauds him. They praise the exertions of a man who apprehends the criminal after the crime has been committed. Why, then, should the conduct of this man be condemned?... There are some observations made by my learned friend Sir Charles Russell to which I must refer. I do not suppose, however, that my learned friend meant exactly what he said. If he did, I am sure he had not the facts of the case fully in his mind. He said: "Here we have a man about whose odious profession

I will not waste breath in talking. Surely the state of society has something faulty in it when the employment of such a man as Le Caron can be defended or can be necessary. His life was a living lie. He was worming himself into the confidence of men presumably honest, however mistaken in their views, only to make money and to betray them."

My learned friend says that the state of society must be faulty that excuses the employment of such men. Well, I first ask who employed Le Caron? He has been employed since 1867. Twenty years have run since he has been engaged in this employment, during which period he has sent home statements of what he has learnt by way of warning to the representatives of the English Government. If he has been paid it has been with the acquiescence, if not by the very hands, of English statesmen. During those twenty years, Ministers of State, men of high honour, unblemished reputation, acting upon to the best of their judgment, and seeking to protect their country, were asking from him and receiving from him the results of his inquiries in America. Does my learned friend attack these men, some of whom have been his colleagues and associates in the administration of the country's affairs?

What would be said of a statesman, indeed of any human being, who, being told, "Through such a man you can obtain information as to how a contemplated raid upon Canada is to be carried out, and as to a plan for blowing up the public buildings of London, including the House of Commons itself when the representatives of the nation are actually in session"—I wonder what would be said of a statesman who should reply, "No; we will run the risk of execution of these acts, involving, as they must, a deplorable loss of life." . . .

As Le Caron's character was debated, Patrick Egan was appointed as American ambassador to Chile, replacing fellow Irish rebel William Randall Roberts, who helped lead the 1866 Fenian invasion of Canada. The posting was a high public honour for one of the architects of the Phoenix Park murders.

Ultimately, the revelations about Pigott's forgeries made it impossible for the judges to rule on the side of the Times. The newspaper was forced to pay a libel fine to Parnell of £5,000, plus the staggering added cost of more than £200,000 for the commission of inquiry (about twenty million dollars today).

Worse yet for government allies of *The Times* was the enormous outpouring of public sympathy for Parnell. Even the National Liberal Club reached out to him and gave him a lifetime membership, confident that this somehow was a great honour for an Irish nationalist.

For Henri Le Caron, the intense newspaper coverage of the inquiry meant he was suddenly catapulted from virtual anonymity into the unforgiving glare of fame. Sketches and photos of him were circulated on both sides of the Atlantic, forever limiting his hiding places. He lived under false names in a series of suburban London hotels, guarded by two police detectives, while his family hid out in Brixton. The persona of General Henri Le Caron of the Clan na nGael was forever dead. The fugitive realised that his former targets lusted to kill him as well.

CHAPTER 25

MURDER IN CHICAGO

January 1889

It strikes me that your funeral would be a very nicely attended one.

**—Dr. Patrick Henry Cronin predicts
his own death in a work of fiction**

A rumour crossed the ocean that Henri Le Caron had told British authorities that there were at least four more British spies in Irish-American ranks. When the story reached Chicago lawyer Alexander Sullivan, he was excited, sensing an opportunity. It might be bad for the Irish independence movement, but could prove useful for his own ends. He promptly accused Dr. Patrick Henry Cronin of being one of these British spies, and repeated this accusation so often and so enthusiastically that the smear took on a reality of its own.

Lost amid the verbal assault upon Cronin was the fact that it was Sullivan who had sponsored Le Caron into the Clan na nGael. The spy had pretended to support Sullivan—not Cronin—for years, including at Sullivan's secret trial for misappropriating funds. None of the Clan na nGael members knew that yet another of Sullivan's backers, the late General Francis Millen, had also been a British spy.

The constant shelling on Cronin's reputation took an ugly toll on his nerves. In January 1889, Cronin published a pamphlet entitled, *"Is It a Conspiracy?"* that featured a strange imaginary interview between himself and a reporter, in which they discussed a report that Cronin had been shot and killed. In the fictitious interview, Cronin mentioned "one William Starkey, formerly of New Haven, Conn.," as one of the conspirators in his slaying.[1]

"It strikes me that your funeral would be a very nicely attended one," the imaginary reporter commented to Cronin in the article.

"Yes, and the cause of death very extensively inquired into," Cronin replied.

Luke Dillon of Philadelphia first saw Cronin's strange pamphlet at the corner of Clark Street North and Randolph Streets in Chicago, close to the doctor's office. He showed it to his friend Henry Jordan who dismissed it with the comment, "That is one of Dr. Cronin's circulars. He's crazy. Pay no attention to him."

Shortly afterwards, Dillon and Jordan walked past the doctor.

"I am informed that you are sent here to assassinate me," said Cronin, mixing anger with paranoia. Then he exploded with a string of vile epithets that shook the battle-hardened Dillon.

"He had me all worked up," Dillon later said. "I asked several other people why he used such language toward me. They told me to pay no attention to him."

Cronin didn't let up, and also sent Dillon a nasty letter. Dillon later said, ". . . it stated that it knew what my business in Chicago was. It ordered me to leave the city at once or he would have me arrested on charges preferred by his friends here. It said he would have my pedigree traced up and that I would be fully exposed."[2]

Cronin packed a revolver now, in part because of an incident from the previous year when he was called into a room to talk with a man who claimed he needed medical treatment. The doctor quickly concluded the man was feigning illness and planning bloodshed. "My God, have you called me here to murder me?" Cronin shouted, running out of the examining room.

Cronin wasn't invited to an emergency meeting on 8 February 1889 for Camp 20 of the Clan na nGael, also known as the Columbia Literary Society. The meeting was called while Le Caron was still on the witness stand in the London commission. Not surprisingly, all the talk in Chicago Clan na nGael circles was about spies in their midst. Among those addressing the Camp 20 meeting was Detective Daniel ("Big

Dan") Coughlin, one of Sullivan's many friends in the Chicago police department. Now in his mid-thirties, Coughlin was spared a lifetime of toil in the iron mines of northern Michigan by Sullivan, who found him more agreeable employment above ground as a Chicago police officer.

Nine days after the secret meeting of Camp 20, a dark-eyed man with a long, drooping moustache, derby hat, and short-nap chinchilla coat bought $45.50 worth of furniture, including a large, cheap trunk, at a shop near Cronin's office.[3] The man called himself J.B. Simmonds and volunteered that he was setting up accommodations for his brother, who was coming from the east to have his eyes treated. The deal complete, Simmonds arranged for the furniture to be delivered to rooms 12 and 13 at 117 South Clark Street in Chicago, directly across the street from Cronin's medical office.

The next day, a man who called himself Frank Williams rented a weather-beaten, three-room, white-frame cottage at 1872 Ashland Avenue on Chicago's outskirts, for just $12 a month. The cottage backed onto open prairie and faced a cabbage patch, and it was even more lonely and isolated at night when the only light came from a kerosene street lamp, filtered through two rows of willow trees. One of the few neighbours was Patrick O'Sullivan, a former Chicago streetcar conductor, who was in his mid-thirties and ran a business that supplied blocks of ice for cooling food. Williams told the owners of the cottage, a couple named Carlson, that his invalid sister would be moving there soon to live with him. Not long after that, the furniture that J.B. Simmonds had purchased at the shop near Cronin's office was moved into the Ashland Avenue cottage.

Another secret, late-night meeting of Camp 20 was called for 22 February. It was chaired by Detective Coughlin, who announced there was "another Le Caron" in their ranks. That spy, the detective pronounced, was Dr. Patrick Henry Cronin.

Dr. Cronin was in his office a couple of weeks later when Justice John A. Mahoney introduced him to O'Sullivan, noting that the ice merchant was active in city and Democratic Party politics. O'Sullivan told Cronin that he wanted to arrange medical care for his employees. Quickly a deal was struck, with the men agreeing upon a retainer of $8 monthly, plus medical costs. Then O'Sullivan gave Cronin some business cards, and said his workers would present similar cards if they needed medical treatment. "I may be out of town and my card will be presented," O'Sullivan said.

Had Cronin thought much about it, he might have considered the arrangement to be odd. O'Sullivan's ice business was not particularly dangerous, and there were no reports of accidents there previously. Also, there were several doctors between O'Sullivan's place of business and Cronin's office, nearly an hour's carriage ride away. But even a paranoid man has to believe someone, and Cronin trusted Judge Mahoney.

On 20 April the man who identified himself as Frank Williams offered to pay another month's rent in advance for the Carlson cottage, even though his invalid sister still hadn't appeared. The Carlsons felt uneasy about the arrangement, but agreed to go along with it after the iceman, Patrick O'Sullivan, gave Williams a character reference.

In the first few days of May, Detective Coughlin was overheard bragging in a Chicago saloon that a leading Irishman would soon "bite the ground." On 4 May the detective visited the livery stable of Patrick Dinan, at 360 North Clark Street, a short walk from the East Chicago Avenue police station where Coughlin was based, and five blocks south of Cronin's office. "I want you to reserve a rig for a friend of mine who will call for it tonight," Coughlin said. "Say nothing to anyone about it. I will be responsible."

A little after 7pm, a man called for the rig, and became flustered because it was drawn by an old white horse. He didn't object to the horse's age, or the fact that its knees were knobby. However, he wasn't at all happy with its distinctive colouring, and insisted that he needed a darker animal without explaining why. He also wanted a buggy with side curtains, so that no one could see inside. The stable master said that only the white horse was available, and that there were no buggies with curtains. The man grumbled, but nonetheless accepted the rig, and drove off in the direction of the Windsor Theatre Building, where Cronin lived.

About 7.20pm, Cronin gathered with some friends in his flat, preparing to attend a meeting of directors of the Celto-American Society. His bell rang, and a rough-looking man rushed in, asking for the doctor.

"O'Sullivan is out of town. And here is his card," the man said, gasping for breath in the doctor's parlour. It was a matter of life and death as a workman's leg had been crushed. A horse and buggy waited outside, and there was no time to waste. As Cronin gathered his instruments into a satchel, his landlord looked out the window and saw a buggy hitched to a white horse. Moments later, Cronin jumped into the carriage and the driver whipped the white horse as it ran off into the night.

Later that evening, washerwoman Pauline Haertel saw a white horse and buggy arrive at the Carlsons' cottage. A tall man with a black satchel jumped out and ran into the cottage. Seconds later, she heard blows, the thud of a fall, and a cry of "Oh God!" Later she also recalled, "I heard the faraway cry of 'Jesus!'"

The washerwoman looked toward the direction of the cries and saw the silhouette of a man who looked like he was standing guard outside the cottage in the moonlight.

The white horse and buggy were returned to Dinan's stable at about 9.30pm that same night. The driver tossed the reins to the hosteller, and then rushed away. Clearly, the horse had been driven hard as its mouth was covered with lather.

When Dr. Cronin didn't rejoin his friends that evening, they feared the worst. The next morning, when he still hadn't appeared, they told police that they suspected violence from Alexander Sullivan.

Two days after Cronin's disappearance, sewer worker Martin Burke asked a local tinsmith to solder up a large box for him. Burke wouldn't say what was in the container, or where it was being shipped. When the tinsmith tried to raise the lid, Burke abruptly stopped him, and made him complete the job without ever looking inside. As he worked, the tinsmith asked Burke what he thought of the well-publicised disappearance of Dr. Cronin. Burke swore about Cronin, called him a spy, and then cryptically said he would "turn up alright."

There was no shortage of sightings of the missing doctor. One account had him in New York City, while a man named Charles T. Long, the son of a Toronto publisher, reported that he had just spoken with Cronin on Clan na nGael business in Canada. Long published what he claimed was an account of an interview with Cronin on 11 May in which Cronin allegedly described a threatening conversation with enemies of the Irish independence movement. Cronin reportedly said:

> Their next move was to introduce me to Le Caron under the name of Beach, in order that he might pump me and damage me in any way that he could. Beach was introduced to me by a reporter named Conwell, a man whom I had always considered my friend, but since the recent developments in the London Times case I know he was against me and that Le Caron was introduced to me for no good purpose. He got little out of me, however, and that means failed. I have been warned several times to get out of the country, and assured that my life was in danger.

The few people who recalled Cronin's unsettling "*Is It a Conspiracy?*" pamphlet of January 1889 might have been jarred to read Long's name. He was a former Chicago reporter, and an associate of the man Cronin described in his pamphlet as "one William Starkey, formerly of New Haven, Conn." In Cronin's work of fiction, Starkey was a conspirator in his murder.

Reports surfaced in the press that Cronin was alive and well in England, readying himself to testify for *The Times* at the Parnell Inquiry, like Le Caron. There was even a published story quoting an unidentified source who said that a coded communication had been intercepted, revealing that Cronin was in London with a stack of documents. According to this report, Cronin was eager to testify at the inquiry for a sum of $100,000.[4]

There was also a false news report from England, which allegedly quoted Le Caron himself: "Le Caron, the man who acted as a spy for the British Government on the movements of the Irish leaders in America, and who testified for *The Times* before the Parnell Commission, declares that he and Dr. Cronin were the closest friends. Le Caron believes that

Dr. Cronin has been killed, and that the friendship of the murdered man may account for his removal."[5]

Other published stories reported that the missing doctor had fled Chicago to escape prosecution after accidentally killing a woman named Alice during an illegal abortion. Another yarn suggested the bachelor doctor was involved in a bizarre and unprintable love affair. Yet another rumour was that the doctor staged a vanishing act in a childish bid to win attention. To hear these stories, one could easily conclude that Dr. Cronin was an accomplice of Le Caron, as well as a traitor, spy, one of the city's many sloppy abortionists, a sex fiend, or a pathetic attention seeker, but certainly not a murder victim.

Cronin's friend, John F. Scanlan of Chicago, wrote Devoy on 10 May about his anger and frustration with other Irish nationalists in America: "We are met on street corners by the gang with their faces wreathed in leers, not smiles, offering to bet 'he will turn up all right; he is off in a spree; it's a love affair; he was a companion of Le Caron; he's gone to England to testify against Parnell,' ad libitum, lies, lies, lies; and every morning we meet new batch of lies in the press. Of course, the gang do not speak to me or other men like me, but they are continually moulding public opinion, so that nine out of ten of the citizens seem to forget the serious side and think it a joke."[6]

Devoy himself alluded to Le Caron when he concluded that Cronin had been murdered as "the direct result of branding all critics as British spies."[7] Luke Dillon went from Philadelphia to Chicago, where he and Cronin's friends scoured woods and cemeteries, dredged the ponds of Lincoln Park and searched every house they could enter.

Back at the Ashland Avenue cottage, old Mrs. Carlson was visited by two strangers on 13 May who offered her yet another month's rent for the empty property. The rent wasn't due for a week, and Williams's invalid sister still hadn't arrived, but the men at her doorstep were eager for her to accept the money. Something obviously wasn't right, and she balked at the offer. Not long after that, the Carlsons received an odd letter from their tenants saying they were sorry, but they had painted the floor for Williams's sister.

The tenants didn't return the key to the Carlsons, who entered their cottage through a window on 20 May the date of the expiry of Williams's lease. They were horrified by what they saw: the sloppy attempt to repaint failed to cover the blood smeared over the walls and floor. A rocking chair arm was torn off, and a key, smeared with blood and paint, was found under a bureau. Throughout the cottage, there were bloody fingerprints.

Across the Atlantic, Irish Party MP Tim Healy claimed to have obtained a letter from Le Caron about Cronin's disappearance. The letter was supposedly written to a lawyer for *The Times* newspaper named Soames, and read:

> Dr. Cronin is a man shrewd, intelligent, well educated, possessing a fine tenor voice, known amongst his enemies as the "Singing Doctor," a good forcible speaker always desiring to be foremost in all-aggressive and quarrelsome to an eminent degree. He is tall, possessing a fine presence, married, and has no family.
>
> He is chronically hard up. He was sued for rent by Dr. L. Burlingham, owner of his late residence, 351 North Clark Street, Chicago, in December, 1887, the suit being settled by his brother-in-law, T.H. Conkwin [sic], who is one of the wealthy saloon-keepers of Chicago, since which date he has resided with his brother-in-law in the Windsor Block, same street.
>
> He was elected Junior Guardian of Camp 96, Chicago, in 1881, and became Senior Guardian. He is Superintendent of the Dynamite School. Being a good chemist, he made it a study and gave lectures on explosives to a class weekly. He was a delegate to the Dist., v.c. Convention in 1883, at which Sullivan and William Mackey Lomasney were elected, made a lying report to his "camp" thereon, and charges were preferred against him through Sullivan, and he being a Senior Guardian at the time, his trial-committee were all Senior Guardians, of which I was one (vide evidence).
>
> They unanimously found him guilty and expelled him from the organization.
>
> While I know that the Chicago "gang" would like to see, and are bad enough to put him out of the way, he has enough friends to post him and thwart their murderous designs.

I don't think him dead. . . His whole conduct for years past shows him to be bitterly opposed to the acts and administration of the Irish Party in power. Yes, even on both sides of the water, by Parnell and Co., endorsing and not opposing the corrupt party in America.

He is so bitter that, in my opinion, for a money consideration he would be willing to pose as a real friend of the Irish Cause by exposing the true inwardness and corruption of the administration. He is an egotist of the first water.[8]

Perhaps Le Caron wrote the letter, but it's more likely a forgery. Le Caron didn't have qualms about writing letters to the editor of *The Times*, and yet he declined to write of the doctor's disappearance to the newspaper. Certainly, it advanced nationalist interests to have Le Caron dismiss Cronin as a bitter egotist, ready to sell out the "Irish Cause."

On 22 May 1889 Chicago workmen smelled something putrid as they cleaned ditches along Evanston Avenue, near Lake Michigan at 59th Street. "I guess there's a dead dog in there," a worker said. "Let's take a look."[9]

Curled up in a catchbasin, in about four feet of water, was the nude, badly decomposed body of a man, with slash marks and bruises across the head. His knees were pressed up against his chest, as if in the fetal position, and he wore nothing but a cloth around his neck and a heart-shaped religious medal called an Agnus Dei, Latin for "Lamb of God." Apparently, whoever beat, cut, and stripped him didn't want to offend the Almighty any further by stealing his sacred medallion.

A sketch of the body soon appeared in newspapers with speculation it was the missing doctor, and the headline "THE SEWER'S TERRIBLE SECRET."[10] A crowd gathered outside the city morgue, where doctors were examining the man's "vegetable clock," or the decomposing food inside his stomach, to estimate a time of death. In many ways, this was bigger news than the city's 1886 Haymarket Square riots, when four police officers and an undetermined number of workers and anarchists were killed in a rally for an eight-hour workday. Four more anarchists were hanged the next year for their alleged roles in the rioting. The Haymarket story clearly had a higher death count, but far less mystery than the Cronin murder. Cronin's slaying remained a local whodunit, since the doctor's killer or killers had yet to be tracked down, and were presumably still living in the community. One book that was rushed to print declared that the murder "startled the civilized world," and a rival author, equally breathless, called it "a crime that shocked the civilized world."[11]

Cronin's dentist visited the morgue and said the corpse's gold fillings matched those of the missing doctor. It wasn't a great surprise when other friends of Cronin also identified him. Cronin's old ally, John Devoy, did everything but directly accuse Sullivan in a 24 May *Times of London* report: "Cronin's death is the result of a conspiracy by certain men accused of embezzling large sums from the Parnell fund collected in Chicago and elsewhere. Cronin, myself, and others know their dishonesty, and as they feared exposure they resolved to enforce silence by murder." Then Devoy hinted that other murders would likely follow, saying, "Cronin was the first victim."

For his part, Sullivan told the newspaper "that he was horror-stricken when told of the findings of Dr. Cronin's body, as he had believed all along that the missing man would turn up." "Mr. Sullivan had no theories to advance, and did not think the promised exposure of the alleged crookedness in the Irish organisation had caused the murder," the report continued. "He treated with contempt all stories of his knowing more about it than he cared to tell. He denied that he knew anything about Dr. Cronin's death or the causes leading to it, and said he would do anything and everything in his power to help to convict the guilty persons."

Another news report quoted Cronin's friends as saying that he was about to expose the theft of $200,000 from "an Irish organization." The story also suggested that Chicago police weren't really trying to find the killers. "Indeed, throughout the inquiry they [police] manifested the utmost indifference." The news agency was duped by the repeated lie that Cronin worked with Le Caron as a paid British agent, continuing, "Cronin's friends indignantly deny the charges but it is certain that Cronin was a friend of Major le Caron [sic]."

An ornate hearse carried Dr. Cronin's body to Holy Name Cathedral, amid floral tributes that included the sentiments "The Philadelphia Clan na nGael mourn their patriot brother," and the word "Martyr" spelled out in blue violets. Father Muldoon, a friend of Cronin's, told mourners they should all be prepared for death, although hopefully not in such a grotesque form: "Let us always be prepared for God to strike, for his angel is always going forth from him to touch the young and the old, the strong as well as the infirm, and to call them from this earth to the land above."[12]

On 25 May Sullivan's bitter enemy, Dr. M'Cahey of Philadelphia, telegraphed Patrick Egan, care of the *Irish World* newspaper at 17 Barclay Street, New York. He wanted to know—one way or the other—whether Le Caron had given the inquiry in London Cronin's name as that of a fellow spy. That rumour had apparently already cost one man his life, and threatened to cause more bloodshed within revolutionary ranks. "Will you either affirm or deny the truth of the rumor that Dr. Cronin's name was on the list of spies made known to Sir Charles Russell?" M'Cahey asked. "If you have not this knowledge no other man in the United States has, and I hope you will state so publicly."

The newspaper's editor sent back a sharp telegram the same day: "P.E. [Patrick Egan] has not knowledge whatever of the list referred to, and it would be an outrage to mix his name up in the matter."

A mutilated, nude body dumped in a sewer was suspicious even by Chicago standards, and finally the city's police were moved to investigate. One of the detectives assigned to the case was "Big Dan" Coughlin, the same man who chaired the emergency Camp 20 meeting of the Clan na nGael, in which he declared Dr. Cronin to be "another Le Caron." It was common knowledge that Coughlin and his partner and fellow Clan na nGael member, Michael Whelan, like many others at the East Avenue Station, owed their jobs to Cronin's enemy, Alexander Sullivan.

After the discovery of Cronin's body, Detective Coughlin was visited at the police station by Dinan, the livery man. Dinan wanted answers about the man who rented the white horse and buggy the night Cronin went missing.

"Keep quiet about it," Detective Coughlin advised. "Me and Cronin have not been good friends and if you go to talking, you may get me into trouble."

Getting Detective Coughlin into trouble didn't bother Dinan, who now spoke directly to the chief of police. Despite Coughlin's efforts to stifle the investigation, police were now getting co-operation from Clan na nGael members who didn't support Sullivan. Thomas F. O'Connor, a friend of Cronin and member of Camp 20, told police that Detective Coughlin told him he suspected Cronin had slipped off to London to follow in the footsteps of Le Caron as an informer to the British at the Parnell Inquiry. A man known as Major Sampson told police that Detective Coughlin had once approached him, saying he should waylay Cronin for money.

Meanwhile, there was no shortage of alibi witnesses for suspects. There was even a cover story for the knobby-kneed old white horse. A visitor from Hoboken, New Jersey, said he was across the street from the cottage when the rig arrived, and it was drawn by a dark speckled grey with white legs. Clearly, this could not be the same animal that was rented from Dinan's stable, the man assured police.

A troubling story drifted out of the booze and smoke of Sol Van Drag's gambling house at 363 South State Street about Frank J. Black, a.k.a. Woodruff, who moved to the city about five weeks before Cronin's murder. Black, who had served time in several penitentiaries for petty crimes, including horse theft, told fellow gambling house patrons he was paid $25 to drive a wagon with a trunk the night of the murders, and that he dumped a body into a manhole by the lakeshore.

William Niemann, a saloon keeper on North Clark Street, said that the iceman O'Sullivan, Detective Coughlin, and another man were in his establishment around 10.30pm on 4 May the night Cronin was lured from his home. They were "talking, whispering, like they had a great secret."

CHAPTER 26

"ANOTHER LE CARON"

A spy has no rights.

—Poet William Butler Yeats, 25 July 1889

Luke Dillon was considered a "hard man" in revolutionary circles. Fellow extreme nationalists respected how he fought in the cavalry as a teenager and had enough sand in his stomach to personally plant bombs at Scotland Yard and inside the British House of Commons.[1] No matter how much someone despised his methods or his politics, it was impossible to ignore the determination or sense of purpose in his voice as he testified at the coroner's inquest into the death of Dr. Philip Cronin. "His voice was full, resonant and well modulated, and he spoke fluently and yet in a measured way that indicated caution," a journalist noted. "In answer to the questions of the Coroner he said that he was a member of the Clan na nGael, but that there was nothing in the obligation which he had taken that conflicted with the laws of the United States."[2]

"He began his testimony in a low yet clear voice, but in a few minutes there were tears in his eyes," John T. McEnnis wrote. "From the moment he took the stand every person present expected that startling revelations would be made. This expectation was more than realized."

Dillon's voice was drenched in emotion as he told the inquest that Cronin and many other Irish nationalists felt that they had lost men who were sent to England on bombing missions because of Alexander

Sullivan's close association with British spy Henri Le Caron. Dillon was speaking of betrayal, not honest mistakes. Perhaps he was also thinking of how close he came to ending his life in a British cell himself, just a few years before, when he was stopped by a guard while fleeing Westminster.

Despite Cronin's frequent bouts of paranoid ranting, Dillon still respected the man and felt he was true to the independence movement.

"He [Cronin] has told me that he believed men had been betrayed through the intimacy of Alexander Sullivan with Le Caron," Dillon testified.

"Was Le Caron a member of a camp in Illinois?"

"Yes sir, in Braidwood, Illinois.

"Who is Le Caron?"

"Well," Dillon said, and a smile could now be seen under his moustache, "I wish they had tackled him instead of Dr. Cronin. I didn't know him personally."

"What position did he hold?"

"He held the position of chief officer—what would be the same as president in an ordinary society."

"Was he once considered a good member of the order?"

"Yes sir."

"Is he considered such now?"

"Not at all, certainly not."

Dillon continued in his testimony to say that he thought Cronin's death was a direct result of "the abuse heaped upon him by the friends of Alexander Sullivan. He has been denominated a spy and a traitor, perjurer, and in fact all the invectives that have been piled upon him that could have been heaped upon the head of any man by the friends of Sullivan, all because of Cronin's enmity to Sullivan."

"Why did Cronin have any enmity toward Sullivan?"

"Because he believed, as I do, that he was a professional patriot, sucking the life-blood out of the Irish organisations, and we tried to purify the organization by removing from its head such men as Alexander Sullivan."

Shortly before Cronin's murder, Dillon continued, the doctor had told him that Sullivan's goal was to head the nationalist movements in both Ireland and America. Cronin predicted that he would lose his life because of Sullivan's ambitions "for he felt that the man had no more blood than a fish and would not hesitate to take his life."

On 11 June 1889 Sullivan was among a half dozen men whose names were offered to a U.S. grand jury as suspects in the murder of Dr. Cronin. Prosecutor Joel M. Longenecker clearly adopted Dillon's theory about the murder as he told the jury that Cronin was dead because of a smear campaign falsely connecting him with the spy Le Caron:

> [Detective Dan] Coughlin went along the street saying that Cronin was a traitor and Le Caron a spy. Men would whisper, too, and state that Cronin would turn up on the other side [of the Atlantic Ocean]. In Camp 20, on the night of February 8—to show you how far back this education began—they began to educate the rank and file that Cronin was another Le Caron; they led them to believe that this patriotic Irishman who was demanding an investigation of these men—a man who stood up and demanded the rights of those Irish people belonging to the order, who demanded a prosecution, who demanded that these men be exposed who were the real traitors to the cause—was a spy; that he was a Le Caron, and was waiting to go to England to testify as did Le Caron.

It was now clear that Burke had tried unsuccessfully to decoy Cronin several times by sending him messages to call on bogus patients. Each false message had been bait to a murder trap. It was also duly noted that Burke and his co-accused, Michael ("The Fox") Cooney, both belonged to Camp No. 20 of the Clan na nGael, with Burke's number being 108 and Cooney's 109. On 21 June *The Times* reported: "Each man is described as an enthusiast on Irish matters, and as 'bitter on the British spy system.'"

Burke had fled as far as Winnipeg, Canada, before he was captured, and police there found a small flat satchel key on him. That key raised questions about his strange encounter with the tinsmith two days after the murder when he ordered a large trunk to be hermetically sealed. Had Cronin's clothes been sent to England? Did Burke's associates in England plan on finding or creating a disfigured corpse in London, and dressing him in Cronin's clothes? The discovery of an otherwise unrecognisable corpse in Cronin's clothing would support the allegation that Cronin went to England to testify before the Parnell Inquiry, and was murdered there as a spy. It would forever damn Cronin as another Le Caron.

The grand jury poured over some 150 Western Union Telegraph dispatches to Alexander Sullivan, including some written in a code that police couldn't crack. It was certainly suspicious but not, in the opinion of the grand jury, enough to compel Sullivan to stand trial for Cronin's murder. The grand jury indicted six men for the murder—Martin Burke, a.k.a. Martin Delaney/Frank Williams; John Beggs; Detective Daniel ("Big Dan") Coughlin; ice-merchant Patrick O'Sullivan; Patrick ("The Fox") Cooney; and John Kunze, a young German jewellery swindler and good friend of Coughlin's.

As the six men awaited trial, newspaper readers were told that a fear of spies was at the heart of the Cronin murder. The accusation that someone was a British spy, even if untrue, was potentially lethal. "It has been proved that many members of the Clan have little compunction about killing an enemy of Ireland, while regarding spies as the most hateful of such enemies," *The Times of London* reported on 25 June. "There is little reason to doubt the impression prevalent in Chicago that Cronin was removed because his enemies declared him to be a British spy."

The Cronin murder was a common topic for thundering from pulpits across Chicago. What had happened the night of the doctor's death wasn't just immoral. It was also un-American, as Methodist clergyman Reverend Robert M'Intyre earnestly told his flock in a discourse on the duties of foreign-born citizens: "I believe that Uncle Sam intends there shall be peace. I think I see the feathers of the American eagle ruffle; and he will clutch his talons in the spines of these political assassins!"

In an effort at public relations, Dillon, James Tierney of Brooklyn, Edward O'Meagher-Condon of York, and Mortimer L. Scanlan of Chicago circulated a statement about the Clan na nGael on 26 June headlined "Not a 'Murder Society,' But an Association of Liberty-Loving, Crime-Hating American Citizens, Determined to Bring Dr. Cronin's Brutal Murderers to the Gallows."

In early July, a convention in Chicago of junior and senior guardians of the Clan na nGael resolved that the "active" policy of dynamiting would be dropped. The association, at least for the time being, would exist solely to support Parnell's parliamentary movement in Britain.

At a mass rally in the city, Judge Richard Prendergast called out to a crowd of thousands, "Was Dr. Cronin a spy?"

"No!" they chorused.

"Was he known to be such before Le Caron testified?" the judge continued.

"No!" the crowd shouted, and a reporter noted that it felt like the entire building was shaking.

As the prisoners awaited trial, prominent Irish associations continued to pass resolutions condemning murder and secret societies, while urging the state and federal government to punish anyone connected with secret societies. The jury selection was like a massive trial in itself as a reporter wrote: "No fewer than 1115 [sic] unfortunate citizens of Cook County were exposed to the rigid scrutiny of counsel for the State and counsel for the defence."[3]

On 25 July William Butler Yeats wrote to fellow poet Katharine Tynan. The great Irish poet couldn't accept that Cronin had been murdered, or that Sullivan was the crime's author: "I have seen such a good deal of Mrs. Alexander Sullivan. She is looking much better than when I wrote last and seems to have quite recovered her spirits. . . She is not yet sure that he [Cronin] is dead at all. He seems to have been great rascall [sic]. It was really a very becoming thing to remove him—if he be dead and the man found in Chicago be not someone else. A Spy has no rights."[4]

On 24 October Prosecutor Longenecker finally began his opening remarks in the trial of the six accused men. He offered a history of the Clan na nGael, and noted the importance of what Le Caron had called "The Great Dynamite Convention" at the Palmer House in Chicago in 1881.

"They then adopted," the state's attorney said, "what is called the dynamite policy. They called it 'active work.' They adopted a policy to blow up property and individuals, and that policy was adopted immediately after they got possession of the executive board of the organisation." The new executive body also inserted a provision in the oath of the organisation which bound all members to obey the Executive Body without question. "If they directed a man to go and kill another man in England it had to be done, and they had no right to question the order."

The real object of this faction was to steal organisation funds, Longenecker continued. He accused them of pretending that great sums were being spent on "active work." Some work was done, but only enough to "lend colour to this fiction."

In effect, the prosecutor was carrying on the very work that got Cronin killed, using Cronin's own papers to give him a posthumous voice in the proceedings. Reports in the doctor's own handwriting were read into evidence, detailing how dynamiters sailed below-deck in ships in steerage class, while their leaders luxuriated in opulent hotels like the Gresham in Dublin and Hotel Brighton in Paris. Among Cronin's handwritten notes made public was this record of the questioning of a dynamite attacker from the secret United Brotherhood trial:

Q. How many operations did you perform?
A. Three. We always bade each other good-bye after each meeting, thinking it might be our last meeting on earth. I have learned that, in order to get back, the other man who went over with me had to sell his clothes to get passage-money. He came with a sprained ankle. In July or August 1885, he received seven dollars from Moroney.

The best the defence could do was offer up thin alibis. In the end, Beggs and Cooney ("The Fox") were acquitted and Detective Coughlin and the iceman O'Sullivan and Burke were found guilty of murder. When Kunze heard he was found guilty of the reduced offence of manslaughter, he cried out, "God knows I am innocent!"

The jury determined that Kunze should spend three years in prison, while Coughlin, Burke, and O'Sullivan were hit with life terms. Within a few years, Burke and O'Sullivan had died behind bars of tuberculosis.

In 1893, former detective Coughlin won a new trial on the grounds that the jurors were prejudiced by arguments about secret societies and that the prosecution had failed to show that the Clan na nGael was unlawful or that it had anything to do with the Cronin murder. His second trial heard from a new prosecution witness, Lizzie Foy of Chicago, whose husband Andrew was a Camp 20 member. She testified that Burke and Cooney often met with Coughlin at her home on Oak Street near Market Street, where a frequent topic of conversation was Cronin and his alleged treason. On the evening of the killing, she said, Cooney rapped his brickmason's chisel, saying he would remove "another Le Caron."

Despite her testimony, Coughlin was acquitted. The former Chicago police officer quietly slipped away for a time to his childhood home of Hancock, Michigan. The pull of Chicago proved too strong, however, and he moved back and opened a saloon. Soon, he was supplementing his income with jury-tampering.[5]

CHAPTER 27

MESSY DIVORCE

1889–1890

He refused to bow to "English hypocrisy," whatever the cost to his country or his cause.

—Sir Winston Churchill on Charles Stewart Parnell

The pressure wasn't letting up on Le Caron's British spymaster. On 25 July 1889 a letter arrived at Scotland Yard, which began "Dear Boss" and was signed "Jack the Ripper." The writer taunted police, and said he would soon be murdering different targets than English prostitutes. "I will give the foreigners a turn now," he wrote.[1]

British Prime Minister William Gladstone personally knew some of the strange paths men can wander when following sexual desire. Since 1840, when he was 31 years old, he was in the habit of walking the streets of London at night, approaching prostitutes and urging them to reform. Four decades later, he was still drawn to the Soho district of downtown London, within walking distance of Whitehall, for what he considered "rescue" work of prostitutes.[2] His aides worried about embarrassing public fallout should his Soho strolls—or what his private secretary, Edward Hamilton, euphemistically called his "night walks"—become widely known.

Le Caron also wondered if Gladstone's fascination with streetwalkers might have international ramifications. It was natural to also wonder if it was altruism alone that attracted the prime minister to the prostitutes. Le Caron had heard of a Russian agent named Anna Popova, who was as beautiful as she was mysterious, and who also knew of Gladstone's midnight rambling. What Le Caron didn't know was whether Popova was more sympathetic to the English or the Irish, or how she might handle this potentially explosive information to the benefit of her government.[3]

For his part, Gladstone certainly knew of Parnell's affair with Katharine O'Shea, now in its tenth year. The Irish leader had been under close watch by detectives for years, who may have even deciphered the personal code between Parnell and Katharine, which grew from geological terms, with William O'Shea as "Tailings," and others "Crude," "Gas," and "overseer."[4] They might also have noticed that when Parnell held his handkerchief in his hand in the House of Commons, it was his signal to Katharine to meet him at Charing Cross station, a few minutes' brisk walk from Whitehall. Home Secretary Harcourt had a pronounced fascination with police reports, especially when they concerned Ireland, as well as an acute taste for racy stories and gossip. It defies belief that he wasn't drawn to this file, or that he somehow managed to keep the intelligence about the relationship to himself.

Finally, on Christmas Eve 1889, a fuse was lit that threatened to explode the private world that Parnell and Katharine so cherished. Captain Willie O'Shea filed divorce papers, naming Parnell as a respondent, with a full appreciation of the havoc this would wreak for his party's leader, both politically and personally. Formal divorce proceedings meant that the private affair was now about to become public fodder. Looking back, Katharine said she and Parnell were to be punished because they had breached the unwritten social commandment that stated, "Thou shalt not be found out."[5]

For years, Willie O'Shea had reaped side benefits from the affair between his wife and Parnell. The odd arrangement had given the captain an entree with Gladstone and other high-level Liberals as he acted as a go-between for the government and the Irish Party. It had also given him leverage to pressure Parnell to back him as an Irish Party candidate for Galway city in 1886, enraging many party loyalists. In many respects, O'Shea was less an aggrieved spouse than a pimp in the matter.

What finally pushed him to make the decade-long affair public was the death of Katharine's wealthy aunt Ben. The grand old lady was in her nineties when she drew her last breath in 1889, leaving behind a carefully crafted will that left Katharine some £20,000 and not a penny for O'Shea.[6] Horrified and infuriated, O'Shea challenged the will in court, alongside Katharine's brothers and sisters. Aunt Ben might have been old and eccentric, but her will was strong, both literally and figuratively, even from the grave. O'Shea and Katharine's siblings reasoned that their leverage in court would be stronger if Katharine could be shown to be an adulteress.

On 13 November 1890 the case of O'Shea v. O'Shea and Parnell opened in Divorce Court in the same sprawling legal complex on the Strand where Le Caron had come in from the cold. True to his aloof nature, Parnell offered no defence, and O'Shea's allegations of adultery went uncontested. It was a humiliating spectacle for the intensely private Parnell as the court heard he was spotted climbing from Katharine's room on a ladder in his nightclothes. Soon afterwards, replicas of his Brighton home, complete with a tiny doll-like Parnell figure and a miniature fire escape, went on sale. Music hall comedians lapped up the affair as fodder for new acts, and cartoonists loved it as well.[7] The public heard how Parnell and Katharine privately called each other "King" and "Queen" and that she sometimes also called him "Mr. Fox." Soon, newspapers began referring to her as "Kitty," slang for a prostitute. *Vanity Fair* magazine was a little more delicate, writing of her under the headline, "O'Shea Who Must Be Obeyed." American newspapers primly observed that there was a historical context for such behaviour, as Lord Nelson and Lady Hamilton were other notable English adulterers.

Irish Party MP T.P. O'Connor noted the flood of negative publicity wasn't just a shock for Parnell, but also had enormous implications for his party and the entire independence movement, which had been basking in the afterglow of the Special Commission of Inquiry. As O'Connor wrote, "It was a staggering thunderbolt and from a sky of blazing sunshine."[8]

Katharine urged Parnell to go to the London courts and fight the action, but instead he stayed in Brighton, reasoning, "What's the use? We want the divorce." Other times, he would walk with her to the ocean and stare out upon it, saying, "Isn't this glorious, my Queenie? Isn't it alive?"[9]

Former defenders of Parnell now stampeded to distance themselves from him. People who could condone terrorism with a wink could not abide the thought of love, however devoted, outside of marriage. English Protestants in London and Irish Catholics in Dublin professed to be equally shocked by the union of the Irish Catholic leader and the already-married Protestant Englishwoman. Candidates who were backed by Parnell found themselves out of office. True to form, Parnell ignored his advisers, refusing to resign from politics or to leave Katharine's side. Sir Winston Churchill later wrote that "His friend and admirer Cecil Rhodes telegraphed, 'Resign-marry-return.' It was wise advice. But Parnell was not to be moved; the passion which had burned for so long beneath his cold exterior burst into flame. His pride revolted. He refused to bow to 'English hypocrisy,' whatever the cost to his country or his cause."[10]

John Devoy wrote from America to James J. O'Kelly, MP for the Irish Party, urging him to hang tough behind Parnell: "If Parnell yields to English clamour will destroy American movement. No other man or men can keep it together."[11]

In the end, Parnell and Katharine lost custody of their six and seven-year-old children to Willie O'Shea as the divorce courts were in the practice of giving custody rights to the partner who was considered the "injured party." Parnell and Katharine's relationship proved unbreakable. They continued to take their long walks by the sea at Brighton, where he found peace amid the pounding waves. "The storms and thunderings will never hurt us now, Queenie, my wife," he told her, "for there is nothing in this wide world that can be greater than our love; there is nothing in all the world but you and I."[12]

On 25 June 1890 Parnell married Katharine near Brighton in Steyning, West Sussex, in a civil service in the registry office after local clergymen refused to conduct the ceremony. There was a thunderstorm that day and no wedding cake as Parnell's many phobias included one about rich pastry. The scandal of his loving relationship with Katharine, public for less than a year, had done immeasurably more damage to him than dozens of dynamite attacks inside England and a quarter-century of Le Caron's spying. [13]

CHAPTER 28

AFTERMATH

1889–1894
11 Tregunter Road, South Kensington, London

> I have done what I thought right to do and I will bear the consequences.
> —**Henri Le Caron**

Every breath that Henri Le Caron drew after he walked away from the Special Commission was an insult to Clan na nGael members and extreme Irish nationalists around the world. He was alternately credited with, and damned for, putting some twenty Irishmen into prison, and throwing the American wing of the movement into chaos. He left the Royal Courts of Justice on the Strand flanked by guards and exposed as a spy, knowing full well that he was under a death sentence with no hope of pardon.

Luke Dillon knew that killing Le Caron would be a quick and efficient way to exact some measure of revenge, and send a message to others who might be considering following Le Caron's lead. Le Caron likely didn't know the specifics of how Dillon and a party of his trusted companions were trying to track him down, but he did know his life was in danger. Dillon's men met in Berne, Switzerland, away from the eyes of British agents who watched vessels at English and Irish ports. Dillon then travelled to Paris, but Le Caron's trail was cold, and the would-be assassin was ordered home to Philadelphia. There would be fresher trails, and better chances to kill.

Given the task of guarding Le Caron from such threats was Detective-Inspector John Sweeney of Scotland Yard. Le Caron assumed the name of Dr. Howard and Sweeney became Dr. Simpson as they checked into a succession of hotels and a villa near Crystal Palace on the outskirts of London. Sweeney later noted that he was struck by Le Caron's "ferret eyes," what he considered Le Caron's "distinct lack of education," and his continual unease that Clan na nGael agents would "put his lights out." Sweeney also noted that his charge had an exceptionally powerful memory, and much pride over what he felt he had done for the governments of England and Canada. Le Caron spent some fleeting time with his family, but commonplace activities like a relaxed and unguarded family picnic were now out of the question. "Of course, we went about a little; on these journeys he was certainly a good deal frightened," Sweeney later recalled. "Especially at railway stations he would go peering anxiously about, fearing that anyone he saw might be his enemy. If by chance he saw the same man twice in one day he would insist that this stranger must be following him. For a man whose education was so limited, his conversational powers were great. He was one of the most inveterate smokers that ever cut off the end of a cigar, seeming never to leave off except at meal times. He had a very agreeable family; one of his daughters distinguished herself by winning a prize at a beauty show."[1]

Perhaps his enemies couldn't find Nannie and the children. More likely, they weren't so ruthless that they would kill Le Caron's family to punish him. Le Caron was a different case. His murder was a requirement for face-saving. While Le Caron was afraid for his life, he did not want to give his would-be assassins the satisfaction of knowing this. He surfaced in February 1889 to give an interview with the *New York Herald*. In it, Le Caron said that Parnell lost much of his revolutionary fervour after his brief imprisonment in Kilmainham Gaol in 1881:

> *I will tell you briefly what I think of Mr. Parnell. There can be no question that up to the time of his imprisonment in 1881 he was exceedingly revolutionary in his ideas, believing in the most extreme measures against the English Government, but iron bars had a singularly happy effect in moderating his views. Since that time I do not believe that he has deliberately encouraged any of the outrages which have been committed by his followers, and in the case*

of the Phoenix Park murders I do believe that this dreadful crime might have been averted had Mr. Parnell shown proper vigilance and discretion.

I do not believe him to have been aware of the intention to commit this crime, much less to have encouraged it, but I have positive and unquestionable means of knowing that his most intimate advisors were both cognizant of and parties to those murders.[2]

In that interview, Le Caron spoke proudly of his past and nervously of his future:

You ask me how I feel about the moral aspect of my case. I say without hesitation that I feel I have done my duty as a man who loves his country and sees it threatened by a deadly and unscrupulous foe. I did what I could to save it. I consider myself a military spy, and my conduct justifiable under the same ethical considerations which justify all military spies. As to danger in the future, I am prepared for anything that may happen. I have done what I thought right to do and I will bear the consequences.

Where I shall go and what measures I shall take to protect myself against assassins is a subject on which I have the best reason in the world for keeping silent. It is needless, for me to say that I shall not settle in Chicago, nor shall I make a visit to Ireland.

Le Caron was thinking a lot about his mortality now. He was also worrying about his finances and the financial future of his family when, on 24 March 1891, he filed a codicil to his will. His bodyguard, Sweeney, who listed his address as 53 Yeldham Road, Hammersmith, and George Newman, a merchant at 121 Newgate Street, London, were the official witnesses as he revoked leaving £20 each to his surviving siblings.[3] Money had obviously become tight for him. Nannie, whom he referred to in the document as "my dear wife," would now be the sole beneficiary if she outlived him. She was the one who ran almost all of the risks with him during decades of deception. She had been brave, strong, clever, and understanding, and he didn't want her to be neglected.

Le Caron generally didn't like talking about the extent of his "black ops," or black operations, for the British government. When he did talk, he maintained he was proud of his efforts. He stressed that he was never an agent provocateur, or motivated by greed. "I allied myself with

Fenianism in order to defeat it," he stated. ". . . True, I had to take many oaths. But what of that? By the taking of them I have saved many lives."[4] Anyone seeking to judge him, he said, should judge him by his inner life and not his "outward show."

He remained contemptuous of his former Clan na nGael associates, as if taunting them to try to exact revenge. He was also fiercely loyal to Robert Anderson, commenting on him only in glowing terms: "To him, and to him alone, was I known as a Secret Service agent during the whole of the twenty-one years of which I speak. Therein lay the secret of my safety." Anderson's son, Arthur Ponsonby Moore-Anderson, noted that the respect was mutual, and wrote that his father had the highest regard for Le Caron and his "sterling integrity." "He was one of the most truthfully accurate men I have known," the spymaster had commented in one of his many publications. ". . . Though he deserves well of his country he will never get a statue. But if he is to be pilloried I will take my place by his side."[5]

Le Caron wasn't so complimentary when writing about what he considered the British government's "miserable pittance doled out for the purpose of fighting such an enemy as the Clan na nGael," which he considered "perfectly ludicruous." Clearly, he was smarting from a lack of funds now as he noted that Dr. Thomas Gallagher had £1,400 on him when arrested in 1883, while Joseph Melville (a.k.a. Moroney) arrived from New York in 1887 to help with the Jubilee explosion plot while carrying £1,200. Was Le Caron playing an inside joke for Anderson, and pretending he never learned that Millen was a fellow spy, when he wrote, "It is the Millens and the Moroneys of the conspiracy who should be in government pay—and they have no mean price. . . Imagine offering these men a retainer of £20 per month. . . The idea is ridiculous."[6]

The former agent noted that there were some thirty men given the task of circumventing political crime in London, compared to the thousands in the Irish revolutionary movement. "All praise and honour to them for the work they have done. . . But these policemen have succeeded more by chance than anything else."[7]

Hopefully, Le Caron had grown as a person since 1868 when he had spewed his racist comment to Anderson, saying he hated associating with

Irish who were "a pack of low dirty foul mouthed beings—worse than niggers." However, no record can be found in which Le Caron described his command of an African-American unit in the Civil War. For a man who wasn't shy to brag, it's easy to conclude from the omission that he was embarrassed by the association.

He did comment, in rather patronising terms, about the Irish. After the commission made him a public figure, Le Caron maintained that he truly cared for the Irish people, even though he attacked leaders espousing Irish nationalism: "For these poor weak people, animated by the purest, if the most mistaken of patriotic motives, who give their little all in the hope and trust that the day will come in their lives when Ireland will be a land flowing with milk and honey, I have the deepest and most sincere sympathy... But for the blatant loud-voiced agitator, always bellowing forth his patriotic principles, while secretly filling his pockets with the bribe or the consequences of his theft, there can be no other feeling but that of undisguised loathing."[8]

Le Caron also apparently didn't reflect in his post-commission life about how love, not spying, spelled the demise of his nemesis, Charles Stewart Parnell. In the wake of the O'Shea divorce, Parnell sank fast and deep into a quagmire of false and deadly accusations, including one that he embezzled money from the Land League to finance his life with Katharine. It was perhaps expected that he would be shunned by Gladstone's Liberals, but support also bled from his Irish Party. Parnell pleaded with them to hang tough and continue to support him as their leader. At one particularly emotional meeting, he asked, "Who's the master of the party?" Sharp-tongued Irish MP Tim Healy fired back, "Who's the mistress of the party?"[9] Soon afterwards, Parnell's Irish Party abandoned him as well.

There were more shadows than usual under Parnell's dark eyes as he spoke in the rain in the fall of 1891 in Creggs, County Roscommon, and his eyes seemed even deeper-set than before. But their fire still burned with a fury as he exhorted his party members to hang tough and remain focused on their true enemy, the British government. "I would rather die than give in now—give in to the howling of the English mob," he wrote Katharine. "But if you say it I will do it, and you will never hear of it again from me, my love, my own wife."[10]

Katharine didn't push him to quit when he returned home to rest at their home facing the sea at 10 Walsingham Terrace in the Brighton district of Hove. She heard him mutter something about the Conservative Party as his eyelids finally closed. "Late in the evening he suddenly opened his eyes and said, 'Kiss me, sweet Wifie, and I will try to sleep a little,'" she recalled. "I lay down by his side, and kissed the burning lips he pressed to mine for the last time. The fire of them, fierce beyond any I had ever felt, even in his most loving moods, startled me, and as I slipped my hand from under his head he gave a little sigh and became unconscious. The doctor came at once, but no remedies prevailed against this sudden failure of the hearts action, and my husband died without regaining consciousness, before his last kiss was cold on my lips."[11]

The cause of Parnell's death on 6 October 1891, was given as exhaustion. He was just 45-years-old. In his essay, "*The Shade of Parnell*," James Joyce wrote of the irony of Parnell's final years: "In his final desperate appeal to his countrymen, he begged them not to throw him as a sop to the English wolves howling around them. It redounds to their honour that they did not fail this appeal. They did not throw him to the English wolves; they tore him to pieces themselves."[12]

Spurned as he lay dying, Parnell was deified in death. Some one hundred and fifty thousand people attended his funeral in Dublin, with radical Fenians leading the procession to Glasnevin cemetery, where the bodies of Irish patriots like Daniel O'Connell already lay. Parnell's sister Fannie objected to his burial in such hallowed ground and didn't attend the funeral, never forgiving him for his rapprochement with Gladstone in the early 1880s. After the burial, Parnell's mother slipped deep into confusion, alternately believing her son was either still alive or the victim of an assassination plot by English agents. In the years that followed, many supporters of the Irish cause considered Parnell's death to be far more than a personal tragedy, but rather one that set back Irish nationalism for a couple of generations.

For her part, Katharine didn't attend the very public funeral, choosing instead to stay home by the English seashore, where she and

Parnell had walked together on so many rough days. She never once set foot in the country that so consumed her husband. However, before she released his body for its burial in Ireland, she placed upon his breast a rose, a reminder of the flower they had exchanged, the first time their eyes met.[13]

Katharine never remarried, and slipped into near poverty, embezzled of her sizable inheritance by her solicitor. In her final years before her death in Littlehampton on 5 February 1921, she found some measure of comfort in recalling how Parnell often said he gave his life to Ireland, but reserved his love for her. It also lifted her spirits to think of how, on the day Parnell died, a new planet was discovered.[14]

O'Donovan Rossa, the wildest of the Fenians, somehow survived into his eighties, and gave an interview to the *New York Telegram* at his Staten Island home in 1911, four years before his death. His wife greeted the reporter, saying Rossa was feeling out of sorts: "It's a cloudy day, you see. He likes to gaze out of his window at the Statue of Liberty and the sky has been overcast all day. I think the sunshine cheers everyone up, don't you?" Talk of England and Ireland drew Rossa out of his funk and his bed, and into a lively rant. "Before I was even able to read a book I heard stories of Irish women being ripped open with English bayonets, and of Irish infants being taken on the points of English bayonets and then dashed against the walls. I've heard fathers and mothers and neighbours rejoice whenever they heard of a landlord shooting in any part of the country." He continued that he was sure the English understood violence more than debate, making them sound oddly like himself. "It's not blarney and soft soap that appeals to England. It's dynamite, cold steel and flames that talk a language they understand. They used black powder in Kaffirland and Zululand to bring the natives to their knees—not alone to their knees, but to their graves." The old man was in full rhetorical flight now, as lively as the day he threw his latrine bucket into his English jailor's face decades ago. "They talked to the Boers with lyddite and melnite shells," he continued. "The Irish must fight them with their own weapons."[15]

Alexander Sullivan, always resilient, remained a backroom force in Chicago politics, running what amounted to a labour exchange for Irish-Americans throughout the 1890s. His profile had dropped, however, after the frequent mention of his name in the trials of Dr. Cronin's killers. He became even more of a public liability on 22 December 1901, when he was convicted of helping a jury briber to jump bail. For this, he was fined $2,000. Two years later, he won a new trial and the case against him was tossed out of court on a technicality. He remained with his wife Margaret until her death in 1903, and lived another decade alone.

Le Caron had quietly reunited with Nannie and their daughter May after the inquiry. He continued to be compensated financially, and Anderson's records show that he received £600 from Secret Service funds on 16 August 1892, and a further £400 on 22 August.[16] Anderson's son, Arthur Ponsonby Moore-Anderson, wrote that Le Caron spent much time now in the Hyde Park area of London, close to Buckingham Palace:

> *I remember more than once, when walking there with my father, his saying that he had to go and see a sick friend, never giving the slightest hint of his identity even to us. . . Afterwards he [Robert Anderson] wrote: 'With all his cynicism and coldness of manner he [Le Caron] was a remarkably attractive man. . . At first we used to talk over his adventures, but later on we often spoke on subjects of which I will make no mention here.[17]*

Those subjects, which Anderson would never publicly discuss, were of a religious nature. Le Caron's health was failing now, no doubt sapped by his constant fear of assassins as his relationship with Anderson shifted from that of spy and spymaster to something like that of parishioner and priest. Moore-Anderson was struck by the profoundly religious tone of this undated letter from Le Caron to Anderson:

> *I fully appreciate and will always endeavour to keep in my mind the pith, the main principle of what you have impressed upon me in reference to God's goodness and my duty to Him; and if I live to get well again my earnest desire*

is that I may ever keep uppermost in my mind what I owe to Him and what He is willing to do for me.

Believe me to be,

Yours sincerely,
H. LE CARON[18]

On 14 September 1891 Le Caron reflected again on life's great questions as he wrote Anderson from 44 Castletown Road, West Kensington, London:

My Dear Sir

If I have been neglectful in not writing you before I have not been unmindful of you and your kindness to me. I have before me your favor of April 8th last and I want to say that I have not forgotten your kind visits to me and the counsel you gave me upon religious duties. I try to be thankful to the ruler of all things for his goodness in sparing me to write this letter to you, and try to be ever mindful of the many mercies shown to me.

For the first time in my life in my feeble way I try to thank God with all earnestness and sincerity for all the blessings and mercy shown to me, and so long as I live I hope to never forget that I am in his hands, and that it is in his hands to save and bless me.

I am thankful to say that my health has much improved. I am not well and I have periodical attacks of pain which prevent me from growing strong, yet upon the whole I ought to be content.

Now I want to ask you for a little advice. Mr. Johnston ever kind and thoughtful sent for me that Tuesday in part for the purpose of again inviting me to take a trip upon one of his Steamers. The trip he suggests would occupy about two months and cover Mediterranean ports Constantinople and take me from London during winter cost me nothing and I am advised be likely to do me good.

If you know any reason why it would be unadvisable to accept his offer would you kindly advise me.

Another thing, any relations with the Times are exactly as when I saw you last. The lease of the house I occupy expires Oct. 4th. Had I better continue as now in furnished house or try to move. . . my family in permanent home?

You perhaps will remember the advice you gave me to save money in case of emergency. When taken ill I had over 200 pounds in bank, and what I would

have done this year without that "nest egg" to draw upon I do not know. The
advice was excellent.

Mr. Johnnston MP has espressed a desire to assist me in any way and to
secure the cooperation of ther MPs if needed. I mention this in case you might
know of any way in which he might be of service.

The continual newspaper notices which I get cannot be prevented. Wherever
I go I find it difficult in fact almost useless to try and hide myself and escape
recognition. In this section I am generally known and. . . nothing unpleasant
has even occurred but to the contrary much that has been pleasant.

Mr. Houston I am confident has had nothing to do with publishing
anything about me. If able I hope to run down to Liverpool next week to meet
my eldest Daughter who visits us from the United States. Many and varied are
the communications I continue to receive from Mr. Soames the latest has been
arranging for response of and dispatches to paper of Chicago convention Oct.
1st and 2nd.

I hope that you are quite well and with an apology for troubling you.
I am faithfully
H. Le Caron[19]

By 18 November 1893 Le Caron was settled into a new home with
Nannie and May on a posh row of tan-coloured stuccoed townhomes
on Tregunter Road, near the Boltons in South Kensington, London,
and walking distance of Anderson's Notting Hill Gate home.[20] It was
a charming, well-to-do, tree-lined neighbourhood, where Victorian
children's author Beatrix Potter was born and drew inspiration for her
gentle stories like *The Tale of Peter Rabbit*. The move to the leafy, restful
section of London brought the ailing former spy close to the Royal
Hospital, which had been designed two centuries earlier by Christopher
Wren for Charles II to provide comfort for veterans of Britain's many
wars. Le Caron wrote Anderson that day, referring to his family doctor,
S.F. Harvey, and signing the letter with one of his earliest code names:

My best Friend
I write a line to say that I am still as when you last saw me, no better no
worse. I still hope and Doctor Harvey must think I will recover for the good
fellow has just got for me a splendid furlined overcoat which he says I shall
want this winter.

> *I am ever mindful of the goodness of God in that I am alive at all. My only*
> *trust now is in him, that he will look with favor upon me, and care for me, a*
> *humble sinner.*
>
> *hope you are well*
> *Yours gratefully*
> *J.R. Howard*[21]

Money, or the lack of it, was the theme for Le Caron's 6 February 1894 letter to Anderson, also under the name J.R. Howard. He asked for a loan of £20, writing, "I need this money at once, hence my request. . . I am progressing slowly and shall be very pleased to see you, if you have an opportunity. . . I detest begging but necessity knows no law."[22]

Le Caron's 16-year-old daughter, May, was with him in their home on Tregunter Road on 1 April 1894, when he was confined to his bed. His health didn't prove as strong as his optimism. That day, the man who had escaped countless potential disasters drew his last breath in the privacy of his own home. He was fifty-two years old, and his death certificate, registered the next day, said he had suffered from "Typhlitis, (recurrent) 3 years Exhaustion." His occupation was given as "Major in Army (United States) MD." and he was identified by his nomme de guerre, Henri Le Caron.[23] "His end was probably hastened by his anxieties," speculated his bodyguard, Detective-Inspector Sweeney.

Le Caron's bank accounts and stocks were worth a little more than £523, which was not a small sum, but certainly no fortune.[24] It was nowhere near what he had been seeking for his commission testimony from *The Times*, which ran a lengthy obituary:

> *It is with much regret that we record the premature death of the remarkable*
> *man whose evidence before the Special Commission concerning the work of the*
> *Irish-American conspiracy against Great Britain was one of the most dramatic*
> *episodes of that inquiry. Major Henri Le Caron—to speak of him by the name*
> *by which all the world knew him—passed away in London yesterday shortly*
> *before noon. For some time he had been suffering from a most painful malady*
> *which placed his recovery beyond hope, and at the end death came as a happy*
> *release from pain borne with the fortitude and iron resolution characteristic of*
> *his whole career. . .*

. . . Had he nodded for a moment, had a single letter miscarried, had a post-office official betrayed him, he would have perished inevitably. This deadly peril, nevertheless, he faced, and faced successfully for a quarter of a century. There is something almost superhuman in this spectacle of a man who could devote his life to so terrible a duty, keeping his secret locked up from all companions except his devoted wife.

The *St. James Gazette* was also quick and fulsome in its praises, noting on 2 April that:

To-day is recorded the death of a brave, able and resolute man, who had done much good to the service of his country. We mean Thomas Beach, otherwise Henri le Caron [sic], the Spy. The term is sometimes one of reproach; in a case like this it ought to be one of the highest praise. If you honour a soldier for risking his life in the excitement of the battlefield, what are you to say of the cool daring of the man who for five-and-twenty years slept and waked, so to speak, with a rope around his neck and a knife at his breast?

Ironically, news of his death infuriated his enemies in the Irish underground. They noted the supposed date of his death and fumed that the death announcement was an April Fool's prank played against them by the British government. Writers at the pro-Clan na nGael journal, the *Chicago Sunday Times*, clearly had trouble believing that nature somehow got to Le Caron before Irish assassins, running a story on 8 April 1894, headlined "IS LE CARON DEAD/? RUMORS IN LONDON THAT HE HAS GONE TO ONE OF THE COLONIES/ It is alleged the Spy Left England to Avoid a Fenian Conspiracy to Kill Him—His Supposed Body Buried at Norwood." The writer for the Irish nationalist newspaper simply couldn't accept that Le Caron wasn't hiding somewhere, cowering as he thought of Clan na nGael assassination teams:

It is added that this disappearance of the British spy is due to the fact that the detectives who have been guarding Le Caron ever since he was brought so strongly into public notice discovered some time ago that a Fenian plot, having its ramifications in New York and other American cities, existed of killing him. When informed of the danger to which he had been exposed, Le Caron is said to have petitioned the British government to enable him to leave England for some distant portion of the Queen's Dominions where he would be safer from the vengeance of the Fenians. Prominent Irishmen who were questioned upon the subject of Major Le Caron's alleged disappearance said that they would not be astonished if the report circulated by the Admiralty and Horse Guards Gazette was true, but they claim to know absolutely nothing about the alleged Fenian conspiracy to kill him. A body said to be that of Maj. Le Caron was buried today in Norwood cemetery. The registrar of deaths ridicules the idea that Le Caron was not dead and that he is on his way to some distant colony. . .

Instead of convincing the Irishmen of advanced opinions that Le Caron had gone to his long home it has confirmed them in the opinion that the death and burial of Le Caron is a British government "fake" designed to divert attention from him while spiriting him off to some other country, or again starting him in a second career of duplicity either in America or Ireland, where he is almost completely unknown. A number of Irish nationalists interviewed today were unanimous in their opinion that Le Caron is still on earth.

The sympathetic hometown Essex Review enjoyed the fury of "Irishmen of advanced opinions," while lauding Le Caron as "the distinguished spy." The newspaper from his boyhood hometown continued that he had an "extraordinary and unique career," and that he was paid more by his enemies than by the British government. He was treated as a war hero of sorts in the review's funeral coverage:

The remains of Major le Caron [sic], whose death we announced last week, together with a summary of his remarkable career, took place on April 7, at Norwood Cemetery. The weather was beautifully fine, but, as the funeral had apparently been kept secret, very few outside members of the public were present. The cortege left the late residence of the deceased at Tregunter Street [sic], Kensington, at half-past twelve, and arrived at the cemetery at two o'clock. The service was held at the chapel in the cemetery, and was conducted by the Rev. St. Maur Willoghby. Among those present were the widow of the deceased, the two sons and daughter, deceased's mother, brother, and aunt and uncle, Mr. Heinemann [the publisher of Major Le Caron's book] Dr. Harvey, who attended the deceased during his illness, and Mr. Soames and Mr. Houston, who acted for the Times during the Commission. There were many beautiful wreaths. One was sent by the Times, and another "From his old friend." This latter came from Paris, but no name was attached. A pretty cross bore the pathetic inscription, 'To our Darling Father.' The body was placed in a leaden coffin, which was enclosed in an oak case, the plate bearing the inscription, Henri Le Caron, died April 1, 1894. Aged 51.

On 11 April 1894 W.M. Heinemann, who had published Le Caron's memoirs two years earlier, wrote to another of his authors, James Abbott McNeill Whistler. Whistler had written *The Gentle Art of Making Enemies*, but was best known for his painting "Arrangement in Grey and Black," popularly referred to as "Whistler's Mother." Heinemann wrote that many people still believed that Le Caron hadn't really died: "As for poor Le Caron, we buried him on Saturday, and now the papers declare that he is not dead at all, but that we are keeping him somewhere locked up—in a box, I suppose."[25]

Frank M. Crawford, Le Caron's old friend from the Anderson Cavalry in the American Civil War, also had trouble accepting the fact that Le Caron was actually dead, and not simply crafting another deception. More than a decade after Le Caron's death, Crawford wrote:

> *I do not know what became of him. They tell me that he is dead, but he fooled me so well before that I'll try not to be surprised if he walks in to see me some day. I do not care to glorify the actions of anyone who seeks friends that he may do them an injury, but there was something in the personality of the man I could not help liking. Had the ability which he showed in his chosen profession been used in some other sphere of life, he would have achieved great success, financially and socially.*[26]

After reading reports of Le Caron's death, John Devoy commented with a potent mixture of contempt and respect for the man whom he had never really liked or trusted: "[W]ith twenty millions of a race that hates informers as does no other in the world supposed to be thirsting for his blood not a hostile hand is raised against him, and he dies peacefully in his bed... the champion spy of the century... That Le Caron fooled me, as he fooled others, goes without saying, but I admit the fact."[27]

Devoy acknowledged that Le Caron's death was one final victory for the superspy. It was a grudging compliment, but often those are the most sincere. Henri Le Caron would have been pleased.

CHAPTER 1: INFORMANT B

1. Henri Le Caron's birthname was incorrectly given as Thomas Willis Beach in *The Times* coverage of his testimony at the Special Commission. However, he was listed as Thomas Beach on his birth certificate, which was reproduced in A.J. Coxhead, "The Colchester Choirboy Who Turned Spy." He was also listed as Thomas Beach and Thomas Willis Beach in Wilson, *The History of the Times*, vol. III, and T.B. Beach in the index to *The Times* Special Commission report, vol. IV, which is known as *Special Commission Act, 1888: Report of the Proceedings Before the Commissioners Appointed by the Act*, reprinted from *The Times, The Times*, Four vols. (London, 1890). He was called Thomas Miller Beach in John MacDonald, *Diary of the Parnell Commission*. The 1861 census lists Le Caron's father, John Joseph Billis Beach, as born about 1816 in Southwark, London, England, and employing two men and two apprentices, all coopers, while Le Caron's mother, Maria Beach (née Passmore), was born around 1820 in Truro, Castleshire Cornwall, England.

As an interesting aside, Andrew Parnaby and Gregory S. Kealey's "The Origins of Political Policing in Canada: Class, Law, and the Burden of Empire" suggests that Le Caron's name may have influenced David Cornwell in choosing his *nomme de plume*: John Le Carré. However, a spokesperson for the official John Le Carré website says there is "no truth whatever" in this. The spokesperson could not clear up the mystery of the name, saying she does not know how the Le Carré *nomme de plume* was chosen.

2. My description of Le Caron draws heavily from page 47 of the collection of his correspondence, entitled *Devoy's Post Bag: 1871–1928* by William O'Brien and Desmond Ryan. On page 48, there's this quote from Le Caron's 10 February 1889 interview with the *New York Herald*: ". . . the interviewer notes that Le Caron both in tone and gesture is more like a shrewd far-seeing Yankee than an Englishman: 'There is nothing stolid about Major Le Caron, nor is he constructed on a roast beef plan . . . his memory is marvelous, neither dates, names nor details escaping, and beginning with a youthful escapade, when he robbed his sister's missionary box of pennies and fled to France, he deliberately traced his life up to the present. . . He boasts of having accepted pay from both the English Government and Irish societies at the same time.'" It's also notable that Le Caron repudiated this interview in a page 6 article in *The Times* of 18 February 1889.

I also benefited from MacDonald, *The Daily News Diary of the Parnell Commission*, which notes on page 2: "Major Le Caron is short and slightest in build; erect like a soldier—and imperturbably cool; he has a lofty forehead, and smallest, alert eyes, which look straight. The major's is one of the boniest faces in or out of the New World, like a death's head with a tight skin of yellow parchment. With his arms foldest *[sic]* across his chest—like another short man, the great Napoleon—he raps out his answers, short, sharp. 'Yes, yes,' he says, snappishly, sometimes pronouncing it 'yus.'"

3. I visited Colchester in June 2006 as part of my research.

4. The fact that he was the oldest son is from the *Essex Review*, Vol. 3 (1894), page 162.

5. Ibid.

6. Henri Le Caron's own book, *Twenty-five Years in the Secret Service: The Recollections of a Spy*, helped greatly with his childhood. The comment about "foolish boys" drawn to London is from page 2.

7. Le Caron's autobiography was also the source of the description of his meeting with President Johnson and his childhood. This begins on page 2.

J.A. Cole's *Prince of Spies: Henri Le Caron* was also useful. William D'Arcy's *The Fenian Movement in the United States: 1858–1886* was also a valuable reference. These two books provided valuable starting points for research throughout this story.

8. D'Arcy, *The Fenian Movement*; *The Essex Review*.

9. Alistair Horne, *Seven Ages of Paris: Portrait of a City*, page 262.

10. Ibid, page 277.

11. Le Caron, *Twenty-five Years in the Secret Service*, page 8. I also visited Paris as a cheerful part of my research, and visited the neighbourhood of the British Embassy and the site of the old St. Michael's Church on the Rue d'Aguesseau. In the 1960s, the church would gain much unwanted attention when Anthony Blount, one of the notorious "Cambridge Four" Russian gay spy ring, was revealed to be the son of its pastor, the Reverend Stanley Blount. The Faubourg St. Honoré district where Anthony Blount lived is now known for such haute couture boutiques as Gucci, Hermés, and Versace.

CHAPTER 2: WAR FEVER

1. Charles Dickens's description of Five Points in New York appears on pages 86 and 87 of *American Notes for General Circulation.*

2. Jeff Keshen, "Cloak and Dagger: Canada West's Secret Police, 1864–1867," page 373. He also notes that people with Irish blood made up about 5% of the American population.

3. Richard Hil and Gordon Tait, eds. *Hard Lessons*, pp. 17–18.

4. There were numerous sources on the Civil War and the Irish Brigades, notably Craig A. Warren, "Oh, God, What a Pity!?"

5. Le Caron, *Twenty-five Years in the Secret Service*, page 23.

6. The mutiny is extremely well covered in www.swcivilwar.com/15MutinyStan tonQueriesMitchell.html

7. Ibid.

8. Ibid.

9. Le Caron's Civil War record draws from several sources. There's Samuel P. Bates' *The History of the Pennsylvania Volunteers, 1861–65, Vol. 4.*

I benefited from the *History of the Fifteenth Pennsylvania Volunteer Cavalry, Which Was Recruited as the Anderson Cavalry in the Rebellion of 1861–1865*, edited by Charles H. Kirk, First Lieutenant Company E., assisted by The Historical Committee of the Society of the Fifteenth Cavalry. Philadelphia: 1906. I particularly enjoyed a sketch on pp. 328–330 in Frank M. Crawford, "Henri Le Caron? One of Our Characters."

10. Le Caron, *Twenty-five Years in the Secret Service*, page 23.

11. Crawford, "Henri Le Caron."

12. Bates, *The History of the Pennsylvania Volunteers.*

13. Le Caron, *Twenty-five Years in the Secret Service*, pp. 18–19.

14. Crawford, "Henri Le Caron?" Ambrose Bierce's wonderfully haunting Civil War stories can be found in *The Complete Short Stories of Ambrose Bierce.*

CHAPTER 3: A SPY IS BORN

1. Library and Archives Canada website, www.collectionscanada.ca/primeministers/h4-3031-e.html

2. Patricia Phenix, *Private Demons: The Tragic Personal Life of John A. Macdonald.* This book does an excellent job of detailing Macdonald's sad private life, and how he battled his own demons. The mention of enjoyment of the London theatre is on page 262.

3. Ibid.

4. Cheryl MacDonald, "Gilbert McMicken, Spymaster: Canada's Secret Police," page 44.

Anyone interested in the beginnings of Canada's spy service should also read Gregory S. Kealey's, "*The Empire Strikes Back: The Nineteenth-Century Origins of the Canadian Secret Service.*" On the Canadian Security and Intelligence Service (csis) website www.csis-scrs.gc.ca, there's Backgrounder No. 5, "A Historical Perspective on csis," revised January 2001.

5. MacDonald, "Gilbert McMicken," pp. 45–46.

6. Keshen, "Cloak and Dagger," page 353.

7. Ibid., page 359.

8. C.P. Stacey, "A Fenian Interlude: The Story of Michael Murphy."

9. Keshen, "Cloak and Dagger," page 356.

10. Barbara Tuchman, *The First Salute: A View of the American Revolution*, page 75.

11. I found a copy of the letter written by John J.B. Beach to Edward Cardwell on 28 March 1866, in the archives of the Historical Society of Pennsylvania, with the Balch Institute for Ethnic Studies, Dennis Clark Papers (Mss 37-Box 1a). It is also quoted in D'Arcy, *The Fenian Movement in the United States*. This is an excellent reference for Le Caron's final year in Canada, with 43 letters written by him from early 1888 until December 1888. There are no names of the people to whom Le Caron was writing, although it's highly likely that many were to Robert Anderson.

Le Caron's memoirs, *Twenty-five Years in the Secret Service*, are invaluable. The Canadian Encyclopedia online listing; Parnaby and Kealey, "*The Origins of Political Policing in Canada*"; and MacDonald, "Gilbert McMicken," were all useful in putting McMicken's work in context.

CHAPTER 4: "ON TO CANADA"

1. T.W. Sweeny's thoughts and plans are from pp. 201–202 of his article, "The Fenian Invasion of Canada, 1866."

2. Stacey, "A Fenian Interlude," page 136.

3. Le Caron, *Twenty-five Years in the Secret Service*, page 31.

4. Keshen, "Cloak and Dagger," page 367.

5. Le Caron, *Twenty-five Years in the Secret Service*, page 32.

6. Keshen, "Cloak and Dagger," page 377.

7. There's a description of Richard Anderson in "Representative Men at Home: Dr. Anderson at New Scotland Yard," (from *Cassell's Saturday Journals*, 11 June 1892) and extracts of several journalists' descriptions of him in Ponsonby Moore-Anderson, *Sir Robert Anderson and Lady Agnes Anderson* (www.newble. co.uk/anderson/biography/preface.html). The *Yorkshire Weekly Post* called him, "warm-hearted and jocular, ever ready with a quip and a joke, and on the whole impressing one as a sane and delightful man of the world."

The Home Office's collection of his correspondence at HO 144/1538/5 [Papers of Sir Robert Anderson Advisor on Political Crime, Home Office, 1868: Assistant Commissioner of Metropolitan Police 1888–1901] 5. Papers [1867–1894] relating to Thomas Beach (alias Major Henri Le Caron) was invaluable throughout, as was the massive collection of the Public Archives of Canada, Ottawa, Sir John A. Macdonald font, volume #234, Ref. #MG26a.

8. Le Caron enrolled in Rush Medical College in Chicago in April 1867.

9. Le Caron, *Twenty-five Years in the Secret Service*, page 39.

10. HO 144/1538/5.

11. When 27-year-old Michael Barrett of County Fermanagh, Ireland, was arrested for the Clerkenwell explosion, he strongly protested that he was innocent. His denials weren't enough to prevent his trip to the gallows outside Newgate Prison in London on 26 May 1868, where a crowd of 2000 sang "Rule Britannia" and jeered. Some of the spectators had paid the considerable sum of £10 to rent rooms at the Magpie and Stump Tavern facing the prison, where they could enjoy a "hanging breakfast" and a prime viewing spot for Barrett's drop to eternity.

CHAPTER 5: CANADIAN SPY

1. HO 144/1538/5.

2. This quote is from a 8 February 1868 letter by Macdonald to a colonel in the Canadian military. I found it and other Macdonald letters on Le Caron in the Public Archives of Canada (PAC), Ottawa, Sir John A. Macdonald font, vol. 234, Ref. #MG26A; 1864, Reel: C1660; 1865, Reel: C1660, C1662; 1866, Reel: C1508, C1660, C1663, C1664; 1867, Reel: C1665; 1868, Reel: C1507, C1508, C1509, C1513, C1586, C1666; 1869, Reel: C1514, C1522, C1667, C1668, C1669; 1870, Reel: C1509, C1668, C1669; 1870, Reel: C1509, C1670; 1881, Reel: C1509, C1671; 1885, Reel: C1670; 1889, Reel: C1692, C1795.

There were also numerous references to Macdonald's correspondence on Le Caron and the Fenians in D'Arcy, *The Fenian Movement in the United States*.

3. Le Caron, *Twenty-five Years in the Secret Service*.

4. D'Arcy, *The Fenian Movement in the United States*, notes on pp. 285–286 that the quality of Le Caron's information dramatically improved in 1868, and McMicken's 4 September 1868, letter is on page 302. I was able to find copies of most of these letters, as well as scores of others, in reels of correspondence between Judge Gilbert McMicken and Prime Minister Sir John A. Macdonald at the National Archives of Canada, which have been previously cited. I found Le Caron's letter of 9 March 1868, signed with the alias Donald Mackay, to

Macdonald about a plot to kill the Prince of Wales in these reels, including reels C26 and C1666.

5. PAC

6. Ibid.

7. Pierre Berton, "Drunk or Sober, We Can't Forget John A.," page SA 2.

8. PAC. Also in D'Arcy, *The Fenian Movement in the United States*, page 290.

9. In coming to grips with McGee, I enjoyed the books of T.P. Slattery, *The Assassination of D'Arcy McGee* and *They Got to Find Me Guilty Yet*; and Josephine Phelan, *The Ardent Exile* and *The Ballad of D'Arcy McGee*.

10. *Globe*, 18 April 1868.

11. pac.

11. Ibid.

12. Ibid.

13. Ibid. Also in D'Arcy, *The Fenian Movement in the United States*, pp. 296–297.

14. pac. Also D'Arcy, *The Fenian Movement in the United States*, page 377, gives the different salaries paid to Le Caron for his spying by the Canadian government, as well as noting Sir John A. Macdonald's comment to Judge Gilbert McMicken that "a man who will engage to do what he offers to do, that is, to betray those with whom he acts is not to be trusted." The pay of $60 monthly was worth about seven hundred and eighty U.S. dollars and $100 a month was worth a little more than thirteen hundred U.S. dollars in the early 21st Century.

15. pac.

16. Ibid.

17. Ibid.

18. Ibid.

19. Ibid.

20. Sweeney, "The Fenian Invasion of Canada, 1866."

21. pac, 29 August 1868, McMicken to Macdonald.

22. www.henrilecaron.com/Welcome.html

23. This draws from the description of Sir Richard Anderson in "Representative Men at Home: Dr. Anderson at New Scotland Yard," and extracts of several journalists' descriptions of him in Ponsonby Moore-Anderson, *Sir Robert Anderson and Lady Agnes Anderson*.

24. August Maue's *The History of Will County, Illinois* provided contemporary information on the prison in Joliet, and Le Caron's memoirs helped here to a lesser extent.

25. Le Caron, *Twenty-five Years in the Secret Service*, page 19.

26. Ibid.

CHAPTER 6: IRA ORGANISER

1. Le Caron, *Twenty-five Years in the Secret Service*, page 53.
2. Less than a century later young folk singer Bob Dylan would make his professional New York debut across the street from the site of the old Fenian headquarters at 10 West Fourth Street.

While the Fenian embassy wasn't in a violent neighbourhood, danger came knocking nonetheless, like after P.J. Meehan, a longtime Fenian, was shot outside its doors after being accused of treason when some secret papers in his possession somehow found their way into the hands of British prosecutors. Meehan survived both the bullets and the accusations, rebounding to become editor of the *Irish American* newspaper. The account of his shooting is from John T. McEnnis, *The Clan na nGael and the Murder of Dr. Cronin*, page 231.

3. Le Caron, *Twenty-five Years in the Secret Service*, pp. 55-57.
4. Of particular use here was Sir Robert Anderson, *The Lighter Side of My Official Life* (www.casebook.org/ripper_media/rps.lighterside.html) and Moore-Anderson, *Sir Robert Anderson and Lady Agnes Anderson*.

CHAPTER 7: DAILY DISPATCHES

1. Le Caron, *Twenty-five Years in the Secret Service*, page 61.
2. National Archives of the United Kingdom Home Office file, HO 144/1538/5.
3. Le Caron, *Twenty-five Years in the Secret Service*, pp. 67-69.
4. Ibid., pp. 71-72. There's a nice description of John Boyle O'Reilly in A.G. Evans, *Fanatic Heart*, page 103.
5. Le Caron, *Twenty-five Years in the Secret Service*, page 70.
6. National Archives of the United Kingdom Home Office file, HO 144/1538/5.
7. McEnnis, *The Clan na nGael and the Murder of Dr. Cronin*, 1889, page 140.
Michael F. Funchion's *Chicago's Irish Nationalists, 1881-1890* guided me through Sullivan's Detroit years and those of Margaret Buchanan and explains Buchanan's early rise in Chicago politics, as well as how the Clan na nGael filled the void left by the self-destruction of the Fenians. Henry M. Hunt's *The Crime of the Century* does a solid job of explaining Sullivan's move to New Mexico. My Detroit friend, Roger McCarville, helped with Margaret Buchanan's Detroit roots.
8. T.P. O'Connor, *Memoirs of an Old Parliamentarian*, vol. 2, pp. 193-194.

CHAPTER 8: BLOWN COVER

1. PAC.
2. Ibid.
3. Ibid.
4. Ibid.
5. Ibid.

6. Ibid.

7. Ibid.

8. Ibid.

9. Phenix, *Private Demons*, pp. 197-200.

10. PAC

11. D'Arcy, *The Fenian Movement in the United States*, page 322. Le Caron's salary would have been worth almost twelve hundred U.S. dollars in the early 21st Century.

12. Le Caron, *Twenty-five Years in the Secret Service*, page 77. O'Neill's debt to Le Caron was worth almost fifty-two hundred U.S. dollars in the early 21st Century.

13. Kealey, 'The Empire Strikes Back,' page 11.

14. PAC.

15. HO 144/1538/5.

16. PAC.

17. Ibid.

18. Ibid.

19. Le Caron, *Twenty-five Years in the Secret Service*.

20. In McEnnis, *The Clan na nGael*, pp. 113-115, there's a discussion about how Le Caron's French name was received in Fenian circles.

21. Le Caron, *Twenty-five Years in the Secret Service*, pp. 75-76.

22. Ibid.

23. Ibid., page 86.

24. Ibid., page 87.

25. Ibid., page 88.

26. Ibid., pp. 90-93.

27. Ibid.

28. Ibid.

29. That expense money was worth more than five thousand U.S. dollars in the early 21st Century.

30. Le Caron, *Twenty-five Years in the Secret Service*.

31. Ibid.

32. By early 1870, there were some fifty thousand people involved in the American Fenian movement, after a peak of between one hundred and fifty thousand and two hundred thousand after the Civil War, according to Michael Davitt, *The Fall of Feudalism in Ireland*, page 120.

CHAPTER 9: HEROES' WELCOME

1. Pádraic H. Pearse, "O'Donovan Rossa." http://www.ucc.ie/research/celt/online/E900007-008.html

2. Ibid.

3. Frederick Engels, "Jenny Longuet, Née Marx."

4. Saul K. Padover, *Karl Marx: An Intimate Biography*, page 178, describes Jenny Marx as beautiful and witty. Her favourite motto, 'All for one, one for all,' appears on page 476 and Engel's obituary for her appears on pp. 588-589.

5. In Evans, *Fanatic Heart*, page 42, is a note that Millbank penitentiary stood where the Tate Gallery now stands, and also that its twelve by eight foot cells were considered 'spacious.' Prisoners were forbidden to talk, and the only sounds heard inside were the chimes of nearby Westminster.

6. Pearse, "O'Donovan Rossa," www.ucc.ie/research/celt/online/E900007-008. html

7. Le Caron, *Twenty-five Years in the Secret Service*, page 103.

8. Kenne Fant, *Alfred Nobel*, page 265, quotes Nobel as saying, in 1867, "I should like to be able to create a substance with such a horrific capacity for mass annihilation that wars would become impossible forever." On pp. 265-266, Nobel Prize winner Albert Einstein is quoted as saying, "He invented an explosive that was stronger than any known before-an exceedingly efficient means of destruction. In order to calm his conscience, he created his Nobel Prizes."

9. Terence Dooley, *The Greatest of the Fenians*, page 81.

10. In ibid., Devoy gives the location of Rossa's bar on page 329 and a nice description of William Mackey Lomasney on pp. 210-211. Tyler Anbinder's *Five Points* describes Rossa's saloon and his political rivalry with Boss William M. Tweed.

11. PAC.

12. Ibid.

CHAPTER 10: PRAIRIE RAID

1. A.H De Trémaudan, "Louis Riel and the Fenian Raid of 1871," pp. 132-144.

The prime source of Gilbert McMicken's frantic rush to Manitoba, including the quotes, is his article, 'The Abortive Fenian Raid on Manitoba.' There was a sharp reply to it from Alexandre-Antonin Taché, *Fenian Raid: An Open Letter from Archbishop Taché to the Hon. Gilbert McMicken*.

2. Ibid., page 136.

3. Ibid., page 142.

4. Taché, *Fenian Raid*.

5. Ibid., page 114.

CHAPTER 11: DR. MORTON

1. McEnnis, *The Clan na nGael*, page 114.

2. *History of Reed Township*.

3. Ibid.

4. Ibid.

5. www.henrilecaron.com/Welcome.html. That health board pay was worth about sixteen hundred U.S. dollars in the early 21st Century.

5. *History of Reed Township.*

6. Ibid.

7. Ibid.

8. Le Caron, *Twenty-five Years in the Secret Service*, page 110.

9. Ibid., pp. 111-117.

10. *History of Reed Township.*

11. Home Office Papers (HO) 144/1538/5.

12. O'Brien and Ryan, *Devoy's Post Bag*, quotes the 10 February 1889 *New York Herald* interview in which Le Caron states: "In order to successfully carry out my plans I was obliged to adopt various devices. As a physician I started drug stores in various places. I had two in Braidwood, Ill., and one in Brace Hill, same State. Then in order to have an excuse for traveling about the United States I assumed the position of an agent for a large wholesale drug house and had business cards printed bearing its name. Another device was to have my wife live in a different city from myself, it being understood that we had agreed to disagree, whereas in reality there never was the slightest trouble between us. By such devices as this I was able to move about rapidly from one place to another without exciting comment or suspicion. I practised medicine in the State of Illinois during my residence there and made money."

13. Robert L. Blakely and Judith M. Harrington, *Bones in the Basement*, pp. 166-167, 197.

14. J.F. Baldwin, a Columbus, Ohio, surgeon and writer on medical matters in the early 20th Century, was also useful with his article, "Grave Robbing."

15. Ambrose Bierce, *The Unabridged Devil's Dictionary*, page 100.

16. Curt Dalton's *The Terrible Resurrection* did an entertaining and thorough job of describing the Harrison body theft Nannie's bribe of a $100 was worth almost nineteen hundred U.S. dollars in the early 21st Century.

17. Ibid.

18. Donald F. Huelke, *The History of the Department of Anatomy.*

19. Dalton, *The Terrible Resurrection.*

20. Ibid.

21. Ibid.; Harry J. Sievers, *The Harrison Horror*; Kevin Grace and Tom White, *Cincinnati Cemeteries*. Le Caron's grave-robbing is noted in Funchion, *Chicago's Irish Nationalists, 1881-1890*, page 33.

22. Dalton, *The Terrible Resurrection.*

23. Le Caron, *Twenty-five Years in the Secret Service*, page 233.

24. W.J. Herdman, "Report on Graverobbing to the Board of Regents."

25. Herbert Asbury, *The Gangs of Chicago.*

26. *The Special Commission Act, 1888*, page 233.

Chapter 12: Uncrowned King

1. Tom Corfe, *The Phoenix Park Murders*, page 53.

2. An excellent, thorough biography of Parnell is F.S.L. Lyons's *Charles Stewart Parnell*, which describes his superstitions on pp. 22-33. Katharine O'Shea's *Charles Stewart Parnell: His Love Story and Political Life* offers an insightful, thoroughly loving look into the man by his wife.

3. Lyons, *Charles Stewart Parnell*, and O'Shea, *Charles Stewart Parnell: His Love Story and Political Life* are particularly useful here, with O'Shea describing his various superstitions in vol. 2 on pp. 232-233.

4. Lyons, *Charles Stewart Parnell*, pp. 184, 235.

5. O'Connor, *Memoirs of an Old Parliamentarian*.

6. Davitt, *The Fall of Feudalism in Ireland*, page 110.

7. Kealey, "The Empire Strikes Back," pp. 16-17; Keshen, "Cloak and Dagger," page 376; Wayne A. Crockett, "The Uses and Abuses of the Secret Service Fund.'"

8. Moore-Anderson, *Sir Robert Anderson and Lady Agnes Anderson*, Chapter 3.

9. Le Caron, *Twenty-five Years in the Secret Service*.

10. Davitt, *The Fall of Feudalism in Ireland*, page 254.

11. The $60,000 raised was the equivalent of more than U.S. $3.9 million in the early 21st Century.

12. O'Connor, *Memoirs of an Old Parliamentarian*.

13. O'Shea, *Charles Stewart Parnell: His Love Story and Political Life*, page 126.

14. Ibid.

Chapter 13: Skirmishing

1. *Kilmainham Gaol Document Pack; Parnell.*

2. *The Special Commission Act, 1888; Report of the Proceedings*, pp. 613-614. The amount paid to harvest his crop came to the equivalent of almost eight hundred-seventy thousand dollars U.S. in the early 21st Century.

3. Moore-Anderson, *Sir Robert Anderson and Lady Agnes Anderson*.

4. Ibid.

5. Davitt, *The Fall of Feudalism in Ireland*.

6. Funchion, *Chicago's Irish Nationalists, 1881-1890*, page 67.

7. PAC. The $75 monthly came to almost fourteen hundred U.S. dollars in the early 21st Century.

8. In D'Arcy, *The Fenian Movement in the United States*, page 402, there's a report that things could erupt in Canada if Parnell was convicted, as well as a description of the activities of the spy Mrs. E. Forest. She is also mentioned in Kealey, "The Empire Strikes Back," page 17; and PAC.

9. PAC. Also in D'Arcy, *The Fenian Movement in the United States*, page 404. That $1,000 figure was equal to more than U.S. $18,450 in the early 21st Century.

10. Le Caron, *Twenty-five Years in the Secret Service*, page 119.

11. Ibid, page 117.

12. HO144/1538/5; I was aided in my description of Archibald by Leslie Harris's entry in *The Canadian Encyclopedia*. Christy Campbell's *Fenian Fire* deals with Millen's undercover work, and I highly recommend it. This incident is described on page 65. Archibald was also one of the few people who knew of Le Caron's undercover work, and had written a letter about him in November 1868 to English officials, saying, "His true name is Beach."

Less than a century after Millen met Archibald, the brick apartment building on 4th Street would be the address of young folk singer Bob Dylan, who would make the street a metaphor for social betrayal and ill will with the song, "Positively 4th Street."

13. Le Caron, *Twenty-five Years in the Secret Service*, page 129.

14. Sir Winston Churchill, *A History of the English-Speaking Peoples*, vol. 4.

15. Ibid.

CHAPTER 14: BOMBSHELL

1. Le Caron, *Twenty-five Years in the Secret Service*, page 156.

2. Ibid, page 158.

3. This note was cited in *The Special Commission Act, 1888* report and news coverage.

Years later as he looked back on that meeting, Devoy would protest that he wasn't fully duped by Le Caron, writing in *Devoy's Post Bag*:

> I never suspected him of being a British spy, but I never liked or trusted him. The true story of his receiving a letter of introduction from me to Patrick Egan in Paris is this. . . I was sitting one day in the Palmer house writing letters when Major Clingen, the ex-district officer and then a member of the district military board, walked into the room with Le Caron. He said that Le Caron was going to France and that the man who had succeeded him as head of the district thought it was a good opportunity to send over any important message I might not like to send by mail. I was at that time the officer in charge of such matters, but Le Caron was not supposed to know it. I told Clingen that I had a system that had worked very well and that I had no message to send over. He then suggested that I should give him introductions to the heads of the organization in Ireland, but I told him that we were under pledges not to do that in the case of men going over on pleasure trips. Clingen was very disappointed and Le Caron stood by with an air of unconcern, but evidently very much interested. They went away, but returned in less than an hour and informed me that the district officer was very anxious that the doctor should have an introduction to "somebody on the other side," and, as he himself knew nobody, he asked me as a personal favour that I should give Le Caron a letter. I then wrote

on the Palmer house paper the letter which he called a "sealed packet," but which was a mere line of introduction. It merely said that he was "a good Irishman, barring the bull, and a member of the Land League, and that as he had been kind to Davitt when in his town I knew he would receive him kindly while in Paris"... Mr. Egan was not then a member of the "home organization," and my introduction contained no recommendation that Le Caron be trusted.

4. In O'Brien and Ryan, *Devoy's Post Bag*, page 47, there's Le Caron's false belief that Devoy suspected him of being a spy after Devoy stated, "that there was clear and incontrovertible evidence that there was at least one spy in the general convention held in the Palmer House in 1881; that its proceedings had been fully reported to the British consul in New York; that the said spy had never been found out; that he was an officer in the organization after the convention, and was probably a delegate listening to me in that convention." There's also the anecdote about Devoy giving Le Caron "a little tongue thrashing." From the Chicago *Sunday Times* on 8 April 1894, there's Devoy's description of Le Caron having "Dark hair, sallow complexion, and long nose, all doubtless due to a strong strain of gypsy blood, which is common around Colchester."

5. In HO 144/1538/5, there's a 23 May 1881, letter from Le Caron to Anderson, in which he tells of his meetings with Egan and Parnell, and that Egan felt there could be a viable revolutionary movement in Ireland within 12 months.

6. It was my pleasure to take this walk with my wife, Barbara, during my research.

7. Le Caron, *Twenty-five Years in the Secret Service*, pp. 160-161.

8. Ibid. and *The Special Commission Act*, page 142.

9. Le Caron, *Twenty-five Years in the Secret Service*, pp. 163-164.

10. Ibid., page 166.

11. *The Special Commission Act*, page 146.

12. Ibid., page 146.

13. In Davitt, *The Fall of Feudalism in Ireland*, page 610, there's his disbelief that Le Caron interviewed Parnell, saying, "His alleged interview... was a palpable yarn engrafted upon a probable interview." In the newspaper *Gaelic American* on 8 September 1923, Devoy states: "Parnell, with his invariable caution, did not confide anything to him, and the statements to that effect in Le Caron's book are all inventions. Parnell gave no message for me. When I met him on his return, Le Caron told me verbally that Parnell wanted me to go over to Ireland, but he had not a line in writing to show that the message was genuine."

14. T.M. Healy, *Letters and Leaders of My Day*, vol. 1, page 136.

15. Le Caron, *Twenty-five Years in the Secret Service*, page 181.

16. O'Shea, *Charles Stewart Parnell: His Love Story and Political Life*, vol. 1, page 194. In O'Brien and Ryan, *Devoy's Post Bag*, page 50, there's the notation from Sir

Robert Anderson, Le Caron's British handler: "General warnings of the dynamite plots, he gave me repeatedly"; while the *Times'* Special Commission report, part XII, page 202, contains Le Caron's very candid admissions that he had taken part in later discussions with Dr. Gallagher and Lomasney on dynamiting.

17. I learned this on an excellent guided tour of Kilmainham Gaol, which I highly recommend.

18. O'Shea, *Charles Stewart Parnell: His Love Story and Political Life*, vol. 1, page 211.

19. Ibid.

20. Davitt, *The Fall of Feudalism in Ireland*, page 350.

21. Ibid., page 501.

22. Ibid., page 362.

CHAPTER 15: THE GREAT DYNAMITE CONVENTION OF 1881

1. The 18 June 1881 letter to Devoy is from O'Brien and Ryan, *Devoy's Post Bag*, page 88. Le Caron, *Twenty-five Years in the Secret Service*, also describes his return to America after his visit with Parnell in London.

2. Le Caron, *Twenty-five Years in the Secret Service*, page 183.

3. I greatly enjoyed visits to the Palmer House during my research.

4. Le Caron, *Twenty-five Years in the Secret Service*, pp. 188-203.

5. Ibid., page 188.

6. Alfred Nobel made his fortune through dynamite, but was at heart a pacifist, and the will he left after his 1896 death led to the establishment of the Nobel Prize for Peace, which was offered to "those who, during the preceding year, shall have conferred the greatest benefit on mankind." Nobelprize.org notes that one of his aphorisms was "We build upon the sand, and the older we become, the more unstable the foundation becomes."

7. The observation that Parnell needed Devoy is from Robert Kee, *The Green Flag*, page 369.

CHAPTER 16: MURDER IN THE PARK

1. HO 144/1538/5. That was equivalent to more than twenty-nine thousand U.S. dollars in early 21st Century terms.

2. Exactly how much Anderson agreed to pay Le Caron isn't clear, but it was enough to keep him on as a spy. In the Home Office papers, HO 144/1538/5, there's an 30 April 1883 letter regarding Le Caron signing a five year contract with Archibald, starting 1 January 1883.

3. Moore-Anderson, *Sir Robert Anderson and Lady Agnes Anderson*, Chapter 3.

4. Corfe, *The Phoenix Park Murders*, does an excellent job of describing the slayings.

5. Davitt's reaction to the Phoenix Park murders is from Healy, *Letters and Leaders of My Day*. In Davitt, *The Fall of Feudalism in Ireland*, page 455, there's a description of James Carey, including how he and others were part of a plot to kill Forster and also of Carey's death on the high seas.

6. O'Shea, *Charles Stewart Parnell: The Love Story and Political Life*, vol. 1, pp. 247-248.

7. In Weintraub, *Victoria: An Intimate Biography*, pp. 451-452, there's a description of Queen Victoria receiving news of the Phoenix Park murders and the monarch's frustrations with Gladstone's policies on Ireland.

8. Moore-Anderson, *Sir Robert Anderson and Lady Agnes Anderson*, Chapter 3.

9. The money raised by Ford was equivalent to more than nine hundred and forty thousand U.S. dollars in early 21st Century terms.

10. Irish literary great James Joyce later relegated James Carey to infamy as a Judas, and in *Ulysses,* the character Leopold Bloom comments on: "That fellow that turned queen's evidence on the invincibles he used to receive the, Carey was his name, the communion every morning. This very church. . . Wife and six children at home. And plotting that murder all the time." The *Chicago Citizen* reported on 13 February 1886 about how John Devlin was greatly annoyed by rumours that he was related to James Carey.

CHAPTER 17: BOMB SCHOOL GRADUATES

1. Funchion, *Chicago's Irish Nationalists, 1881-1890*, describes the hard bargaining between Sullivan and Egan in Paris, and how League funds wound up in Sullivan's bank account.

2. HO144/1538/5.

3. The idea that McDermott was denounced by many suspicious members of his movement is from Desmond Ryan, *The Fenian Chief*, page 202, while on page 203 he is described as handsome, quick with comebacks, smart, free of principles, and the son of a Dublin coachman. On page 310 of *The Fenian Chief* is the mention that McDermott's life was threatened if Davis was arrested. A warning by James Stephens about 'Red Jim' McDermott is from D'Arcy, *The Fenian Movement in the United States*, page 41, while the June 9, 1894, *Chicago Citizen* describes McDermott's career as an informer in the 1880s.

4. Le Caron, *Twenty-five Years in the Secret Service*, page 230.

5. Terry Golway, *Irish Rebel*.

6. HO144/1538/5. There's a receipt here and also a handwritten contract. That figure amounts to almost 23, 625 U.S. dollars in early 21st Century terms.

7. Le Caron, *Twenty-five Years in the Secret Service*, page 221.

8. Ibid., page 222.

9. The Historical Society of Pennsylvania, with the Balch Institute for Ethnic Studies, papers. Le Caron letter of 13 March 1888.

10. Davitt, *The Fall of Feudalism in Ireland*, pp. 428-433 and 435.

11. *The Special Commission Act,* vol. 2, page 166.

12. Campbell, *Fenian Fire*, was very useful in explaining Scotland Yard intrigues.

13. The phrase saying the bomb struck "the street that governs England" is from McEnnis, *The Clan na nGael and the Murder of Dr. Cronin.*

14. The Historical Society of Pennsylvania, Dennis Clark Papers (Mss 37), Box 2, Folder 8, 'Luke Dillon Research Materials.'

15. Ibid. In these papers, there is a poem by Irish nationalists called "The Ballad of Luke Dillon; The Hardest Man of All," which ends, "Here's to old Luke Dillon! He's the hardest man of all!"

16. Le Caron, *Twenty-five Years in the Secret Service,* page 228.

17. Ibid., page 231.

18. The 9 February 1889 *Chicago Citizen* notes on page 5 how Alexander Sullivan felt Gallagher exceeded his orders and gave himself away, and how future candidates for bombing wouldn't have families. In Le Caron, *Twenty-five Years in the Secret Service,* page 230, Le Caron says he asked Egan to expand about Gallagher, and Egan replied, "Why, he got in with some of Rossa's men, and MacDermott (the suspected informer) got it from them, and gave him away."

19. John Devoy, *Recollections,* page 211, there's an explanation of Lomasney's attempts at non-violent terrorism.

20. Le Caron, *Twenty-five Years in the Secret Service,* page 244.

21. The Historical Society of Pennsylvania, Dennis Clark Papers (Mss 37), Box 2, Folder 8, 'Luke Dillon Research Materials.'

CHAPTER 18: BLACK BAG IN PARIS

1. The headlines about Rossa's shooting are from Danny Conlon's article, "New York City, Jubilee Plot. . ."

2. Ryan, *The Fenian Chief,* page 262.

3. In O'Connor, *Memoirs of an Old Parliamentarian,* on page 135, I found this description of Pigott: "A look at the man betrayed his essentially epicurean character; he was rather stout, and had a full, rather bloated face; he looked, as he was, a thorough sensualist; and perhaps this impression was increased by his constant wearing of a single eye-glass."

4. *The Times'* official history, *History of the Times,* pp. 63-64 contains the passage: "Almost anyone with a few years' experience of the political and journalistic life of Dublin would have had something to say about this Pigott, but to young Houston his name was as yet quite unknown."

5. In Davitt, *The Fall of Feudalism in Ireland,* page 565, I found: "Mr. Pigott was perfectly impartial in his scheming propensities," while on page 561 were details about Houston being born in Dublin, about 27 years of age in 1889, and that he worked for the pro-landlord *Daily Express.*

6. That's the equivalent of more than U.S. $9.3 million in early 21st Century terms.

7. *The Special Commission Act,* vol. 2, page 305.

8. Ibid., page 336.
9. That's about U.S. $6,740 in early 21st Century terms.
10. Le Caron, *Twenty-five Years in the Secret Service*, page 246.

CHAPTER 19: DELUSION

1. *The Special Commission Act*, vol. 2, page 190.
2. Le Caron, *Twenty-five Years in the Secret Service*, page 248.
3. *The History of the Times*.
4. Campbell, *Fenian Fire*, was again extremely useful in understanding the workings of Scotland Yard. He is the undisputed authority on the plot to blow up Queen Victoria.
5. O'Shea, *Charles Stewart Parnell: His Love Story and Political Life*.
6. In Davitt, *The Fall of Feudalism in Ireland*, pp. 533-534, there was the note: "Our information was that the late Mr. W.H. Smith and the then Home Secretary were both privy to the intended publication of this letter."
7. Ibid., page 535.
8. Barbara Tuchman, *The Proud Tower*, page 60.
9. O'Connor, *Memoirs of an Old Parliamentarian*, page 131.
10. In O'Brien and Ryan, *Devoy's Post Bag*, Luke Dillon of Philadelphia writes to John Devoy on 7 February 1887: "Friend John" and continues, "General Millen returned from his excursion to Paris, and has drawn on his imagination for facts as usual."
11. Le Caron, *Twenty-five Years in the Secret Service*, pp. 251-252.
12. Ibid. On pp. 255-256, Le Caron writes of Millen and the Jubilee Dynamite Plot: "The whole undertaking was shrouded in mystery, but it is pretty certain that it was not a Clan na Gael affair alone. The best description that could be given of it would be that it was in its inception a Rossa undertaking financed by the Clan na nGael. Millen. . . on his return to American fell in with the scheme. ."
13. Stanley Weintraub, *Victoria*, page 450, contains this quote by Queen Victoria.

CHAPTER 20: STRESS LEAVE

1. Le Caron, *Twenty-five Years in the Secret Service*, page 253.
2. Ibid., pp. 272-273.
3. Dennis Clark, "Letter Book on an English Spy." Florence Sullivan's death is mentioned in Le Caron's 20 February 1888 letter. The core of this chapter comes from Le Caron's 1888 letter books, which were discovered in Philadelphia, copies of which were kindly forwarded to me by the Historical Society of Pennsylvania. They are a treasure trove of unpublished letters, which were deposited with the Historical Society of Pennsylvania by Dennis Clark. Clark's *The Irish Relations* is

an intelligent, thoroughly researched study of Fenianism.

4. Ibid.

5. Physician's Certificate of Death for William Le Caron.

6. The Historical Society of Pennsylvania, with the Balch Institute for Ethnic Studies papers, Le Caron's letter of 3 April 1888.

7. Ibid.

8. Ibid.

9. Ibid.

10. Le Caron, *Twenty-five Years in the Secret Service*, pp. 67-68.

11. The Historical Society of Pennsylvania, with the Balch Institute for Ethnic Studies.

12. Ibid.

13. Ibid.

14. Ibid.

15. Ibid.

16. The $30 monthly rent was the equivalent of slightly more than 580 US dollars in the early 21st Century.

17. Anderson, *The Lighter Side of My Official Life*.

18. An excellent and highly recommended study of the relationship between Millen and other spies and the British government during this time is Campbell's *Fenian Fire*. On page 303, Campbell touches on the mystery of Anderson's visit to Paris in the fall of 1888.

19. *Jack the Ripper*, page 12.

20. Anderson, *The Lighter Side of My Official Life*.

21. In Davitt, *The Fall of Feudalism in Ireland*, page 535, there's a discussion of Egan's role in discovering the Pigott forgery, while on page 388 there's a note about Parnell's compulsion for proper spelling, which details how he wouldn't read a letter because the word 'agriculture' was spelled wrong. It also describes Parnell's face as cheerful when he saw spelling mistakes in *The Times* letter.

22. HO 144/1538/5.

23. The Historical Society of Pennsylvania, with the Balch Institute for Ethnic Studies.

CHAPTER 21: SURFACING

1. It was my pleasure to visit this area along the Strand myself, and if I won the lottery, I would be back there tomorrow. The Royal Courts of Justice is a short walk away from Charing Cross station and the Temple Church. The Temple was built in the 12th Century by the Knights Templar, an order of monks whose mission was to guard pilgrims heading to and from Jerusalem. In earlier days at the Temple Church, one could take communion without leaving the saddle of one's horse, in a medieval version of drive-through religion.

In the massive demolition to create the Law Courts, two roads were lost but mourned: Cursitor Street, grimly immortalized by Charles Dickens in *Bleak House*, and Shire Lane (dubbed Rogue Lane), former home of the Kit-Kat Club.

2. *The Royal Courts of Justice.*

3. Tuchman, *The Proud Tower*, pp. 433-434.

4. Davitt, *The Fall of Feudalism in Ireland*, page 547.

5. Ibid.

6. MacDonald, *The Daily News Diary of the Parnell Commission*, page 2.

7. Ibid.

8. HO 144/1538/5.

9. The Historical Society of Pennsylvania, with the Balch Institute for Ethnic Studies.

10. That fee would be the equivalent of almost U.S $961, 960 in the early 21st Century.

11. Le Caron, *Twenty-five Years in the Secret Service*, pp. 267-268.

12. That's more than U.S. $1.72 million in the early 21st Century.

CHAPTER 22: TRUE COLOURS

1. Davitt, *The Fall of Feudalism in Ireland*, pp. 405-406 and 550.

2. The *Times* report on the Special Commission inaccurately reported his middle name as Billis on page 130 of volume 2.

3. Le Caron, *Twenty-five Years in the Secret Service*, page 269.

4. In O'Connor, *Memoirs of an Old Parliamentarian*, page 142, Le Caron is described in this way: 'He was a very thin man, with black hair, piercing black eyes, small, pallid face, with regular features and a waxed moustache,' while on page 143, there's a description of how Le Caron laughed when he read Egan's letters about how he deserved confidence.

5. Moore-Anderson, *Sir Robert Anderson and Lady Agnes Anderson*, Chapter 3.

6. MacDonald, *The Daily News Diary of the Parnell Commission*, was particularly useful throughout this chapter, and offered a nice description of Le Caron's first day on the witness stand on page 120. *The Chicago Citizen* of 16 February 1889 describes how Le Caron's appearance suddenly ended boredom at the inquiry, and how he responded to the lightly veiled threat of a spectator.

7. That's the equivalent of almost U.S. $190,000 in early21st Century terms.

8. O'Brien and Ryan, *Devoy's Post Bag.*

CHAPTER 23: SPELLING BEE

1. In Davitt, *The Fall of Feudalism in Ireland*, page 576, Parnell is quoted as saying of Pigott: "The rat is caught in the trap at last," and there's also Davitt's description of Pigott's appearance being "more in keeping with the bearing and presentment of a secretary..."

2. This pitiful exchange is well covered in a variety of sources, including MacDonald, *The Daily News Diary of the Parnell Commission*; R. Barry O'Brien, *The Life of Lord Russell of Killowen*; *The History of the Times*; and Lyon, *Charles Stewart Parnell*.

3. Davitt, *The Fall of Feudalism in Ireland*, page 591, deals with Pigott's flight to Paris and then Spain; and Joyce Marlow, *The Uncrowned Queen of Ireland*, page 205, raises the question about why Pigott fled to Spain when he was unfamiliar with that country. The *Times* coverage was extremely useful in dealing with Pigott's flight.

4. Sullivan, *Recollections of Troubled Times in Irish Politics*, page 274.

5. MacDonald, *The Daily News Diary of the Parnell Commission*, page 165.

6. Ibid., pp. 165-166.

CHAPTER 24: LIVING LIE

1. O'Connor, *Memoirs of an Old Parliamentarian*, page 211, notes how Asquith said Le Caron had a "sinister personality."

2. Davitt, *The Fall of Feudalism in Ireland*, page 426.

CHAPTER 25: MURDER IN CHICAGO

1. Hunt, *The Crime of the Century*, page 59; McEnnis, *The Clan na nGael*, page 231. The online archives of the *Chicago Tribune* were also valuable in this section, especially "Famous Mystery Cases in Review No. 4—The Staging of Dr. Patrick H. Cronin of Chicago in a Bitter International Strife $10,000 in Cash Prizes for Solutions! 4 Found Guilty, but Case Never Entirely Solved," *Chicago Tribune* (May 5, 1929).

2. McEnnis, *The Clan na nGael*, page 234.

3. The furniture would have cost slightly more than U.S. $940 in early 21st Century terms.

4. That would have amounted to slightly more than U.S. $2 million in early 21st Century terms.

5. Hunt, *The Crime of the Century*, page 118.

6. Devoy, *Recollections of an Irish Rebel*, page 312.

7. In Dooley, *Greatest of the Fenians*, on page 124, Devoy is quoted as saying Cronin's death was "the direct result of branding all critics as British spies."

8. Healy, *Letters and Leaders of My Day*. For people interested in such things, a site further up North Clark Street was where gangster Al Capone had seven of his rivals murdered in 1929 in what became known as the St. Valentine's Day Massacre.

9. McEnnis, *The Clan na nGael*, page 197; Hunt, *The Crime of the Century*, pp. 127-132.

10. McEnnis, *The Clan na nGael*, page 199.

11. McEnnis, *The Clan na nGael*; Hunt, *The Crime of the Century*.

12. McEnnis, *The Clan na nGael*, pp. 204-209; Hunt, *The Crime of the Century*, pp. 220-235.

CHAPTER 26: "ANOTHER LE CARON"

1. The Historical Society of Pennsylvania, Dennis Clark Papers (Mss 37), Box 2, Folder 8, "Luke Dillon Research Materials." There is a poem by Irish nationalists called "The Ballad of Luke Dillon; The Hardest Man of All," which ends 'Here's to old Luke Dillon! He's the hardest man of all!'

2. Hunt, *The Crime of the Century*, pp. 253-257.

3. Ibid., page 1091. McEnnis's *The Clan na nGael* was also key for this chapter.

4. Brown, *The Politics of Irish Literature*, www.astonisher.com/archives/mjb/irishlit/irishlit_ch23.html Chapter Twenty-three, page 11.

5. In 1899, Coughlin was charged with offering a diamond to a juror in a damage suit against Illinois Central Railroad. He jumped bail and fled to Mobile, Alabama, and then Puerto Cortes, Honduras. He assumed the name James E. David and worked as a foreman until dying out of custody of tuberculosis on 29 December 1910.

CHAPTER 27: MESSY DIVORCE

1. www.casebook.org/timeline.html; it's notable for some that Anderson suspected that Jack the Ripper was Polish immigrant Aaron Kosminski, who died in the Colney Hatch lunatic asylum.
Useful websites regarding Parnell for this chapter include www.historyhome.co.uk/peel/people/parnell2.htm and www.nndb.com/people/901/000092625

2. In O'Shea, *Charles Stewart Parnell: His Love Story and Political Life*, vol. 2, page 153, is a note that Gladstone had known of Parnell's affair with Katharine O'Shea.

3. John Hughes-Wilson, *The Puppet Masters*. I know the phrase "Midnight Rambler" was coined by The Rolling Stones, but I'm a huge fan and feel "midnight rambling" works wonderfully here. This passage of the book was written while listening to an extended version of the tune.

4. O'Shea, *Charles Stewart Parnell: The Love Story and Political Life*, page 109. In O'Connor, *Memoirs of an Old Parliamentarian*, there's the information that Parnell signalled with a handkerchief to meet Katharine O'Shea in Charing Cross.

5. O'Shea, *Charles Stewart Parnell: His Love Story and Political Life*, vol. 1, page 83.

6. Katharine O'Shea's inheritance was equivalent to more than U.S. $2million in early 21st Century terms.

7. The information that replicas of Parnell's Brighton home were sold, and that music hall comedians and cartoonists enjoyed the scandal, is from Marlow, *The Uncrowned Queen of Ireland*, page 239. The *Vanity Fair* headline is from page 239.

8. O'Connor, *Memoirs of an Old Parliamentarian*, page 189.

9. O'Shea, *Charles Stewart Parnell: His Love Story and Political Life*, vol. 2, pp. 108 and 242.

10. Churchill, *A History of the English-Speaking Peoples*, vol. 4, page 361.

11. In O'Brien and Ryan, *Devoy's Post Bag*, page 316.

12. O'Shea, *Charles Stewart Parnell: His Love Story and Political Life*, vol. 2, page 103.

13. O'Connor, *Memoirs of an Old Parliamentarian*, page 245.

CHAPTER 28: AFTERMATH

1. Sweeney, *John Sweeney, at Scotland Yard*.

2. Devoy, *Recollections of an Irish Rebel*, page 48.

3. That comes to about U.S. $2,200 per sibling in early 21st Century terms.

4. Le Caron, *Twenty-five Years in the Secret Service*, page 287.

5. Moore-Anderson, *Sir Robert Anderson and Lady Agnes Anderson*, Chapter 3.

6. Campbell, *Fenian Fire*, calls this comment by Le Caron "a last conspiratorial wink to Whitehall."

7. Le Caron, *Twenty-five Years in the Secret Service*, page 275. Gallagher's money comes to more than U.S. $2,300 in early 21st Century terms.

8. Ibid., page 278.

9. O'Connor, *Memoirs of an Old Parliamentarian*, page 233.

10. O'Shea, *Charles Stewart Parnell: His Love Story and Political Life*, vol. 2, pp. 248-249.

11. Ibid., pp. 164, 225, 248-249, and 258.

12. Richard Ellmann's *James Joyce* discusses the profound influence Parnell had on Joyce and the poet's father, including a poem written by nine-year-old James on Parnell, which is reprinted on page 33. Also useful is Ellmann's *Selected Joyce Letters*. In Suzette Henke, *James Joyce and the Politics of Desire*, page 90, there's an interesting reference to Richard Rowan, the artist character in Joyce's work *Exiles*: "But Richard, like Christ or Nietzsche, speaks in the metaphorical language of riddle and paradox. He lays claims to a stronger and stranger emotional union, the 'faith of a master in the disciple who will betray him.' (*Exiles*, page 44) Richard feels convinced that like Christ and Charles Stewart Parnell, he will be betrayed by friends and disciples and, eventually, by the woman he loves."

13. O'Shea, *Charles Stewart Parnell: His Love Story and Political Life*, vol. 1, page 127.

14. Ibid., page 172. In ibid., vol. 2, there's the note that she was also comforted by the belief that on the day he died, a new planet was discovered. In O'Connor,

Memoirs of an Old Parliamentarian, page 326, Katharine O'Shea's final years are recounted, including the facts that she had more than twenty houses after his death and that she spent two years in an asylum.

15. The quotes from Rossa and his wife are from "The Last of the Fenians," a *New York Telegram* article that was widely reprinted, including in the *Washington Post* (26 February 1911), page 1.

16. HO 144/1538/5. Those secret service funds for Le Caron are the equivalent of almost U.S. $59,000 in early 21st Century terms.

17. Moore-Anderson, *Sir Robert Anderson and Lady Agnes Anderson*, Chapter 16.

18. HO 144/1538/5.

19. Ibid. That amount in his bank amounts to almost U.S. $19,420 in early 21st Century terms.

20. Ibid.

21. Ibid.

22. Certified copy of an entry of death, Registration District, Kensington, 1894, death in the sub-district of Brompton in the County of London. DYB 108039.

23. Researcher Glynis Morris found the will for me at: The Postal Searches & Copies Department, York Probate Sub-Registry, Castle Chambers, Clifford Street

York YO1 9RG.

24. Permission to quote from Heinemann's letter was kindly granted to me by Glasgow University Library, where the letter is filed under Call Number: MS Whistler H187. That figure works out to slightly more than U.S. $39,700 in early 21st Century terms.

25. Crawford, "Henri Le Caron."

26. Nannie Le Caron was said to have moved back to Tennessee, but by 1907 she was living in New York, as is shown by her application for a pension for Le Caron's Civil War service. She appears in the 1910 census, living in Manhattan Ward 12, New York. Her son Charles S. Le Caron, then 27, also lived in Ward 12 with his wife, Victorie, 26, and their children, Victorie, 6, and Charles, 4. By the 1920 census, Charles, Victorie, Victorie Jr., and Charles Jr., as well as a daughter Harriet, 9, lived in the Brooklyn Assembly District 1, Kings, New York, while Nannie does not appear.

In Marlow, *The Uncrowned Queen*, page 311, is the comment that if Parnell had lived longer, Gladstone would likely have succeeded in having a Home Rule bill passed in the House of Commons in 1893, and that her daughter Norah Parnell said she was sustained by the belief that "Parnell comes to her at night, when things are worst and draws her out of the dark waves."

27. *The Chicago Sunday Times*, 8.April 1894, as quoted in Cole, op. cit., page 201.

SOURCES

DOCUMENTS

Canadian Security and Intelligence Service (CSIS) website
www.csis-scrs.gc.ca/en/newsroom/backgrounders/backgrounder05.asp,
Backgrounder no. 5, "A Historical Perspective on CSIS." Revised January 2001.

Clark, Dennis. "Letter Book on an English Spy: Major Le Caron and the Clan na Gael, 1888." Dennis Clark papers, The Pennsylvania Historical Society. Unpublished paper.

Cole, J.A. *Prince of Spies: Henri Le Caron*. London and Boston: Faber and Faber, 1984.

Crawford, Frank M., "Henri Le Caron—One of Our Characters." In *History of the Fifteenth Pennsylvania Volunteer Cavalry, Which Was Recruited as the Anderson Cavalry in the Rebellion of 1861-1865*, edited by Charles H. Kirk, First Lieutenant Company E., assisted by The Historical Committee of the Society of the Fifteenth Cavalry. Philadelphia: 1906.

Crilly, Nancy Bruce. *Selections from Early Will County, Illinois Newspapers*. Will County, Ilinois genealogical registers. Wilmington, Illinois, 1997.

D'Arcy, William. *The Fenian Movement in the United States: 1858-1886*. Ph.D. thesis, Catholic University of America Press, 1947.

"Eleventh Annual Announcement of the Chicago Medical College, Chicago, Ill. For the College Session of 1869-70." Chicago: Robert Fergus' Sons, Printers, 1869. Chicago Historical Society collection.

Federal American Census of 1880, 1900, 1910.

Herdman, W.J. "Report on Graverobbing to the Board of Regents," 28 June 1880, the University of Michigan.

History of Reed Township. Chicago: Wm. Le Baron, Jr. & Co., 1878.

Physician's Certificate of Death for William Le Caron, State of Illinois, Cook County, Chicago City Board of Health, 4 April 1888.

Rauch, John H., MD. "Illinois State Board of Health. Report on Medical Education, Medical Colleges and the Regulation of the Practice of Medicine in the United States and Canada, 1765-1889." Springfield: R.W. Rokker, Printer and Binder, 1889. Chicago Historical Society collection.

The Special Commission Act, 1888; Report of the Proceedings before the Commissioners Appointed by the Act, vols. 1 and 2. London: George Wright, at the *Times* Office, Printing House Square, 1890.

Taché, Alexandre-Antonin. *Fenian Raid: An Open Letter from Archbishop Taché to the Hon. Gilbert McMicken* (n.p., 1888). National Archives of Canada, Alexandre-Antonin Taché collection, file #61794.

CONTEMPORARY SOURCES

Anderson, Sir Robert. *The Lighter Side of My Official Life*. Originally published as articles in *Blackwoods* magazine, 1910.

Bierce, Ambrose. *The Complete Short Stories of Ambrose Bierce*. Compiled with commentary by Ernest Jerome Hopkins. Lincoln and London: University of Nebraska Press, 1984.

D'Arcy, William. *The Fenian Movement in the United States, 1858-86*. Washington, D.C.: Catholic University of America Press, 1947.

Dasent, Arthur Irwin. *John Thadeus Delane; Editor of "The Times," His Life and Correspondence*, vols. 1 and 2. London: John Murray, 1908.

Davitt, Michael. *The Fall of Feudalism in Ireland or the Story of the Land League Revolution*. London and New York: Harper & Brothers Publishers, 1904.

Devoy, John. *Recollections of an Irish Rebel*. Shannon: Irish University Press, 1969.

Dickens, Charles. *American Notes for General Circulation* from *A Tale of Two Cities and American Notes*. London: Oldams Press Ltd., 1933.

Donna, Modesto Joseph. *The Braidwood Story*. Braidwood: Braidwood History Bureau, 1957.

Ellmann, Richard, ed. *Selected Joyce Letters: The Editor's Choice of the Best Letters from James Joyce's Three Great Volumes, with Important Editions of Previously Unpublished Letters*. New York: The Viking Press, 1975.

Ford, Patrick. "The Criminal History of the British Empire." Pamphlet. New York: The Irish World, 1915.

Healy, T.M., K.C. *Letters and Leaders of My Day,* vols. 1 and 2. New York: Frederick A. Stokes Company, 1929.

Herdman, W.J. "Report on Graverobbing to the Board of Regents," June 28, 1880, the University of Michigan.

The History of the Pennsylvania Volunteers, 1861-65, vol. 4. Newberry Library Collection, Chicago.

The History of Will County, Illinois. Chicago: Wm. Le Baron, Jr. & Co., 1878.

Hunt, Henry M. *The Crime of the Century or, the Assassination of Dr. Patrick Henry Cronin: A Complete and Authentic History of the Greatest of Modern Conspiracies.* H.L. & D.H. Kochersperger, 1889.

Le Caron, Major Henri. *Twenty-five Years in the Secret Service: The Recollections of a Spy,* 5th ed. London: William Heinemann, 1892.

Longstreet, James, Lieutenant-General, Confederate Army. *From Manassas to Appomattox: Memoirs of the Civil War in America.* New York: Mallard Press, 1991.

Lytton, Constance, and Jane Warton, Spinster. *Prison and Prisoners: Some Personal Experiences.* London: William Heinemann, 1914.

Macdonald, John. *The Daily News Diary of the Parnell Commission.* London: T. Fisher Unwin, 1890.

McEnnis, John T., ed. *The Clan na nGael and the Murder of Dr. Cronin.* 1889.

McGee, Thomas D'Arcy. *A History of the Irish Settlers in North America, from the Earliest Period to the Census of 1850.* Baltimore: Clearfield Company, reprints and remainders, 1989. (Originally printed 1852.)

McMicken, Gilbert. "The Abortive Fenian Raid on Manitoba: Account by One Who Knew Its Secret History." *Manitoba, Historical and Scientific Society, Trans.* (Winnipeg), no. 32 (1887-1888): 1-11.

O'Brien, William, and Desmond Ryan, eds. *Devoy's Post Bag: 1871-1928.* Dublin: Fallon, 1948.

O'Connor, T.P., MP. *Memoirs of an Old Parliamentarian,* vol. ii. New York: D. Appleton and Company, 1929.

O'Shea, Katharine. *Charles Stewart Parnell: His Love Story and Political Life,* vols. 1 and 2. New York: George H. Doran Company, 1915.

Rossa, O'Donovan. *My Years in English Jails: The Brutal Facts.* Edited by Seán Cearnaigh and Desmond Ryan. Tralee: Anvil Books, 1967. Originally published by the American News Corporation, New York, 1874.

Sullivan, T.D. *Recollections of Troubled Times in Irish Politics.* Dublin: Sealy, Bryers & Walker, M.H. Giull & Son, Ltd., 1905.

Sweeney, John. *John Sweeney, at Scotland Yard; Experiences during 27 Years' Service.* London: Grand Richards, 1904.

Sweeney, T.W. "The Fenian Invasion of Canada, 1866." In *The Journal of the American Irish Historical Society*, vol. xxiii, edited by John G. Coyle, MD, Vincent Fleming O'Reilly, and J. Dominick Hackett. New York: The American Irish Historical Society, 1924.

SELECT SECONDARY BOOKS

Anbinder, Tyler. *Five Points: The 19th-Century New York City Neighborhood That Invented Tap Dance, Stole Elections, and Became the World's Most Notorious Slum.* New York: The Free Press, 2001.

Asbury, Herbert. *The Gangs of Chicago: An Informal History of the Chicago Underworld.* New York: Thunder Mouth Press, 1986.

Bierce, Ambrose. *The Unabridged Devil's Dictionary.* Edited by David E. Schultz and S.J. Joshi. Athens and London: University of Georgia Press, 2000.

Blakey, Robert L., and Judith M. Harrington, eds. *Bones in the Basement: Postmortem Racism in Nineteenth-Century Medical Training.* Washington and London: Smithsonian Institution Press, 1997.

Bradford, Sarah. *Disraeli.* New York: Stein and Day Publishers, 1982.

Brown, Malcolm. *The Politics of Irish Literature from Thomas Davis to W.B. Yeats.* Seattle: University of Washington Press, 1972.

Campbell, Christy. *Fenian Fire: The British Government Plot to Assassinate Queen Victoria.* London: HarperCollins, 2002.

Carey, Tim. *Mountjoy: The Story of a Prison.* Cork: The Collins Press, 2000.

Catton, Bruce. *A Stillness at Appomattox: The Fateful Last Chapter of the Army of the Potomac's Dramatic Saga.* Garden City: Doubleday & Company, Inc., 1953.

Churchill, Winston S. *A History of the English-Speaking Peoples*, vol. 4, *The Great Democracies.* Don Mills: McClelland & Stewart Limited, 1958.

Clark, Dennis. *The Irish in Philadelphia: Ten Generations of Urban Experience.* Philadelphia: Temple University Press, 1984.

_____. *The Irish Relations: Trials of an Immigrant Tradition*. East Brunswick: Farleigh Dickinson University Press, 1982.

Cole, J.A. *Prince of Spies: Henri Le Caron*. London and Boston: Faber and Faber, 1984.

Corfe, Tom. *The Phoenix Park Murders: Conflict, Compromise & Tragedy in Ireland, 1879-1882*. London: Hodder and Stoughton, 1968.

Costello, Peter. *Dublin Castle in the Life of the Irish Nation*. Dublin: Wolfhound Press, 1999.

Creighton, Donald. *John A. Macdonald, the Young Politician*. Toronto: The Macmillan Company of Canada Ltd., 1953.

Dalton, Curt. *The Terrible Resurrection*. Dayton: Progressive Print on Demand, 2002.

Denney, Patrick. *Images of England: Colchester*. Gloucestershire: Tempus Publishing Ltd., 2004.

Dooley, Terence. *The Greatest of the Fenians: John Devoy and Ireland*. Dublin: Wolfhound Press, 2003.

Dublin Castle: At the Heart of Irish History, 2nd ed. Dublin: Government of Ireland, 2004.

Ellmann, Richard. *James Joyce*. New York: Oxford University Press, 1959.

Evans, A.G. *Fanatic Heart: A Life of John Boyle-O'Reilly*. Nedlands, Western Australia: University of West Australian Press, 1997.

Fant, Kenne. *Alfred Nobel: A Biography*. New York: Arcade Publishing Inc., 1991.

Fenster, Julie M. *Ether Day: The Strange Tale of America's Greatest Medical Discovery and the Haunted Men Who Made It*. New York: HarperCollins Publishers, 2001.

Funchion, Michael. *Chicago's Irish Nationalists, 1881-1890*. New York: Beaufort Books, 1976.

Golway, Terry. *Irish Rebel: John Devoy and America's Fight for Ireland's Freedom*. New York: St. Martin's Press, 1998.

Grace, Kevin, and Tom White. *Cincinnati Cemeteries: The Queen City*

Underground. Chicago: Images of America, Arcadia, 2004.

Hard Lessons: The Child Prisoners of Kilmainham Jail. Pat Cooke, curator. Dublin: Nicholson & Bass Group, 2001.

Healy, T.M., K.C. *Letters and Leaders of My Day.* London: Thornton Butterworth, Ltd., 1928.

Henke, Suzette A. *James Joyce and the Politics of Desire.* London: Routledge, 1990.

Herber, Mark. *Legal London: A Pictorial History.* Chichester: Phillimore & Co. Ltd., 1999.

The History of the Times: The Twentieth-Century Test, 1884-1912. London: The Office of the *Times*, Printing House Square, 1947.

Horne, Alistair. *Seven Ages of Paris: Portrait of a City.* London: Pan Books, 2003.

Huelke, Donald. *The History of the Department of Anatomy: The University of Michigan: Part 1, 1850-1894.* Reprinted from *The University of Michigan Medical Bulletin* xxvii (January-February 1961): 1-27.

Hughes-Wilson, John. *The Puppet Masters: Spies, Traitors, and the Real Forces behind World Events.* London: Cassell Military Paperbacks, 2004.

Hurst, Michael. *Parnell and Irish Nationalism.* London: Routledge & Kegan Paul, 1968.

Jack the Ripper. Norwich: Pitkin Guides, 2004.

Jenkins, Roy. *Gladstone.* London: Macmillan Publishers Ltd., 1995.

Kant, Kenne. *Alfred Nobel: A Biography.* New York: Arcade Publishing Inc., 1991.

Kee, Robert. *The Green Flag: A History of Irish Nationalism.* London: Penguin Books, 2000.

Kilmainham Gaol: Document Pack, Parnell. Dublin: The Office of Public Works, 1992.

Kilmainham Gaol: Document Pack, 1796-1849. Dublin: The Office of Public Works,

Knox, Oliver. *Rebels & Informers: Stirrings of Irish Independence.* New York: St. Martin's Press, 1997.

Lyons, F.S.L. *Charles Stewart Parnell*. Toronto: William Collins Sons Co. Ltd., 1977.

MacCabe, Colin. *James Joyce & the Revolution of the Word*. New York: Harper & Row Publishers, 1979.

Marlow, Joyce. *The Uncrowned Queen of Ireland: The Life of Kitty O'Shea*. New York: Saturday Review Press, E.P. Dutton & Co., Inc., 1975.

Moody, T.W., ed. *The Fenian Movement*. Cork: The Mercier Press, 1968.

Moore-Anderson, Arthur Ponsonby. *Sir Robert Anderson and Lady Agnes Anderson*. London: Marshall Morgan and Scott, 1947.

Morley, John. *The Life of William Ewart Gladstone*. London: Macmillan and Co., Limited, 1922.

O'Brien, R. Barry. *The Life of Lord Russell of Killowen*. London: Smith, Elder, & Co., 1901.

O'Broin, Leon. *Revolutionary Underground: The Story of the Irish Republican Brotherhood, 1858-1924*. Totowa: Rowman and Littlefield, 1976.

Office of Public Works. *Kilmainham Gaol Document Pack: Parnell*. Blackrock: Teachers' Centre, 1992.

Padover, Saul K. *Karl Marx: An Intimate Biography*. Toronto: McGraw-Hill Book Company, 1987.

Pernick, Martin S. *A Calculus of Suffering: Pain, Professionalism, and Anesthesia in Nineteenth-Century America*. New York: Columbia University Press, 1985.

Phelan, Josephine. *The Ardent Exile: The Life and Times of D'Arcy McGee*. Toronto: Macmillan Company of Canada Ltd., 1951.

_____. *The Ballad of D'Arcy McGee: Rebel in Exile*. Toronto: Macmillan Company of Canada Ltd., 1967.

Phenix, Patricia. *Private Demons: The Tragic Personal Life of John A. Macdonald*. Toronto: McClelland & Stewart, 2006.

Phillips, Andrew. *Colchester: A History*. Essex: Phillimore & Co. Ltd., 2004.
Ponsonby, Arthur. *Henry Ponsonby: Queen Victoria's Private Secretary, His Life from His Letters*. London: MacMillan and Co. Ltd., 1942.

Ross, Stephen. *Asquith.* London: Allen Lane, Penguin Books Ltd., 1976.

The Royal Courts of Justice: Illustrated Handbook. London: William Clowes & Sons, 1883.

Ryan, Desmond. *The Fenian Chief: A Biography of James Stephens.* Dublin: Gill and Son, 1967.

Short, K.R.M. *The Dynamite War: Irish-American Bombers in Victorian Britain.* Dublin: Gill and Macmillan, 1979.

Sievers, Harry J. "The Harrison Horror." Booklet prepared by the staff of the Public Library of Fort Wayne and Allen County, 1956.

Slattery, T.P. *The Assassination of D'Arcy McGee: The Life—and Tragic Death—of Canada's Most Colorful Founding Father.* Toronto: Doubleday Canada Ltd., 1968.

_____. *They Got to Find Mee Guilty Yet: Canada's Most Dramatic Murder Case—the Trial of James Whelan for the Murder of D'Arcy McGee.* Toronto: Doubleday Canada Limited, 1972.

St. Aubyn, Giles. *Queen Victoria: A Portrait.* London: Sinclair-Stevenson, 1991.

Swan, Ruth, and Edward A. Jerome. "'Unequal Justice': The Metis in O'Donoghue's Raid of 1871." *Manitoba History* 39 (Spring/Summer 2000), www.mhs.mb.ca/docs/mb_history/39/unequaljustice.shtml

Trefousse, Hans L. *Andrew Johnson: A Biography.* New York: W.W. Norton & Company, 1989.

Tuchman, Barbara. *The First Salute: A View of the American Revolution.* New York: Alfred A. Knopf, 1988.

_____. *The Proud Tower: A Portrait of the World before the War, 1890-1914.* New York: The Macmillan Company, 1962.

Unlock the Treasures of the Palmer House Hilton. Undated short history prepared by Palmer House Hilton Hotel.

Van Deusen, Glyndon G. *William Henry Sewart: Lincoln's Secretary of State, the Negotiator of the Alaska Purchase.* New York: Oxford University Press, 1967.

Weintraub, Stanley. *Victoria: An Intimate Biography.* Toronto: Fitzhenry & Whiteside Limited, 1987.

Wheeler, Richard. *Voices of the Civil War: An Eyewitness History of the War between the States*. New York: Thomas Y. Crowell Company, 1976.

_____. *Witness to Appomattox*. New York: Harper & Row Publishers, 1989.
Wilson, A.N. *The Victorians*. London: Hutchinson, 2002.

SELECT ARTICLES

Arndt, Melanie. "Joyce's Hero Mythicized: Charles Stewart Parnell." Student paper.

"Attempt to Assassinate O'Donnovan *[sic]* Rossa." *Elyria Republican* (5 February 1885): 5.

Baldwin, J.F., MD. "Grave Robbing." The Historian's Notebook. *The Ohio State Medical Journal* (August 1936): 754-757.

Berton, Pierre. "Drunk or Sober, We Can't Forget John A." *Toronto Star* (July 3, 1993): SA 2.

Conlon, Danny. "New York City, Jubilee Plot, Details of Millen Funeral from Double Agent Who Betrayed Fenian Fanatics; Unlocking the Past; Our Weekly Look at Irish History." *The News of the World* (17 October 2004)

Coxhead, A.J. "The Colchester Choirboy Who Turned Spy." *Essex Countryside* (November 1978): pp. 40-43.

Crockett, Wayne. "The Uses and Abuses of the Secret Service Fund: The Political Dimensions of Police Work in Canada, 1864-1877." Unpublished MA thesis, Queen's University, 1982.

De Trémaudan, A.H. "Louis Riel and the Fenian Raid of 1871." *Canadian Historical Review* IV (1923): 132-144.

Edwards, Linden F. "Body Snatching in Ohio during the Nineteenth Century." *Ohio State Archaeological and Historical Quarterly* 59, no. 1 (1950): 329-351.

Engels, Frederick. "Jenny Longuet, Née Marx." *Der Sozialdemokrat* 4 (18 January 1883):

"Famous Mystery Cases in Review No. 4—The Staging of Dr. Patrick H. Cronin of Chicago in a Bitter International Strife $10,000 in Cash Prizes for Solutions! 4

Found Guilty, but Case Never Entirely Solved." *Chicago Tribune* (5 May 1929):

"The Fenian Exiles Formally Received by the President." *New York Herald* (February 23, 1871): 6.

Gormley, Myra Vanderpool. "Shaking Your Family Tree! Irish Migration Offers Clue to Roots." *Los Angeles Times* (18 March 1988): 5.

"Irish Convention Opens at Chicago at Chicago with a Large Attendance." *Edwardsville Intelligencer* (27 September 1895):

"Jeremiah O'Donovan Rossa: Exciting Career of the Agitator Recently Ejected from the House of Commons." *The Marion Daily Star* (8 May 1895): 7.

Kealey, Gregory S. "The Empire Strikes Back: The Nineteenth-Century Origins of the Canadian Secret Service." *The Journal of the Canadian Historical Association* (1999): 3-19.

Keshen, Jeff. "Cloak and Dagger: Canada West's Secret Police, 1864-1867." *Ontario History* 79, no. 4 (December 1987): 353-381.

"The Last of the Fenians." *New York Telegram* article reprinted in the *Washington Post* (26 February 1911): 1.

Lavey, Kathleen. "The Influx from Ireland Has Had Profound Effect on Michigan." *Lansing State Journal* (14 March 2004):

MacDonald, Cheryl. "Gilbert McMicken, Spymaster: Canada's Secret Police." *The Beaver* (June-July 1991): 44-49.

McCarthy, Robert J. "The World at Our Doorstep: Built on the American Dreams of Generations of Immigrants, Buffalo Has Long Been a Melting Pot of the First Order." *Buffalo News* (23 September 1999):

"Mrs. Jeremiah O'Donovan Rossa, Widow of Irish Patriot and Journalist, Died Here Today of Heart Disease." *Chicago Tribune* (18 August 1916):

Murphy, Ross. "After 100 Years City's Irish Still March—in Spirits St. Patrick Day Just as Lusty as in 1843." *Chicago Tribune* (18 March 1943):

"O'Donovan Rossa Dies in Gotham." *Chicago Tribune* (30 June 1915):.

"O'Donovan Rossa Shot! An English Lady Severely Injures Him Last Evening." *Weekly Tribune* (6 February 1885):

"Our New York Letter." *The Oleon Democrat* (3 March 1885): 1.

Parnaby, Andrew, and Gregory S. Kealey. "The Origins of Political Policing in Canada: Class, Law, and the Burden of Empire." *Osgoode Hall Law Journal* 41, nos. 2 and 3 (2003):

"Parnell and Mrs. O'Shea." *The Nation* 099, issue 2575 (5 November 1914):

Pearson, Rebecca. "John Mortimer." *The Independent on Sunday* (11 June 2006):

Pritchett, John Perry. "The Origin of the So-Called Fenian Raid on Manitoba in 1871." *Canadian Historical Review* 10 (1929): 23-42.

"Representative Men at Home: Dr. Anderson at New Scotland Yard." *Cassell's Saturday Journal* (11 June 1892): 895-897.

"Rossa in a New Business. He Dropped Dynamite and Is Selling Tobacco on the Road." *The Daily Northwestern* (2 August 1890): 1.

Stacey, C.P. "A Fenian Interlude: The Story of Michael Murphy." *Canadian Historical Review* 15 (1929): 133-154.

"Sullivan Dead: Leader of Irish Lawyer Succumbs to Blood Poisoning at St. Joseph's Hospital. Was Figure in Politics.Campaigned for Grant and Blaine; Mentioned in Cronin Case; Headed Land League." *Chicago Tribune* (22 August 1913):

Warren, Craig A. "'Oh, God, What a Pity!': The Irish Brigade at Fredericksburg and the Creation of Myth." *Civil War History* 47, issue 3 (1 September 2001):

Williams, J. (pseudonym for Jenny Marx). *La Marseillaise* no. 71 (1 March 1870); no. 79 (March 9, 1870); no. 89 (March 19, 1970) co-written with her father, Karl Marx; no. 91 (March 21, 1870); no. 99 (March 29, 1870); no. 113 (April 12, 1870); no. 118 (April 17, 1870).

Wilson, David A. "The Fenians in Montreal, 1862-68: Invasion, Intrigue, and Assassination." *Eire-Ireland: Journal of Irish Studies* (Fall-Winter 2003):

SELECT WEBSITES
Anderson, Sir Robert
www.whatsaiththescripture.com/Voice/The.Coming.Prince.html
www.whatsaiththescripture.com/Fellowship/Edit_Sir.Robert.Anderson.html
www.casebook.org/ripper_media/rps.lighterside.html

Beach, Thomas Billis
(See Major Henri Le Caron.)

Chicago
History of Chicago from Trading Post to Metropolis, External Studies Program
University College, Module 2, Chapter 1, Political Wars in Chicago, 1873-1886
www.roosevelt.edu/chicagohistory/mod2-chap1.htm

Civil War
http://www.civilwar.org/cwe/AREA003.asp?9003001001000
www.distantcousin.com/Links/Ethnic/Irish/CivilWar.html
www.acsu.buffalo.edu/~dbertuca/155.html
http://archiver.rootsweb.com/th/index/CIVIL-WAR-IRISH/2000-09

Davitt, Michael
www.museumsofmayo.com/davitt1.htm

Devoy, John
www.thewildgeese.com/pages/breview.html

Fenians
http://freepages.genealogy.rootsweb.com/~mruddy/fenian3.htm
www.fremantleprison.com.au/history/history32.cfm
www.irishdemocrat.co.uk/reviews/catalpa/

Glasnevin Cemetery
http://www.vincentpeters.nl/triskelle/attractions/glasnevincemetery.
php?index=100.040.004.020.008

Invincibles
http://www.irelandinformationguide.com/Irish_National_Invincibles

Ireland
http://web.uniud.it/clav/contatti/lettori/bliss/schede_lavoro_varie/ireland/
history/glossary.pdf

Le Caron, Major Henri
www.henrilecaron.com/Welcome.html

London
www.fidnet.com/~dap1955/dickens/dickens_london_map.html

McMicken, Judge Gilbert
C:\ Le Caron, McMicken, Dictionary of Canadian Biography Online, www.
biographi.ca/EN/index.html

O'Neill, General John
www.historicomaha.com/whelan.htm
www.historicomaha.com/oneill.htm
www.geocities.com/CapitolHill/Lobby/8151/oneill.html
Dictionary of Canadian Biography Online.htm

Palmer House
www.travelhero.com/prophome.cfm/id/45181/hotels/reservations/
www.pbs.org/wgbh/amex/chicago/peopleevents/p_ppalmer.html

Parnell, Charles Stewart
www.nndb.com/people/901/000092625/

Prisons
http://digital.library.upenn.edu/women/lytton/prisons/prisons.html

Queen Victoria
die_meistersinger.tripod.com/victoria.html

Rossa, Jeremiah O'Donovan
freepages.genealogy.rootsweb.com/~mruddy/UI.htm
www.ucc.ie/celt/published/E900007-008/text001.html

RECORDS CONSULTED
Civil War Pension Index: General Index to Pension Files, 1861-1934 Record

Communications between Earl Granville to Governor General Sir J. Young respecting Fenian Raid into Canada, Series, sessional papers; volume xlix; paper/ bill number C 185; Start Page (in vol) 331; Publisher HMSO; Source, Cockton England and Wales, Civil Registry Index: 1837-1983

England and Wales, FreeBMD Death Index: 1837-1983 Record

England Census, 1861, 1871, 1881, 1891

HO 144/1538/5, The National Archives, Kew Richmond Surrey, United Kingdom, Sir Richard Anderson papers

Military records of individual Civil War soldiers
New York Passenger Lists Record

Philadelphia Historical Society, Luke Dillon papers

Public Archives of Canada, Ottawa, Sir John A. Macdonald font, vol. 234, Ref. MG26A; 1864, Reel: C1660; 1865, Reel: C1660, C1662; 1866, Reel: C1508; C1660, C1663; C1664; 1867, C1665; 1868, C1507, C1508, C1509, C1513, C1586, C1666; 1869, C1514; C1522; C1667, C1668, C1669; 1870, C1509, C1668, C1669; 1870, C1509, C1670; 1881, C1509, C1671; 1885, C1670; 1889, C1692, C1795

United States Federal Census, 1870, 1880, 1910, 1920, 1930

United States Social Security Death Index Record

World War I draft registration Cards, 1917-1918 record

ARCHIVES/ LIBRARIES CONSULTED
American-Irish Historical Association, Manhattan
Chicago Historical Society
Historical Society of Pennsylvania
National Archives, Kew Richmond Surrey, United Kingdom
National Archives of CanadaNewberry Library, Chicago

PICTURE CREDITS

First page, picture section.
• The Battle of Nashville, Library of Congress, Prints and Photographs Division, LCB-8172639.
• Battle of Ridgeway, Library of Congress, Prints and Photographs Division, LC-DIG-pga-01485.

Second page, picture section.
• Thomas D'Arcy McGee (Protrait), Library and Archives Canada PA-C006109.
• Prime Minister William E. Gladstone, Library of Congress, Prints and Photographs Division, LC-DIG-pga-00481.
• Sir Richard Webster, Mary Evans Picture Library.

Third page, picture section.
• Dublin Castle, Photo by Peter Edwards.
• Serpents above the door to Kilmainham Gaol, Photo by Peter Edwards.
• Kilmainham Gaol cellblock, Photo by Peter Edwards.

Fourth page, picture section.
• Luke Dillon, The Pennsylvania Historical Society.

Fifth page, picture section.
• The Cuba Five, Library of Congress, Prints and Photographs Division, LC-USZ62-72818.
• Diagram of Pedal-powered submarine, Graf Collection: Courtesy of the Paterson Museum.

Sixth page, picture section.
• Robert Anderson's former townhome in London, Photo by Peter Edwards.
• Robert Anderson (Portrait), Mary Evans Picture Library.
• Le Caron's former home, London, Photo by Peter Edwards

Seventh page, picture section.
• Fenian Headquarters NYC, Photo by Peter Edwards.

Eighth page, picture section.
• Artists rendition of the Phoenix Park Murders, Mary Evans Picture Library.
All other photographs are in the public domain.

Index

Note: Page numbers followed by the letter n and a second number (e.g., 304n11) point to references found in endnotes.